Living Physical Geography in the Laboratory

Theodore I. Erski, McHenry County College

for use with

Living Physical Geography

Bruce Gervais, California State University, Sacramento

W. H. Freeman and Company

Macmillan Education

Living Physical Geography in the Laboratory

by Theodore I. Erksi

for use with *Living Physical Geography* by Bruce Gervais

© 2015 W. H. Freeman and Company

All rights reserved.

ISBN 13: 978-1-4641-0957-7
ISBN 10: 1-4641-0957-5

Second Printing

Printed in the United States of America

W. H. Freeman and Company
41 Madison Avenue
New York, NY 10010
www.whfreeman.com/geography

CONTENTS

PREFACE

All the labs in this manual are designed for a broad population of students taking their first physical geography class. The topics are wide-ranging and include subjects as diverse as remote sensing, biogeography, plate tectonics, soils, and glaciation. A total of 30 labs enable faculty and students to explore the comprehensive breadth of inquiry within the field of physical geography. The scientific method is used throughout the manual and requires systematic, evidence-based problem solving.

The manual is structured with flexibility in mind because every lab setting has unique assets, students, and instructors. For this reason, each lab has multiple self-contained modules that can be completed within the time constraints of the lab requirement. Equipment and supplies are kept at a minimum, and where they are needed, they are restricted to specific modules and never apply to an entire lab.

The comprehensive and flexible nature of this manual extends to the modules that require Google Earth. Because few physical geography labs are equipped with computer workstations, these modules are best assigned as homework, thereby allowing students to use their personal computers, or a computer lab, in order to complete the assignment.

Each lab contains the following sections:
- Recommended textbook reading prior to lab
- Goals
- Key terms and concepts
- Required materials
- Problem-solving modules (at least two per lab activity)
- Summary of key terms and concepts

A complete answer key for instructors is available at www.livingphysicalgeography.com.

Acknowledgments

Writing this manual has made me a better thinker and a better teacher. When my editor Steven Rigolosi invited me onto this project, he could not have known how much it would enrich my own classroom experiences. Thank you, Steven.

Thank you, Bruce Gervais, author of *Living Physical Geography*, the textbook that forms the basis for this lab manual. Bruce gave me the freedom to develop these labs as I saw fit, and he was always available to answer my questions.

This finished manual is also the product of the careful scrutiny of external reviewers. My sincere thanks to Josh Durkee, whose comments helped increase the manual's overall readability and structural flow; to Ingrid Luffman, a deeply thorough reviewer who always considered how students might perceive the labs; to Armando Mendoza, whose cartographic comments improved all the maps; and to Thomas Orf, who recognized the importance of soils as an essential topic in any physical geography lab manual.

Theodore I. Erski
McHenry County College

LAB #1 Physical Geographers and the Scientific Method

Recommended Textbook Reading Prior to Lab:
- The Geographer's Toolkit
  - GT.1 Welcome to Physical Geography!
  - GT.5 Geographic Perspectives: The Scientific Method and Easter Island

Goals: After completing this lab, you will be able to:
- Evaluate how physical geography contrasts with other sciences in terms of its fields of inquiry and problem-solving methods.
- Identify anthropogenic influences associated with physical geography problems and challenges on Earth.
- Determine appropriate spatial scales of inquiry necessary to investigate physical geographic phenomena.
- Determine appropriate temporal scales of inquiry necessary to investigate physical geographic phenomena.
- Summarize the steps associated with the scientific method.
- Create a hypothesis.
- Analyze satellite photos to test a hypothesis.
- Recognize that physical geographers are problems solvers who work across many fields of inquiry.

Key Terms and Concepts:
- anthropogenic
- hypothesis
- people and physical geography
- physical geography
- scientific method
- spatial scale
- temporal scale

Required Materials:
- Textbook: *Living Physical Geography*, by Bruce Gervais
- Atlas

Problem-Solving Module #1: Physical Geography and Anthropogenic Factors

1. Define the discipline of physical geography.

_____

_____

_____

_____

2. Why are spatial relationships important in physical and human geography?

_____

_____

_____

_____

3. Describe two different ways that people modify Earth's physical landscape.

_____

_____

_____

_____

_____

4. In your own words, define the term "anthropogenic."

_____

_____

_____

_____

In Figure 1–1, the dark shading identified with arrows represents high concentrations of nitrogen dioxide (NO_2) suspended in Earth's lower atmosphere. The data were acquired by NASA's Aura satellite between 2005 and 2012. Sources of nitrogen dioxide pollution are combustion engines used to power cars and ships.

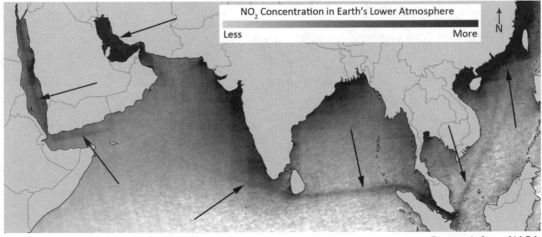

Research from NASA

FIGURE 1–1

© 2014 W. H. Freeman and Company

5. Use an atlas to identify at least two major urban places where Figure 1–1 shows high concentrations of nitrogen dioxide (NO_2) suspended in Earth's lower atmosphere.

_____

_____

6. Explain how Figure 1–1 shows evidence of an anthropogenic factor at work in Earth's lower atmosphere.

_____

_____

_____

_____

7. If you were a NASA scientist on the Aura team, how might you explain the linear nature of some of the nitrogen dioxide concentrations seen in Figure 1–1?

_____

_____

_____

_____

Landsat 7, November 27, 2000   Landsat 7, November 12, 2012

Dubai's Islands

Research from the U.S. Geographical Survey

FIGURE 1–2

Figure 1–2 consists of two Landsat images of the city and coastline of Dubai, United Arab Emirates. The city is located on the Persian Gulf and has experienced significant economic growth over the past several decades.

8. Compare and contrast the two Landsat images in Figure 1–2, and describe any anthropogenic changes between 2000 and 2012.

_____

_____

_____

_____

_____

_____

Problem-Solving Module #2: The Scientific Method

1. Figure 2–1 is a flow diagram with six steps detailing the scientific method of inquiry. Fill in the title of each step (remember that the method does not always follow this order). *Hint: See GT.5 in textbook.*

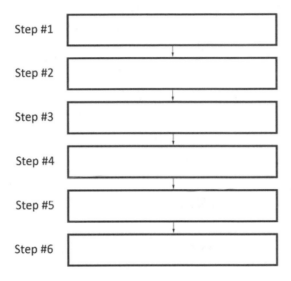

Step #1

Step #2

Step #3

Step #4

Step #5

Step #6

FIGURE 2–1

Figure 2–2 is a map showing the location of Central Asia's Aral Sea (outlined with a black square). In the 1960s the Soviet Union began diverting rivers that flowed into the Aral Sea and using that water to irrigate cotton and rice farms. By the late twentieth century, local fishing communities claimed that the Aral Sea's area was shrinking. Government officials in Moscow, in contrast, claimed that the Aral Sea's area was not shrinking. Assume that you are called in to investigate these allegations using the scientific method.

2. Which one of the above two hypotheses would you adopt, and why?

_____

_____

_____

_____

Research from the Central Intelligence Agency

FIGURE 2–2

© 2014 W. H. Freeman and Company

3. To test your hypothesis, what data would you need to collect?

_____

_____

_____

_____

4. Examine the satellite pictures of the Aral Sea in Figure 2–3 and the data in Table 2–1. Describe what you see and then state if your hypothesis is supported or not supported by the imagery in Figure 2–3.

_____

_____

_____

_____

_____

5. In your own words, compose a sentence or two that corresponds with Step #6 of the scientific method as it relates to the Aral Sea issue.

_____

_____

_____

_____

_____

_____

Aral Sea 1989

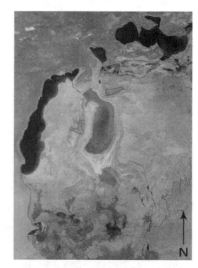
Aral Sea 2011

Research from NASA

FIGURE 2–3

	1960	1990
Surface Area (10³ km³)	65–75	37
Average Depth (m)	15	8
Volume (km³)	1,100	300

TABLE 2–1: Aral Sea Data

Problem-Solving Module #3: Spatial Scale

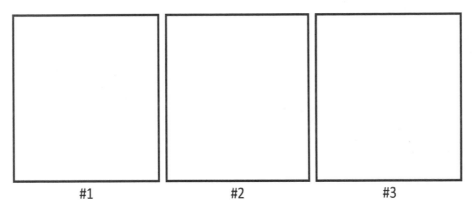

#1   #2   #3

FIGURE 3–1

1. In box #1 of Figure 3–1, sketch a simple outline of Florida. Draw the state as large as possible while staying within box #1.

2. In box #2 of Figure 3–1, sketch a simple outline of the entire contiguous United States. Be sure to make the country's outline as large as possible while staying within box #2. Does Florida get larger or smaller as you move from box #1 to box #2?

   _____

3. In box #3 of Figure 3–1, sketch a simple outline of the entire planet. Be sure to make the planet's outline as large as possible while staying within box #3. Now, sketch a simple outline of the entire contiguous United States on the planet, trying to maintain its scale within the western hemisphere. Does Florida get larger or smaller as you move from box #2 to box #3?

   _____

4. Large scale maps make geographic features _____ to show more detail. Small scale maps make geographic features _____ to cover broad regions.

5. Considering Figure 3–1, is box #1 a large or small scale map?

   _____

6. Considering Figure 3–1, is box #3 a large or small scale map?

   _____

Problem-Solving Module #4: Temporal Scale

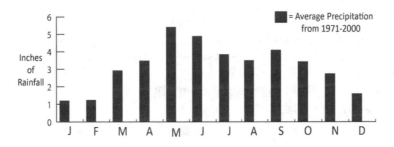

FIGURE 4–1

	J	F	M	A	M	J	J	A	S	O	N	D
Monthly Average	1.2	1.24	2.92	3.48	5.41	4.89	3.84	3.50	4.09	3.43	2.74	1.60
2014	0.3	0.25	1.10	0.95	2.10	1.45	2.07	5.01	1.75	2.50	1.20	0.30

TABLE 4–1: Monthly Average Precipitation (inches) in Any City, USA 1971–2000 and for 2014

1. The term "drought" is difficult to define, but a generally accepted definition is an extended period of months or years with consistently below-average precipitation. Figure 4–1 is a graphical representation of the tabular data in Table 4–1, the monthly average precipitation for Any City, USA, as measured from 1971 through 2000. Finish Figure 4–1 by graphing the hypothetical monthly average precipitation during 2014. (Add the data in a separate bar next to the existing bar for each month.)

Assume you are conducting a study of precipitation in Any City, USA and have completed Step #4 of the scientific method of inquiry. Your hypothesis is: A drought occurred in Any City, USA in 2014. Recall that Step #5 of the scientific method of inquiry is to test your hypothesis by examining data. These data are presented in Figure 4–1.

2. Test your hypothesis by examining only the month of August in Figure 4–1. Is your hypothesis supported or not supported by the data. Why or why not?

_____

_____

_____

3. Now, test your hypothesis by examining the data across all 12 months of 2014. Is your hypothesis supported or not supported by the data. Why or why not?

_____

_____

_____

4. In your own words, explain why careful consideration of temporal scale is important when conducting your study of precipitation in Any City, USA.

_____

_____

_____

_____

Summary of Key Terms and Concepts:

- *Anthropogenic* means made or caused by people.
- A hypothesis is a proposed idea based in reason that can be tested.
- Physical geography is the study of Earth's living and nonliving physical systems and how they change through space and time, naturally or by human activity.
- The scientific method is a systematic procedure for gaining understanding of phenomena and is based on empirical and measurable evidence.
- A spatial scale is the physical size, length, distance, or area of an object or process.
- A temporal scale is the window of time used to examine phenomena. It is the length of time over which phenomena develop or change, from minutes to millions of years.

LAB #2 Globes and Maps

Recommended Textbook Reading Prior to Lab:
- The Geographer's Toolkit
  - GT.3 Mapping Earth

Goals: After completing this lab, you will be able to:
- Identify the utility of the geographic coordinate system.
- Use lines of latitude and longitude to identify locations of physical geographic features.
- Understand the challenges of using globes and maps of various scales to analyze issues and solve problems.
- Use contour lines to analyze elevation and relief differences across topographic maps.
- Create a series of questions to test your peers' knowledge and application of the geographic coordinate system.

Key Terms and Concepts:
- contour lines
- equator
- geographic grid
- latitude
- longitude
- maps

Required Materials:
- Calculator
- Globe (Ward's Natural Science: (80 V 5630)
- High-speed Internet connection (for modules 2, 3, and 4)
- Textbook: *Living Physical Geography,* by Bruce Gervais

Problem-Solving Module #1: The Globe, Latitude, and Longitude

Answer the following questions using a globe.

1. What ocean would you be sailing on if your boat was located at 30° N and 45° W?

   _____

2. What ocean would you be sailing on if your boat was located at 30° S and 135° W?

   _____

3. What country would you be visiting if you stood at 15° N and 80° E?

   _____

4. What country would you be visiting if you stood at 45° S and 175° E?

   _____

5. What continent would you be visiting if you stood at 5° N and 20° E?

   _____

6. What is the approximate latitude and longitude (degrees only, no minutes or seconds) of the city of Tokyo, Japan?

   _____

7. What is the approximate latitude and longitude (degrees only, no minutes or seconds) of the city of Rio de Janeiro, Brazil?

   _____

8. What is the approximate latitude and longitude (degrees only, no minutes or seconds) of the city of Paris, France?

   _____

9. What is the approximate latitude and longitude (degrees only, no minutes or seconds) of the city of Chicago, Illinois?

   _____

10. What is the approximate latitude and longitude (degrees only, no minutes or seconds) of the city of Beijing, China?

    _____

11. Which of the following cities is situated closest to the Tropic of Cancer?
    a. Havana, Cuba   d. Panama City, Panama
    b. Mexico City, Mexico   e. San Diego, California
    c. Austin, Texas

12. Which of the following cities is situated closest to the Tropic of Capricorn?
    a. La Paz, Bolivia   d. Sao Paulo, Brazil
    b. Buenos Aires, Argentina   e. Lima, Peru
    c. Santiago, Chile

13. Which of the following cities is situated closest to the equator?
    a. Ho Chi Minh City, Vietnam   d. Sydney, Australia
    b. Bangkok, Thailand   e. New Delhi, India
    c. Kuala Lumpur, Malaysia

14. Is Italy situated on the east or west side of the prime meridian?

   _____

15. Is Nigeria situated on the east or west side of the prime meridian?

   _____

16. Is the United States situated in the eastern or western hemisphere?

   _____

17. Is the United States situated in the northern or southern hemisphere?

   _____

Meridians on the equator are about 111 km apart. Therefore, if traveling 1° exactly east or west *along the equator*, a person will cover about 111 km. The same is true if one travels exactly north or south along any meridian—again, 1° equals about 111 km. If one is not traveling along the equator, or exactly north or south along a meridian, 1° is never 111 km. This is because as one nears the poles, lines of latitude encircle progressively smaller distances, and lines of longitude steadily converge.

18. If you traveled exactly north, from the origin (0° latitude, 0° longitude) to 15° N latitude, how many kilometers would you have traveled?

   _____

19. If you traveled exactly north, from the origin (0° latitude, 0° longitude) to 90° N latitude, how many kilometers would you have traveled?

   _____

20. How many kilometers would you have traveled if you traveled exactly north, from the origin (0° latitude, 0° longitude) to 90° N latitude along the prime meridian, and then exactly south, back to the equator along the 180° line of longitude?

   _____

Since meridians converge at Earth's poles, the number of kilometers between each meridian shrinks as one nears the North Pole or the South Pole. So, when traveling 1° exactly east or west *along the 15° line of latitude*, a person will cover only 96 kilometers. Similarly, when traveling 1° exactly east or west *along the 60° line of latitude*, a person will cover only 56 kilometers.

Latitude	Approximate Distance Between Meridians from the Equator to the Poles (km)
0	111
15	108
30	96
60	56
90	0

TABLE 1–1

Use Table 1–1 to answer questions 21–23.

21. One person travels a total of 15° east along the 30° N line of latitude, and another travels a total of 15° east along the 60° N line of latitude. Which person travels more kilometers and why?

_____

_____

22. A traveler begins at the origin (0° latitude, 0° longitude) and travels south a total of 15°, then exactly east a total of 165°, then exactly north a total of 45°. What is the traveler's new latitude and longitude?

_____

23. A traveler begins at the origin (0° latitude, 0° longitude) and travels north a total of 45°, then west a total of 210°, then south a total of 30°. What is the traveler's new latitude and longitude?

_____

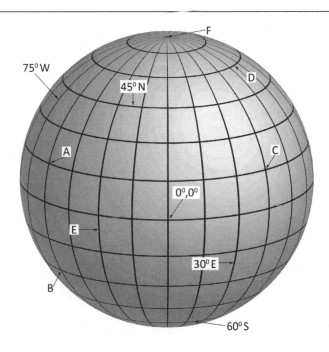

FIGURE 1–1

Use Figure 1–1 to answer questions 24–29.

24. What are the geographic coordinates of location A? _____

25. What are the geographic coordinates of location B? _____

26. If you traveled exactly west, from location C to location A, how many kilometers would you have traveled?

_____

27. If you traveled exactly north, from location C to the parallel identified by letter D, how many kilometers would you have traveled?

_____

28. In what two hemispheres is location E? _____

29. How many degrees separate location 0°, 0° from location F? _____

Problem-Solving Module #2: Map Elements

Download the following two PDF documents from the course companion site that accompanies the *Living Physical Geography* textbook:
- Topographic Map Symbols
- South Lake Tahoe No Contours

Ellipses A, B, C, and D are located at the four corners of the map. There are two geographic grid coordinates within each ellipse—one is a latitude value; the other is a longitude value.

1. What is the latitude value at the top of the map, along letters A and B?

2. What is the latitude value at the bottom of the map, along letters C and D?

3. How many minutes separate the top and bottom latitude values?

4. What is the longitude value of the left side of the map, along letters A and C?

5. What is the longitude value of the right side of the map, along letters B and D?

6. How many minutes separate the left and right longitude values?

7. Ellipse O is the formal title of this map. What are the three parts of this map's formal title?

8. Imagine a longitude line running from E to F, The 55' that is circled on the map is only part of the formal name of this longitude line. What is the complete longitudinal value?

9. Imagine a longitude line running from G to H, The 57' 30" that is circled on the map is only part of the formal name of this longitude line. What is the complete longitudinal value?

10. Imagine a latitude line running from I to J, The 55' that is circled on the map is only part of the formal name of this longitude line. What is the complete latitudinal value?

11. Imagine a latitude line running from K to L. The 55' 30" that is circled on the map is only part of the formal name of this longitude line. What is the complete latitudinal value?

12. Find ellipse M on the map. What two types of scales are present on this map?

13. If you placed an inch on the map, that inch would represent "1 unit" of distance. In the real world, how many inches would you need to cover the same distance as the one you placed on the map?

_____

14. If you placed a paper clip on the map, that paper clip would represent "1 unit" of distance. In the real world, how many paper clips would you need to cover the same distance as the one you placed on the map?

_____

15. Find ellipse N on the map. What is classified within ellipse N?

_____

16. What kind of road is identified by ellipse Q?

_____

17. What kind of road is identified by ellipse S?

_____

18. What kind of road is identified by ellipse T?

_____

19. What kind of road is identified by ellipse U?

_____

20. According to the Topographic Map Symbols PDF, what are contour lines?

_____

_____

_____

21. According to the Topographic Map Symbols PDF, why are contours useful?

_____

_____

_____

22. According to the Topographic Map Symbols PDF, what two kinds of borders are within ellipse V?

_____

23. According to the Topographic Map Symbols PDF, what kind of border is within ellipse R?

_____

24. According to the Topographic Map Symbols PDF, what kind of stream is within ellipse P?

_____

Problem-Solving Module #3: Contour Lines

Download the following PDF document from the course companion site that accompanies the *Living Physical Geography* textbook:

- South Lake Tahoe With Contours

1. Find ellipse A. What is the contour interval of this map?

_____

2. Find ellipse B. Notice that the contour line labeled 9400 is a heavier stroke compared to others—it is an index contour. Index contours logically organize elevation data and enable more efficient and accurate map reading. What is the highest contour line within ellipse B?

_____

3. If you traveled from the index contour in ellipse B to the index contour in ellipse C, would you be traveling downhill or uphill?

_____

4. If you traveled from the index contour in ellipse B to the index contour in ellipse C, how many total vertical feet would you have traveled?

_____

5. Is the stream in ellipse D flowing to the southwest or northeast?

_____

6. One mile is 5,280 feet. If you stood on the index contour within ellipse E, how many miles above sea level would you be?

_____

7. How much elevation difference is there within ellipse F, and how do you know?

_____

8. The sizes of ellipses G and F are identical. Describe what you would expect to see if you visited the area demarcated by ellipse G and how it would compare to the area demarcated by ellipse F.

_____

_____

Problem-Solving Module #4: A Complete USGS Topo

Download the following PDF document from the course companion site that accompanies the *Living Physical Geography* textbook:
- Auburndale Florida

1. What is the northern latitude boundary of this map?

_____

2. What is the southern latitude boundary of this map?

_____

3. What is the scale of this map?

_____

4. What is the contour interval of this map?

_____

5. What lake is located at 28° 05′ N, 81° 47′ 30″ W?

_____

6. What is the value of the contour line located at 28° 02′ 30″ N, 81° 50′ W?

_____

7. What is the name of the road located at 28° 05′ N, 81° 50′ W?

_____

8. Is Route 540 an interstate route, U.S. route, or state route?

_____

9. Is Route 92 an interstate route, U.S. route, or state route?

_____

10. What road must be traveled to get to the highest elevation area on the map?

_____

Summary of Key Terms and Concepts:
- Contour lines are lines of equal elevation in relation to sea level that are used on topographic maps.
- The equator is the line of latitude that divides Earth into two equal halves. The equator is exactly perpendicular to Earth's axis of rotation.
- The geographic grid is the coordinate system that uses latitude and longitude to identify locations on Earth's surface.
- Latitude is the angular distance as measured from Earth's center north or south of the equator.
- Longitude is the angular distance as measured from Earth's center east or west of the prime meridian.
- A map is a flat, two-dimensional representation of Earth's surface.

LAB #3
Google Earth, Topographic Maps, and Remote Sensing

Recommended Textbook Reading Prior to Lab:
- The Geographer's Toolkit
  - GT.4 Imaging Earth

Goals: After completing this lab, you will be able to:
- Differentiate among various remote sensing images and data and determine how such images and data apply to problems that are investigated within physical geography.
- Carry out navigation and measurement activities within Google Earth.
- Use mapping skills within the virtual globe of Google Earth.
- Select and use data layers within Google Earth to solve physical geography problems with USGS topographic maps.

Key Terms and Concepts:
- digital elevation model (DEM)
- Doppler radar
- Google Earth
- Google Earth toolbar, sidebars, sidebar layers, navigation panel, geographic grid coordinates and elevation, eye altitude, historical imagery, and contour lines
- LiDAR (light detection and ranging)
- radar
- remote sensing
- sonar

Required Materials:
- Calculator
- Google Earth tutorials (if needed): http://www.google.com/earth/learn/
- High-speed Internet connection (for all modules) and Google Earth (free download at http://www.google.com/earth/download/ge/agree.html)
- Textbook: *Living Physical Geography,* by Bruce Gervais
- When opening Google Earth, your computer may show the image presented in Figure 1–1. If you see this, simply wait while the selected file is loaded.

FIGURE 1–1

Problem-Solving Module #1: Google Earth and Topographic Maps

Download the following file from the *Living Physical Geography* book companion site and open it within Google Earth:

- Liberty CO Topographic Layers.kmz (Note: This is a large file and may take a few minutes to download. Please be patient.)

1. The kmz file will open with the Liberty, Colorado topographic map boundaries layer already turned on. Fly to marker A by double-clicking A in the Places Sidebar. What is the name of the national forest identified by marker A?

   _____

2. Fly to marker B by double-clicking B in the Places Sidebar. Describe how the boundary of the national forest looks.

   _____

3. In the Places Sidebar, right-click on "Liberty CO Boundaries" and select "Properties." Use the "Transparency" sliding bar to manipulate the map layer. What happens to the map layer when you slide the bar all the way to the left?

   _____

4. In the Places Sidebar, turn off the following map elements: Liberty CO Boundaries, markers A and B. Turn on the following map elements: Liberty CO Hydrography, markers C, D, and E. Fly to marker C by double-clicking C in the Places Sidebar. What is the name of the water source demarcated by marker C?

   _____

5. Fly to marker D by double-clicking D in the Places Sidebar. What is the name of the water source demarcated by marker D?

   _____

6. Fly to marker E by double-clicking E in the Places Sidebar. Is marker E at a higher or lower elevation then markers C and D, and how do you know?

   _____

7. Use the elevation indicator at the bottom of your Google Earth screen and record the elevation of marker E.

   _____

8. Use the elevation indicator at the bottom of your Google Earth screen and record the elevation of marker D.

   _____

9. If you walked from marker E to marker D, how many vertical feet would you travel?

   _____

10. Use the Ruler on the Toolbar to measure the straight-line distance between markers E and D. How many miles (map length) exist between these two markers?

   _____

11. Use the Ruler on the Toolbar to measure a path from marker D, downslope, following the curving line of the river. Proceed to a distance of approximately 3.6 miles. At the end of your path, what happens to the map's graphic element that represents the water source, and what does this mean?

_____

12. In the Places Sidebar, turn off the following map elements: Liberty CO Hydrography, markers C, D, and E. Turn on the following map elements: Liberty CO Contours, markers F, G, 1, 2, 3, and 4. Fly to marker F by double-clicking F in the Places Sidebar. What is the value of the contour line upon which marker F is located?

_____

13. Fly to marker G by double-clicking G in the Places Sidebar. What is the value of the contour line upon which marker G is located?

_____

14. Double-click marker 1 in the Places Sidebar. Notice that this view has both markers 1 and 2 visible and that both are located on an index contour line. According to the contour lines, how many vertical feet separate marker 1 from marker 2?

_____

15. Use the Ruler on the Toolbar to measure a line between markers 1 and 2. How many feet (in map length) are between markers 1 and 2?

_____

16. Double-click marker 3 in the Places Sidebar. Notice that this view has both markers 3 and 4 visible and that both are located on an index contour line. According to the contour lines, how many vertical feet separate marker 3 from marker 4?

_____

17. Use the Ruler on the Toolbar to measure a line between markers 3 and 4. How many feet (in map length) are between markers 3 and 4?

_____

Copy and paste the following coordinates into the Search window on the sidebar and then click the Search button: **37° 41' 23" N 106° 06' 52" W**

Use the above coordinates to answer questions 18–24.

18. What anthropogenic evidence is visible on the landscape?

_____

19. What is the imagery date? *Hint: See the bottom of the Google Earth screen.*

_____

20. What is the elevation of this location?

_____

21. What is the eye altitude?

_____

In the Toolbar, click the icon that looks like a clock with a green arrow wrapping around it in a counterclockwise direction.

22. What is the new imagery date? *Hint: See the bottom of the Google Earth screen.*

_____

23. In the historical imagery slider, slide the marker all the way to the left. What is the new imagery date?

_____

24. How does the 10/22/2005 image differ from the 8/30/2006 image?

_____

25. In the Layers Sidebar, click the "photos" box to turn on pictures posted by Google Earth users. Now double-click "Liberty CO Topographic Layers.kmz" in the Places Sidebar. Investigate the pictures by clicking the photo icons. What is a common desert landscape feature that many people have taken photographs of in this area?

_____

Problem-Solving Module #2: Google Earth and Digital Elevation Models (DEM)

Download the following file from the *Living Physical Geography* book companion site and open it within Google Earth:
- NOAA New Orleans DEM.kmz

1. In the Places Sidebar, expand all the menu items within the Temporary Places folder. Single-click the following layer within the Places Sidebar:
   - NOAA Coastal Digital Elevation Models

   List three things that NOAAs DEMs can be used for.

   _____

   _____

   _____

2. Fly to marker A by double-clicking A in the Places Sidebar. Use the map's legend in the lower left and describe the location of marker A.

   _____

   _____

   _____

3. In the Places Sidebar, right-click on "Path from A to B" and select "Show Elevation Profile." Move the cursor right and left within the elevation profile window. Notice that as you move the cursor within the window, a red arrow indicates that location on the path. Within the elevation profile window, move your cursor to 1 mile (see the bottom of the elevation profile window for distances). What is the elevation at this place?

   _____

4. Within the elevation profile window, move your cursor to 2.50 miles (see the bottom of the elevation profile window for distances). What is the elevation at this place?

   _____

5. Notice that marker B is on the Mississippi River. If you lived in New Orleans near marker A and walked to the Mississippi River along Path A to B, would you walk uphill or downhill to the river?

   _____

6. Click the small X in the elevation profile window and then fly to marker C by double-clicking C in the Places Sidebar. Use the map's legend in the lower left and compare the location of marker C with the location of marker D.

   _____

   _____

7. In the Places Sidebar, right-click on "Path from C to D" and select "Show Elevation Profile." Notice that a wall exists at about 0.45 miles. This is a man-made levee that keeps Lake Pontchartrain (where marker C is located) from pouring into New Orleans (where marker D is located). According to the elevation profile, how high is the highest point on the levee?

   _____

8. In the Places Sidebar, turn off the layer named "NOAA Coastal Digital Elevation Models" (this layer is below marker J). Zoom in to marker D. What do you see?

_____

9. Turn the "NOAA Coastal Digital Elevation Models" layer back on. Click the small X in the elevation profile window and then fly to marker E by double-clicking E in the Places Sidebar. Use the map's legend in the lower left and describe the location of marker E.

_____

_____

10. Fly to marker F by double-clicking F in the Places Sidebar. Use the map's legend in the lower left and describe the location of marker F.

_____

_____

11. Fly to the Path from G to H by double-clicking that path in the Places Sidebar. In the Places Sidebar, right click on "Path from G to H" and select "Show Elevation Profile." If you traveled from marker G to marker H, would you travel uphill or downhill?

_____

12. According to the elevation profile, what is the highest elevation along path G to H?

_____

13. If you wanted to live in Louisiana and were worried about flooding, why would you likely choose location G over location D? (Use both the key as well as the elevation indicator at the bottom of your Google Earth screen to answer this question.)

_____

_____

14. Click the small X in the elevation profile window and then fly to marker I by double-clicking I in the Places Sidebar. Use the elevation indicator at the bottom of your Google Earth screen and record the elevation of marker I.

_____

15. Use the elevation indicator at the bottom of your Google Earth screen and record the elevation of marker J.

_____

16. If you wanted to live in Louisiana and were worried about flooding, why would you likely choose location J over location I? (Use both the key as well as the elevation indicator at the bottom of your Google Earth screen to answer this question.)

_____

_____

_____

Problem-Solving Module #3: Google Earth and Light Detection and Ranging (LiDAR)

Download the following file from the Living Physical Geography book companion site and open it within Google Earth:

- SAF Peninsula LiDAR.kmz

1. Fly to marker A by double-clicking A in the Places Sidebar. From this view you can see markers A and B, as well as a graphic displaying azimuth angle. Imagine standing in the center of this graphic and drawing a circle around your location. Geographic north is 0° or 360° of the circle, geographic east is 90°, geographic south is 180°, and geographic west is 270°. From this view, is location A within sunlight or shadow?

   _____

2. Is location B within sunlight or shadow?

   _____

3. Based on the locations of sunlight and shadow, is the time of day a.m. or p.m., and how do you know?

   _____

   _____

4. Within the Places Sidebar, turn off the following layer: Sunlight from 45 Degrees. Then, hold your cursor over marker A. What happened to the map?

   _____

5. Within the Places Sidebar, now turn on the following layer: Sunlight from 315 Degrees. What happens to the map?

   _____

6. From this view, is location A within sunlight or shadow?

   _____

7. Based on the locations of sunlight and shadow, is the time of day a.m. or p.m., and how do you know?

   _____

   _____

8. Fly to marker C by double-clicking C in the Places Sidebar, and also turn off the following layer: SAF Peninsula LiDAR.kmz. Navigate around at will and then describe what you see.

   _____

9. Turn the following layer back on: SAF Peninsula LiDAR.kmz, and now fly to marker D by double-clicking D in the Places Sidebar. Use the elevation indicator at the bottom of your Google Earth screen and record the elevation of marker C.

   _____

10. Use the elevation indicator at the bottom of your Google Earth screen and record the elevation of marker D.

    _____

11. How high is the dam that creates the reservoir?

_____

12. Fly to marker E by double-clicking E in the Places Sidebar. Also, make sure that one of the following layers is on: Sunlight from 45 Degrees or Sunlight from 315 Degrees. Notice from this view that markers E and F are both visible. The irregular green shapes at marker E are trees. Are there similar irregular shapes at marker F?

_____

13. Turn off the sunlight layer. Are there in fact trees at marker F?

_____

14. Does this LiDAR image see through trees to the ground, or are trees visible?

_____

Problem-Solving Module #4: Google Earth and Radio Detection and Ranging (Radar)

Download the following file from the *Living Physical Geography* book companion site and open it within Google Earth:
- Radar.kmz (Note: This is a large file and may take a few minutes to download. Please be patient.)

The map's legend in the lower-left corner is a graphic reference key for radar reflectivity data. Radar reflectivity is measured in units called "decibels of Z" (dBZ), with higher dBZ values indicating increased amounts of signal that return to a radar dish.

Larger dBZ values indicate stronger rainfall. When light rainfall happens, radar dBZ is typically between 20 and 25, which is colored green on the key. When heavy rainfall happens, radar dBZ is typically between 50 and 55, which is colored red on the key. No rainfall reveals no radar signal, thus no colors on the map.

Markers A, B, C, and D are placed at these cities within Georgia:
- A: Atlanta, Georgia
- B: Augusta, Georgia
- C: Athens, Georgia
- D: Macon, Georgia

Note: Radar image data is displayed most clearly when only one radar image layer at a time is turned on.

1. In the Places Sidebar, notice that the 1:00 p.m. U.S. radar image overlay is already turned on. At this time, what kind of precipitation is Macon experiencing, and how do you know?

_____

2. Keeping the 1:00 p.m. U.S. radar image overlay turned on, what kind of precipitation is Augusta experiencing, and how do you know?

_____

3. Turn off the following image overlay: U.S. Radar 1:00 p.m. Turn on the following image overlay: U.S. Radar 1:10 p.m. What happened to the rainfall over Macon over these 10 minutes, and how do you know?

_____

4. In what direction (N, E, S, or W) did the band of heavy rainfall move between 1:00 and 1:10 p.m.?

_____

5. Between 1:00 and 1:30 p.m., what happened to the weather in Augusta, and how do you know?

_____

_____

6. Between 1:00 and 1:50 p.m., what happened to the weather in Atlanta, and how do you know?

_____

_____

7. Between 1:00 and 1:50 p.m., what happened to the weather in Athens, and how do you know?

_____

_____

Summary of Key Terms and Concepts:

- Digital elevation models (DEMs) are three-dimensional digital representations of surface topography.
- Doppler radar is radar that uses microwave energy to measure velocity of particles of rain or hail within a cloud.
- Google Earth is a virtual globe that provides information about Earth's surface features and allows users to examine spatial relationships among features.
- Google Earth sidebar layers are activated to display different kinds of data, including borders, places, photos, roads, and research activities about oceans, the atmosphere, and water and mineral resources.
- LiDAR (light detection and ranging) operates on the same principle as radar but uses optical light (in the form of a laser) rather than radio or microwave energy.
- Radar is a remote sensing technology that uses radio waves or microwaves to determine the distance, shape, and altitude of surface topography.
- Remote sensing collects information about Earth's physical features without being in direct contact with them. Imaging from satellites, radar, and sonar are examples of remote sensing technologies.
- Sonar works by sending a pulse of sound from a transmitter. The echo of the sound is received and used to create a map of the features of the seafloor.

LAB #4   Atmospheric Composition, Layers, and Pressure

Recommended Textbook Reading Prior to Lab:
- Chapter 1, Portrait of the Atmosphere
  - 1.1 Composition of the Atmosphere
  - 1.2 The Weight of Air: Atmospheric Pressure
  - 1.3 The Layered Atmosphere

Goals: After completing this lab, you will be able to:
- Calculate and summarize permanent and variable atmospheric gases.
- Use steps associated with the scientific method to investigate an atmospheric hypothesis.
- Create and summarize atmospheric graphs illustrating air pressure, temperature, and altitude.
- Identify, use, and interpret different methods of measuring atmospheric pressure.

Key Terms and Concepts:
- air pressure
- environmental lapse rate
- hectopascal (hPa)
- kilopascal (kPa)
- mesopause
- mesosphere
- millibar (mb)
- pascal (Pa)
- pounds per square inch (psi)
- stratopause
- stratosphere
- thermosphere
- tropopause
- troposphere

Required Materials:
- Calculator
- Textbook: *Living Physical Geography,* by Bruce Gervais

Problem-Solving Module #1: Atmospheric Composition

1. The total mass of Earth's atmosphere is 5.6×10^{15} kg. Complete Table 1–1. *Hint: See Section 1.1 in textbook.*

Permanent Atmospheric Gas	Percent of Atmosphere	Total Mass (kg) (Scientific Notation)	Total Mass (kg) (Nonscientific Notation)
Nitrogen (N_2)	78%		
Oxygen (O_2)	21%		
Argon (Ar)	1%		

TABLE 1–1

2. Water vapor is a variable gas, meaning the amount that is in the atmosphere changes. Depending on the season, latitude and local conditions, water vapor may constitute up to what percentage of our atmospheric gas?

_____

Permanent & Variable Atmospheric Gases	Percent of Atmosphere (0% H_2O)	Percent of Atmosphere (1% H_2O)	Percent of Atmosphere (2% H_2O)	Percent of Atmosphere (3% H_2O)	Percent of Atmosphere (4% H_2O)
N_2	78%	77%	76%	76%	75%
O_2	21%	21%	21%	20%	20%
Ar	1%	1%	1%	1%	1%
H_2O	0%	1%	2%	3%	4%

TABLE 1–2

3. According to Table 1–2, what happens to the percentage of nitrogen and oxygen in the atmosphere as the percentage of water vapor increases?

_____

An atom's "atomic mass number" is the number of protons and neutrons within its nucleus. For example, the most common form of nitrogen has an atomic mass number of 14 because it has 7 protons and 7 neutrons within its nucleus (7 + 7 = 14). The most common form of oxygen has an atomic mass number of 16 because it has 8 protons and 8 neutrons within its nucleus (8 + 8 = 16). The mass of any electron is so small that it is not factored into determining an atom's atomic mass number.

A subscript is the little number to the lower right of each letter. Subscripts tell us how many atoms of a particular element are present in a molecule. For example, when you breathe in oxygen (O), you are actually inhaling oxygen molecules (O_2), and each oxygen molecule is composed of two atoms. When you breathe in nitrogen (N), you are actually inhaling nitrogen molecules (N_2), and each nitrogen molecule is composed of two atoms.

Because a single oxygen atom (O) has an atomic mass number of 16, a single oxygen molecule (O_2) has a molecular mass of 32 (16 + 16 = 32). Similarly, because a single nitrogen atom (N) has an atomic mass number of 14, a single nitrogen molecule (N_2) has a molecular mass of 28 (14 + 14 = 28).

4. Complete Table 1–3.

Element	Atomic Mass Number (protons + neutrons)	Atmospheric Gas Formula	Atmospheric Gas Mass
N	14	N_2	
O	16	O_2	32
Ar	40	Ar	
H	1	H_2O	

TABLE 1–3

Suppose someone claims that air with a large percentage of water vapor has less mass than air with a small percentage of water vapor. This sounds strange to you (and possibly wrong) because humid air simply *feels* heavier compared to dry air. You decide to test this claim using the scientific method.

5. In your own words, compose a hypothesis about the mass of humid air versus dry air.

_____

_____

_____

6. To test your hypothesis, what data would you need to collect?

_____

_____

_____

_____

_____

7. Use the data in Tables 1–2 and 1–3 to complete Figure 1–1.

1,000 Molecule Sample of Moist Air (4% H_2O)

Number of N_2 molecules: _____

Number of O_2 molecules: _____

Number of Ar molecules: ___10___

Number of H_2O molecules: ___40__

_____

Mass of all N_2 molecules: __21,000__

Mass of all O_2 molecules: _____

Mass of all Ar molecules: _____

Mass of all H_2O molecules: _____

Mass of all molecules: _____

1,000 Molecule Sample of Dry Air (1% H_2O)

Number of N_2 molecules: _____

Number of O_2 molecules: _____

Number of Ar molecules: ___10___

Number of H_2O molecules: ___10__

_____

Mass of all N_2 molecules: _____

Mass of all O_2 molecules: __6,720__

Mass of all Ar molecules: _____

Mass of all H_2O molecules: _____

Mass of all molecules: _____

FIGURE 1–1

8. Explain why your hypothesis is supported or not supported by the data presented in Figure 1–1.

_____

_____

_____

_____

9. In your own words, compose a sentence or two that corresponds with Step #6 of the scientific method as it relates to the mass of humid air versus dry air (if needed, see Lab #1 to recall this step).

_____

_____

_____

_____

Problem-Solving Module #2: Atmospheric Layers, Temperatures, and Lapse Rates

1. Create a line graph on Figure 2–1 (on the following page) by plotting the data presented in Table 2–1.

Elevation (km)	Temperature (°C)
0	18
11	–58
20	–58
32	–45
50	0
53	0
80	–90
85	–90
100	–70
120	80

TABLE 2–1

2. Complete Table 2–2 using the graph you created on Figure 2–1.

Elevation Range (km)	Temperature Trend (Increases, Decreases, Remains Constant)
0–11	
11–20	
20–50	
50–53	
53–80	
80–85	
85–120	

TABLE 2–2

© 2014 W. H. Freeman and Company

3. Label the four layers of the atmosphere on the lines provided on the right side of Figure 2–1. *Hint: See textbook, Section 1.3.*

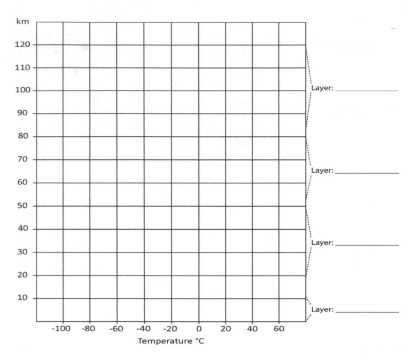

FIGURE 2–1

4. Complete Table 2–3:

   Hints:

   • *Range is the total number of units separating two values.*
   • *Obtain temperatures from your work on Figure 2–2.*
   • *Calculate environmental lapse rate by dividing temperature range by elevation range.*

	Elevations (km)	Elevation Range (km)	Temperatures (°C)	Temperature Range (°C)	Environmental Lapse Rate °C/km
Layer 1	0–11	11	18 to –58		
Layer 2	11–50			58	
Layer 3	50–80	30	0 to –90		3
Layer 4	80–120				

TABLE 2–3

5. In all the above work, it is assumed that Layer 1 of the atmosphere ends at 11 km above Earth's surface—an elevation called the tropopause. Explain why the height of the tropopause varies.

Reason #1: _____

_____

_____

Reason #2: _____

_____

_____

Problem-Solving Module #3: Atmospheric Pressure

Elevation (km)	Millibar (mbar)	Hectopascal (hPa)	Kilopascal (kPa)	Pounds per square inch (psi)	Inches of Mercury (inHg)
0	1013.25	1013.25	101.325	14.69	29.92
1	878.36	878.36	87.836	12.73	25.93
2	761.43	761.43	76.143	11.04	22.48
3	660.07	660.07	66.007	9.57	19.49
4	572.20	572.20	57.220	8.29	16.89
5	496.02	496.02	49.602	7.19	14.64
6	429.99	429.99	42.999	6.23	12.69
7	372.75	372.75	37.275	5.40	11.00
8	323.13	323.13	32.313	4.68	9.54
9	280.11	280.11	28.011	4.06	8.27
10	242.82	242.82	24.282	3.52	7.17
15	118.87	118.87	11.887	1.72	3.51
20	58.19	58.19	5.819	0.84	1.71
30	13.94	13.94	1.394	0.20	0.41
40	3.34	3.34	.334	0.04	0.09
50	0.80	0.80	.080	0.01	0.02

TABLE 3–1

1. Table 3–1 presents five different ways to express average atmospheric station pressure. Examine the millibar and hectopascal values. What is unique about the values in both of these columns?

_____

2. Compare the hectopascal values to the kilopascal values. What is the difference, why does it occur, and how do units of 100 versus 1,000 fit into your answer?

_____

_____

_____

3. Guayaquil, Ecuador is about 10 meters above sea level. If you inflated a balloon in Guayaquil, about how much atmosphere, in pounds per square inch, would press on the outside of your balloon?

_____

4. Assume you took your inflated and sealed balloon up to Quito, Ecuador, which is about 2,850 meters above sea level. Roughly estimate about how much atmosphere, in pounds per square inch, would now press on the outside of your balloon.

_____

5. Predict what would happen to the diameter of your balloon as you drove from Guayaquil to Quito, and why.

_____

_____

Barometers record higher pressure when more air molecules are present at a recording station. They record lower pressure when fewer air molecules are present at a recording station. Early barometers recorded air pressure with mercury (Hg) held within an inverted glass cylinder that was itself held within a pool of Hg. The cylinder was sealed at its top and marked in hundredths of inches. The mercury would rise when more air molecules were present and fall when fewer air molecules were present.

6. Table 3–1 illustrates that as elevation _____, inches of mercury (inHg) _____.
                                          (increases/decreases)   (increases/decreases)

Atmospheric pressure constantly changes as weather systems move through an area (this is studied in a later lab). For questions 7–9 (below), however, assume that weather is held constant and is thus not an issue for consideration at this time.

7. Which of the four locations in Figure 3–1 is located nearest to sea level, and how do you know this?

_____

_____

_____

8. Which of the four locations in Figure 3–1 is located at the highest elevation, and how do you know this?

_____

_____

_____

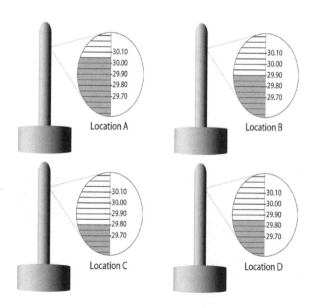

FIGURE 3–1

9. Rank the weather stations in Table 3–2 according to their elevation, with #1 located nearest to sea level. Determine their relative elevations using the data presented in Table 3–1.

Location	inHg	Elevation Rank: 1, 2, 3, 4, or 5 (#1 = nearest to sea level) (#5 = farthest from sea level)
Weather station A	30.71	
Weather station B	30.05	
Weather station C	29.97	
Weather station D	30.52	
Weather station E	30.12	

TABLE 3–2

10. Create a line graph on Figure 3–2 by plotting the data presented in Table 3–1.

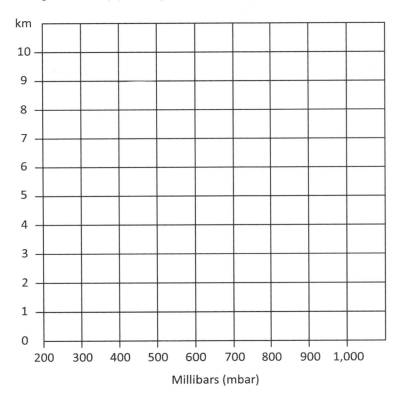

FIGURE 3–2

11. The peak of Mount Everest is 8,848 meters. According to Figure 3–2, what is the predicted average air pressure at its peak?

_____

12. Denver, Colorado is 1,600 meters above sea level. According to Figure 3–2, what is the predicted average air pressure in this city?

_____

Summary of Key Terms and Concepts:

- Air pressure is the force exerted by molecules of air against a surface caused by the weight of air above.
- The environmental lapse rate is the average rate of cooling with altitude in the troposphere (6.5°C per 1,000 meters or 3.6°F per 1,000 feet).
- The following units are commonly used to record and communicate atmospheric pressure: pounds per square inch (psi), pascal (Pa), hectopascal (hPa), kilopascal (kPa), millibar (mb).
- The mesopause is the atmospheric boundary between the mesosphere and thermosphere.
- The mesosphere is the layer of the atmosphere between 50 and 80 km (30 and 50 mi) above Earth's surface.
- The stratopause is the atmospheric boundary between the stratosphere and mesosphere.
- The stratosphere is the atmospheric layer above the troposphere. The stratosphere has a permanent temperature inversion and contains the ozonosphere.
- The thermosphere is the atmospheric layer located from 80 to 600 km (50 to 370 mi) above Earth's surface.
- The tropopause is the atmospheric boundary between the troposphere and the stratosphere.
- The troposphere is the lowest layer of the atmosphere where all weather occurs.

LAB #5　Seasons

Recommended Textbook Reading Prior to Lab:
- Chapter 2, Seasons and Solar Energy
  - ☐ 2.1 The Four Seasons

Goals: After completing this lab, you will be able to:
- Use a protractor and ruler to sketch Earth's various latitudes in relation to the Sun at the two equinoxes and two solstices.
- Determine the subsolar point at various latitudes and various dates using an analemma.
- Determine how "fast" or "slow" the Sun is on a particular date using an analemma.

Key Terms and Concepts:
- analemma
- axial tilt
- equinox
- plane of the ecliptic
- solar zenith angle, also called the angle of incidence
- solstice
- subsolar point
- Tropic of Cancer
- Tropic of Capricorn

Required Materials:
- 180° protractor
- Calculator
- Globe (Ward's Natural Science: 80 V 5630)
- Ruler
- Textbook: *Living Physical Geography,* by Bruce Gervais

Problem-Solving Module #1: The Analemma

The Sun shines directly overhead at only one point on Earth's surface. This point varies from season to season, but it is always within the tropics. The northern boundary of the tropics is the 23.5° N line of latitude called the Tropic of Cancer. The southern boundary of the tropics is the 23.5° S line of latitude called the Tropic of Capricorn. The location on Earth where the Sun shines directly overhead is called the subsolar point. The latitude where the Sun shines directly overhead is called the declination of the Sun.

We often assume that at noon the Sun will have climbed to its highest point in the sky—its zenith. This is not always the case. Sometimes the Sun is not yet at its zenith, and other times it has already passed its zenith. You may therefore experience a "slow" or "fast" Sun compared to what your watch says. A "slow" Sun has not yet reached its highest point in the sky for that day. It is therefore east of its zenith and your watch would display a time before noon. A "fast" Sun has already passed its highest point in the sky for that day. It is therefore west of its zenith and your watch would display a time after noon. The difference between what your watch displays and the Sun's position is called the equation of time.

An analemma (see Figure 1–1) is a graph that illustrates both the declination of the Sun and the equation of time.

Use Figure 1–1 to answer questions 1–10.

1. What is the maximum number of minutes that the Sun might be west of its zenith?

_____

2. During what month is the Sun directly overhead at 23.5° S?

_____

3. If you stood at 5° N on September 5 and your watch displayed noon, would the Sun be directly overhead, past its zenith, or not yet at its zenith?

_____

4. If you stood at 16° S on February 5 and your watch displayed noon, would the Sun be directly overhead, past its zenith, or not yet at its zenith?

_____

5. At what latitude would you need to stand to see the Sun directly overhead on April 10?

_____

6. At what latitude would you need to stand to see the Sun directly overhead on June 20?

_____

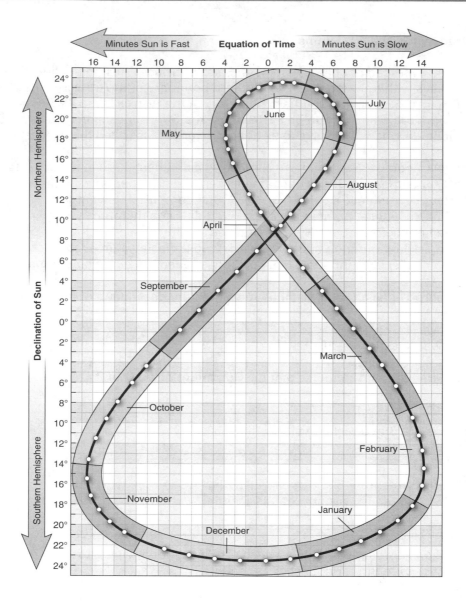

FIGURE 1–1

7. Would you need to be in the northern or southern hemisphere to see the Sun directly overhead during the months of October through February?

_____

8. On what two dates is the subsolar point 0° latitude?

_____

9. What is the declination of the Sun on May 15?

_____

10. Imagine recording the latitude of the subsolar point on February 5. Would the subsolar point have progressed north or south if you recorded its latitude one month later, on March 5?

_____

Problem-Solving Module #2: Solar Elevation

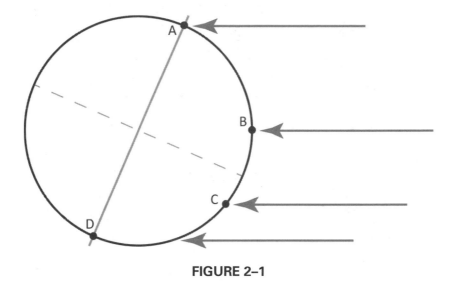

FIGURE 2–1

Figure 2–1 illustrates four different observer locations, at the same date and time. Arrows represent rays of sunlight. Notice that the rays of sunlight are parallel to one another due to the immense size of the Sun compared to Earth. Also, notice that even though it is the same date and time, each observer experiences the Sun at a different place in the sky.

- Observer A (at the North Pole) must look south to see the Sun.
- Observer B (at 23.5° N latitude) must look straight up to see the Sun.
- Observer C (at 15° S latitude) must look in the northern skies to see the Sun.
- Observer D (at the South Pole) cannot see the Sun.

All the observers experience the Sun at different elevations above their respective horizons. For example, observer B experiences the Sun 90° up from his horizon, while observer C experiences the Sun 51.5° above her northern horizon.

The elevation of the Sun, when it is at its zenith, changes from day to day. Sometimes it is higher in the sky, while other times it is lower in the sky. Determining the Sun's elevation requires knowing 1) an observer's latitude and 2) the declination of the Sun. The total number of degrees separating the two values is called arc distance. Subtracting the arc distance from 90° gives us the Sun's elevation.

Example: An observer is located at 40° N and the date is September 15. The analemma tells us that on September 15, the declination of the Sun is 3° N. The arc distance is therefore 37° (40° − 3° = 37°). So, 90° − 37° = 53°. Therefore, for an observer located at 40° N on September 15, the Sun's elevation is 53°.

Complete Table 2–1.

Observer's Latitude	Date	Sun's Declination	Arc Distance	Sun's Elevation
87° S	May 15			−15°
37° S	May 15		55°	
3° S	May 15			
15° N	May 15			87°
37° N	May 15			
82° N	May 15		64°	

TABLE 2–1

Use Table 2–1 to answer questions 2–6.

2. On May 15, is the subsolar point in the northern or southern hemisphere?

_____

3. As one's latitude decreases from 87° S to 3° S, what happens to the Sun's elevation?

_____

4. On May 15, would an observer standing at 37° N latitude need to look in the southern or northern skies in order to observe the Sun, and why?

_____

5. On May 15, would an observer standing at 87° S latitude need to look in the southern or northern skies in order to observe the Sun, and why?

_____

6. On May 15, which latitude experiences the Sun the highest in the sky?

_____

7. Complete Table 2–2.

Observer's Latitude	Date	Sun's Declination	Arc Distance	Sun's Elevation
0°	March 22			
0°	June 22	23.5° N		
0°	September 22		0°	
0°	December 22			66.5°

TABLE 2–2

8. Complete Table 2–3.

Observer's Latitude	Date	Sun's Declination	Arc Distance	Sun's Elevation
38° N	March 22			52°
38° N	June 22			
38° N	September 22		38°	
38° N	December 22			

TABLE 2–3

Problem-Solving Module #3: Earth, Sun, and Solstices

1. Complete the following steps on Figure 3–1 for both solstice scenarios. *Hint: See textbook Figure 2.7.*

   - Draw Earth's axis of rotation. *Hint: This must be tilted 23.5°.*
   - Draw Earth's equator. *Hint: This must intersect the axis of rotation at 90°.*
   - As dashed lines, draw 23.5° N and 23.5° S lines of latitude.
   - Draw rays of sunlight hitting Earth. *Hint: These must be parallel to all other rays.*
   - Shade the hemisphere that is in shadow (this is called the circle of illumination).

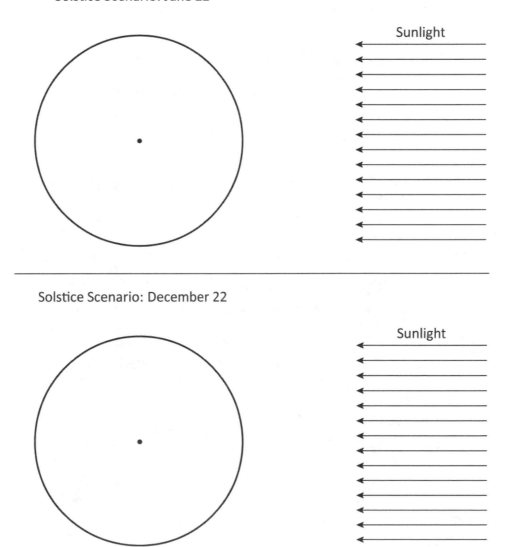

Solstice Scenario: June 22

Sunlight

Solstice Scenario: December 22

Sunlight

FIGURE 3–1

2. Is the northern hemisphere or southern hemisphere receiving more sunlight on June 22?

   _____

3. Is the northern hemisphere or southern hemisphere receiving more sunlight on December 22?

   _____

4. What is the Sun's elevation on June 22 for an observer at 23.5° N latitude?

   _____

5. What is the Sun's elevation on December 22 for an observer at 23.5° S latitude?

   _____

6. June 22 is the first day of what season in the northern hemisphere?

   _____

7. June 22 is the first day of what season in the southern hemisphere?

   _____

8. If Earth had an axis tilt of 41.5° instead of 23.5°, at what latitude would the declination of the Sun be on June 22?

   _____

9. If Earth had an axis tilt of 41.5° instead of 23.5°, at what latitude would the declination of the Sun be on December 22?

   _____

10. If Earth had no axis tilt, at what latitude would the declination of the Sun be on June 22?

   _____

11. If Earth had no axis tilt, at what latitude would the declination of the Sun be on December 22?

   _____

12. The tilt of Earth's _____ determines the farthest extent north or south of the Sun's _____.

Problem-Solving Module #4: Earth, Sun, and Equinoxes

1. Complete the following steps on Figure 4–1. *Hint: See textbook Figure 2.7.*

   - Draw Earth's axis of rotation. *Hint: This will appear as a vertical line.*
   - Draw Earth's equator. *Hint: This must intersect the axis of rotation at 90°.*
   - As dashed lines, draw 23.5° N and 23.5° S lines of latitude.
   - Draw rays of sunlight hitting Earth. *Hint: These must be parallel to all other rays.*
   - Shade the hemisphere that is in shadow (this is called the circle of illumination).

Equinox Scenario: March 22 or September 22

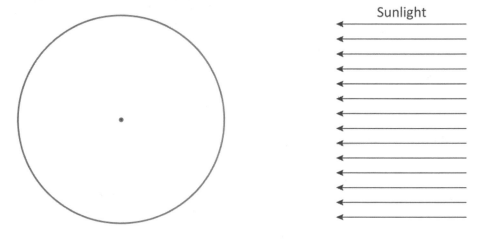

FIGURE 4–1

2. During an equinox, how many hours of daylight does the northern hemisphere receive? (*Hint: See the recommended textbook reading.*)

   _____

3. During an equinox, how many hours of daylight does the southern hemisphere receive? (*Hint: See the recommended textbook reading.*)

   _____

4. During an equinox, at what latitude is the subsolar point? _____

5. During an equinox, at what latitude is the declination of the Sun? _____

6. Earth's axis of rotation is always tilted at 23.5°, so why is it not tilted in Figure 4–1?

   _____

   _____

Problem-Solving Module #5: Solstices, Equinoxes, Duration of Daylight, Perihelion, and Aphelion

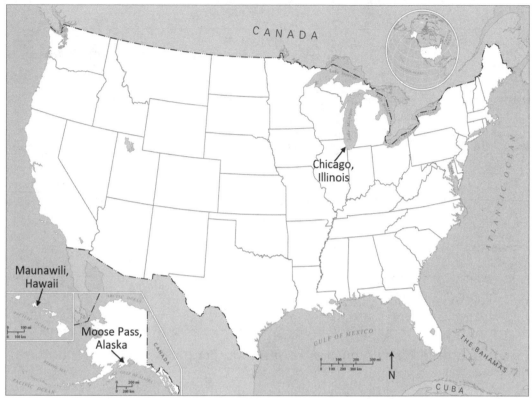

Research from National Atlas/USGS

FIGURE 5–1

	Moose Pass, Alaska (60° 29′ N)	Chicago, Illinois (41° 51′ N)	Maunawili, Hawaii (21° 23′ N)
Duration of Daylight June 22, 2015	19 h, 3 m	15 h, 13 m	13 h, 26 m
Duration of Daylight December 22, 2015	5 h, 43 m	9 h, 8 m	10 h, 50 m
Duration of Daylight March 22, 2015	12 h, 24 m	12 h, 14 m	12 h, 9 m
Duration of Daylight September 22, 2015	12 h, 16 m	12 h, 10 m	12 h, 7 m

TABLE 5–1

Use Figure 5–1 and Table 5–1 to answer questions 1–7. You may also benefit by examining a globe to visualize the latitudinal differences of various locations.

1. During the summer solstice, do higher or lower latitudes receive more hours of daylight?

_____

2. During the winter solstice, do higher or lower latitudes receive more hours of daylight?

_____

3. Which of the three locations in Table 5–1 has the smallest difference in hours of daylight from one solstice to the next?

_____

4. Examining the data in Table 5–1, how can we tell that March 22 and September 22 are equinox dates?

_____

Elliptical Position	Date	Earth's Distance from Sun (km)
Perihelion	First week in January	147,000,000
Aphelion	First week in July	152,000,000

TABLE 5–2

5. In your own words, explain what *perihelion* means.

_____

6. In your own words, explain what *aphelion* means.

_____

7. Using the terms "perihelion" and "aphelion," explain why Earth's elliptical orbit is not the reason for the seasons.

_____

_____

_____

Summary of Key Terms and Concepts:
- The analemma is a "figure-8" pattern denoting the date and latitude of the subsolar point on Earth over the course of an entire year.
- The axial tilt of Earth's axis is 23.5° from vertical in relation to the plane of the ecliptic.
- Equinoxes occur on or about September 22 and March 22. On these dates the subsolar point is over the equator.
- The plane of the ecliptic is the flat plane that the planets in the solar system follow in their orbit around the Sun.
- The solar zenith angle, also called the angle of incidence, is the angle of the noontime Sun above the horizon in degrees. Sunlight on the horizon is zero degrees, and sunlight from straight overhead is 90°.
- The June solstice occurs when the subsolar point is 23.5° north latitude. This occurs on or about June 21.
- The December solstice occurs when the subsolar point is 23.5° south latitude. This occurs on or about December 21.
- The subsolar point is the single point at which the Sun's rays are perpendicular to Earth's surface. The subsolar point is restricted between 23.5° north and south latitude.
- The Tropic of Cancer is the maximum latitude of the subsolar point in the northern hemisphere and is 23.5° north latitude.
- The Tropic of Capricorn is the maximum latitude of the subsolar point in the southern hemisphere and is 23.5° south latitude.

LAB #6 Atmospheric Temperature and Controls on Climate

Recommended Textbook Reading Prior to Lab:
- Chapter 2, Seasons and Solar Energy
  - 2.3 Surface Temperature Patterns
  - 2.5 Earth's Energy Budget

Goals: After completing this lab, you will be able to:
- Create temperature graphs and reflect upon your findings to discuss climate variables using selected NOAA Monthly Station Normals.
- Use selected NOAA data to calculate average annual temperature and temperature range for selected cities.
- Determine how the variables of maritime versus continental location, latitude, elevation, and prevailing winds contribute to the climate of selected locations.
- Employ the scientific method to determine preferred locations based on climate data.
- Judge and graph the insolation value in kWh/m²/day at various locations and dates.
- Employ the scientific method to determine the best location for a photovoltaic power station based on insolation values for selected locations.

Key Terms and Concepts:
- annual average temperature
- annual temperature range
- continental effect on climate
- insolation
- latitude and temperature
- maritime effect on climate

Required Materials:
- Calculator
- Textbook: *Living Physical Geography,* by Bruce Gervais

Problem-Solving Module #1: Temperature Graphs and Latitude as a Climate Control

Assume you are offered a job that allows you to live in one of two places, both of which are located on the same line of longitude but at very different lines of latitude. One location is in North Dakota and the other is in Texas. You want to know about the climate in each place, so you decide to investigate the average surface temperature and the annual temperature range using the scientific method. (Note: Assume for this exercise that both locations are at the same altitude.)

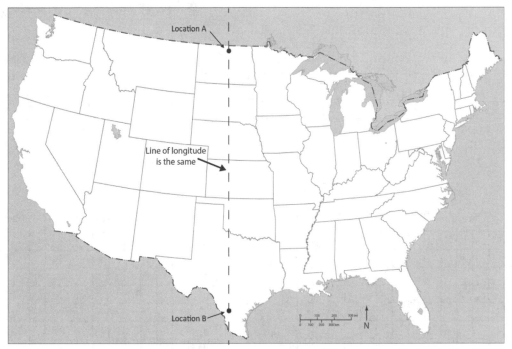

Research from National Atlas/USGS

FIGURE 1–1

Location	Latitude
Location A (North Dakota)	48° 50′ 26″ N
Location B (Texas)	28° 20′ 51″ N

TABLE 1–1

1. In your own words, compose a hypothesis about the average surface temperature and the annual temperature range of both locations.

_____

_____

_____

_____

2. To test your hypothesis, what data would you need to collect?

_____

_____

_____

_____

3. Graph the data in Table 1–2 on the two graphs in Figure 1–2.

Location	Jan	Feb	Mar	Apr	May	Jun	Jul	Aug	Sept	Oct	Nov	Dec
Location A (North Dakota)	–17	–13	–6	3	11	15	18	17	11	4	–6	–14
Location B (Texas)	12	14	19	23	27	29	31	30	28	23	17	13

TABLE 1–2: Average Temperature Normals (°C)

4. Process more data by completing Table 1–3.

Location	Average Surface Temperature (°C)	Annual Temperature Range (°C)
Location A (North Dakota) (48° 50′ 26″ N)		
Location B (Texas) (28° 20′ 51″ N)		

TABLE 1–3

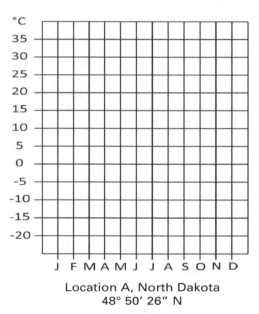

Location A, North Dakota
48° 50′ 26″ N

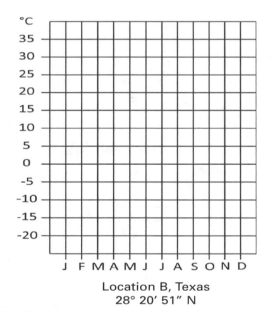

Location B, Texas
28° 20′ 51″ N

FIGURE 1–2

5. Is your hypotheses supported or not supported by the data presented in Figure 1–2 and Table 1–3?

_____

_____

_____

6. In your own words, compose a sentence or two that corresponds with Step #6 of the scientific method as it relates to the average surface temperature and the annual temperature range of both locations (if needed, see Lab #1 to recall this step).

_____

_____

_____

_____

_____

Problem-Solving Module #2: Temperature Graphs and Altitude as a Climate Control

Assume you are offered a job that allows you to live in one of two places, both of which are located on the same line of latitude, but at very different elevations. Location A is high in the mountains of Colorado, while Location B is on the lowland eastern plains of Colorado. You want to know about the climate in each place, so you decide to investigate the average surface temperature of both locations using the scientific method.

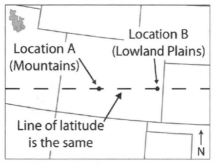

Research from National Atlas/USGS

FIGURE 2–1

Location	Elevation (m)
Location A (Mountains of Colorado)	3,100
Location B (Lowland Eastern Plains of Colorado)	1,287

TABLE 2–1

1. Compose a hypothesis about the average surface temperature of both locations.

_____

_____

_____

_____

2. To test your hypothesis, what data would you need to collect?

_____

_____

_____

_____

3. Graph the data in Table 2–2 on the two graphs in Figure 2–2.

Location	Jan	Feb	Mar	Apr	May	Jun	Jul	Aug	Sept	Oct	Nov	Dec
Location A (Mountains of Colorado)	–8	–7	–4	0	5	10	13	12	8	3	–4	–8
Location B (Lowland Eastern Plains of Colorado)	–3	0	5	9	15	21	24	23	18	11	3	–2

TABLE 2–2: Average Temperature Normals (°C)

© 2014 W. H. Freeman and Company

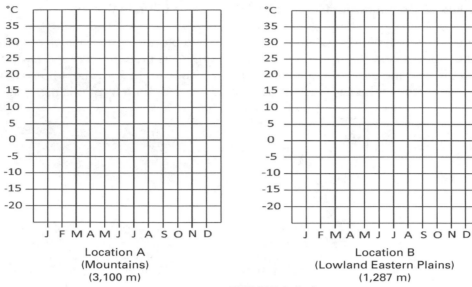

FIGURE 2–2

4. Process more data by completing Table 2–3.

Location	Average Surface Temperature (°C)
Location A (Mountains of Colorado) (3,100 m)	
Location B (Lowland Eastern Plains of Colorado) (1,287 m)	

TABLE 2–3

5. Is your hypotheses supported or not supported by the data presented in Figure 2–2 and Table 2–3?

_____

_____

_____

6. In your own words, compose a sentence or two that corresponds with Step #6 of the scientific method as it relates to the average surface temperature and the two locations (if needed, see Lab #1 to recall this step).

_____

_____

_____

_____

_____

Problem-Solving Module #3: Temperature Graphs and Continental versus Marine Location as a Climate Control

Assume you have a friend that lives in Point Arena, California and another that lives in St. Louis, Missouri. You decide to visit them but are not sure what to pack for the trip. You notice that both places are located near the same parallel, but one location is on the Pacific Ocean coastline and another is in the middle of the continent. How you prepare for the trip depends on the average surface temperature and annual temperature range of a marine location compared to a continental location. Use the scientific method to judge these two variables for each location.

Research from National Atlas/USGS

FIGURE 3–1

Location	Latitude	Relative Location
Point Arena, California	38° 54′ 32″ N	Marine
St. Louis, Missouri	38° 37′ 38″ N	Continental

TABLE 3–1

1. In your own words, compose a hypothesis about the average surface temperature and the annual temperature range of the two locations.

_____

_____

_____

_____

2. To complete Step #3 of the scientific method, what data would you need to collect?

_____

_____

_____

_____

3. Graph the data in Table 3–2 on the two graphs in Figure 3–2.

Location	Jan	Feb	Mar	Apr	May	Jun	Jul	Aug	Sept	Oct	Nov	Dec
Point Arena, California	9	10	10	11	12	13	14	15	15	13	10	9
St. Louis, Missouri	–1	2	8	14	19	24	27	26	21	15	7	1

TABLE 3–2: Average Temperature Normals (°C)

4. Process more data by completing Table 3–3.

Location	Average Surface Temperature (°C)	Annual Temperature Range (°C)
Point Arena, California (38° 54' 32" N)		
St. Louis, Missouri (38° 37' 38" N)		

TABLE 3–3

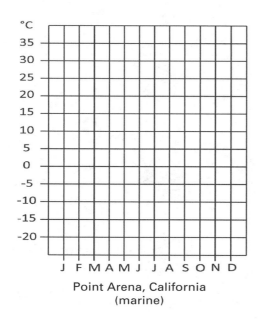

Point Arena, California
(marine)

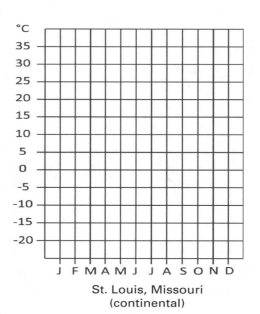

St. Louis, Missouri
(continental)

FIGURE 3–2

5. Is your hypotheses supported or not supported by the data presented in Figure 3–2 and Table 3–3?

_____

_____

_____

6. In your own words, compose a sentence or two that corresponds with Step #6 of the scientific method as it relates to the average surface temperature and the annual temperature range of the two locations (if needed, see Lab #1 to recall this step).

_____

_____

_____

_____

_____

Problem-Solving Module #4: Insolation

Assume you are the CEO of a power company and you need to locate a commercial-scale photovoltaic power station somewhere in California. Two different communities, Daggett and Fresno, are competing for the power station, and both communities have offered exactly the same incentives, tax packages, and employment base. You decide that, since all other variables are equal, the power station must be located in the community with the best average insolation value.

Research from National Atlas/USGS

FIGURE 4–1

Candidate Communities	Grid Coordinates
Daggett, California	34° 51′ 48″ N 116° 53′ 17″ W
Fresno, California	36° 45″ N 119° 46″ W

TABLE 4–1

1. In your own words, compose a hypothesis about the average insolation value of both locations.

   _____

   _____

   _____

   _____

2. To test your hypothesis, what data would you need to collect?

   _____

   _____

   _____

   _____

3. Graph the data in Table 4–2 on the two graphs in Figure 4–2.

Location	Jan	Feb	Mar	Apr	May	Jun	Jul	Aug	Sept	Oct	Nov	Dec
Daggett, California	5.59	6.03	7.10	7.74	7.42	7.42	7.33	7.40	7.34	6.76	5.78	5.20
Fresno, California	3.01	4.55	5.85	6.78	7.04	7.20	7.37	7.47	6.91	6.11	4.45	2.79

TABLE 4–2: Average Insolation (kWh/m²/day)

4. Process more data by completing Table 4–3.

Location	Average Annual Insolation (kWh/m²/d)
Daggett, California	
Fresno, California	

TABLE 4–3

5. Is your hypotheses supported or not supported by the data presented in Figure 4–2 and Table 4–3?

_____

_____

_____

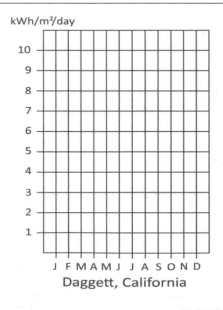

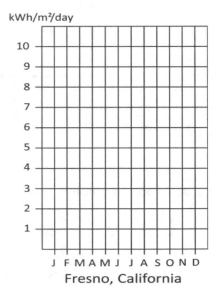

FIGURE 4–2

6. In your own words, compose a sentence or two that corresponds with Step #6 of the scientific method as it relates to the average insolation value of the two locations (if needed, see Lab #1 to recall this step).

_____

_____

_____

_____

_____

Summary of Key Terms and Concepts:

- The annual average temperature is calculated by adding the monthly average temperatures over 1 year and dividing by 12.
- The annual temperature range is calculated by subtracting the lowest annual average temperature from the highest annual average temperature.
- Annual temperature ranges are greater for continental locations and smaller for maritime locations.
- Insolation is a measure of incoming solar radiation and is commonly expressed in Watts per square meter (W/m^2) or kilowatts per square meter (kW/m^2).
- Annual temperature ranges are greater for higher-latitude locations and smaller for lower-latitude locations.
- Maritime areas have lower annual temperature ranges than continental areas due to the moderating effect of water.

LAB #7   Water Vapor and State Change

Recommended Textbook Reading Prior to Lab:
- Chapter 3, Water in the Atmosphere
  - 3.1 The Hydrologic Cycle and Water
  - 3.2 Atmospheric Humidity

Goals: After completing this lab, you will be able to:
- Determine the latent heat that is required to transition selected samples of H_2O into different phases.
- Summarize the saturation vapor pressure table and graph, and determine vapor pressure requirements needed to achieve saturation in selected air samples.
- Determine the relative humidity and dew point temperature of selected air samples.
- Predict the relative humidity and dew point temperature inside a building and outside, and generate a hypothesis about your prediction.
- Carry out temperature data collection using a sling psychrometer.
- Determine the relative humidity and dew point temperatures using psychrometer data and appropriate tables.

Key Terms and Concepts:
- condensation as a warming process
- dew point temperature
- evaporation as a cooling process
- humidity
- latent heat
- relative humidity
- water vapor capacity
- water's phases

Required Materials:
- Calculator
- Sling psychrometer (Flinn Scientific: FB0543)
- Textbook: *Living Physical Geography,* by Bruce Gervais

Problem-Solving Module #1: Specific Heat

Recall that specific heat is the amount of energy required to raise 1 gram of a substance 1°C. Different substances have different specific heat values, as illustrated in Table 1–1.

Substance	Specific Heat (calories/gram) or How many calories it takes to raise the temperature of 1 gram of a substance by 1°C
Water	1
Wet mud	0.60
Water vapor	0.50
Ice	0.50
Dry sandy clay	0.33
Dry air	0.24
Granite	0.19
Dry quartz sand	0.19

TABLE 1–1

The relationship between calories and temperature change can be expressed as follows:

$$Q = cm\Delta T$$

Q = calories added
c = specific heat of substance
m = mass of substance (grams)
ΔT = temperature change

Or, if you prefer, you can express it this way:

Calories added = specific heat of substance × mass of substance × temperature change

Example #1: How many calories must be added to 1 gram of granite to increase its temperature 5°C?
Calories added = 0.19 × 1 × 5
Calories added = 0.95

Example #2: How many calories must be added to 1 gram of wet mud to increase its temperature 5°C?
Calories added = 0.60 × 1 × 5
Calories added = 3

1. True/False: One gram of wet mud requires more calories than 1 gram of granite to raise its temperature by 5°C.

If we need to determine temperature change as a result of adding calories, we simply rearrange the above formula as follows:

$$\Delta T = Q/cm$$

Example #3: What is the temperature change of 1 gram of granite if we add 0.95 calories to it?
Temperature change = (0.95 / 0.19) × 1
Temperature change = 0.95 / 0.19
Temperature change = 5°C

Example #4: What is the temperature change of 1 gram of wet mud if we add 3 calories to it?
Temperature change = (3 / 0.60) × 1
Temperature change = 3 / 0.60
Temperature change = 5°C

2. True/False: Adding 0.95 calories to 1 gram of granite and 3 calories to 1 gram of wet mud will increase the temperature of both substances by an equal amount.

3. Complete Table 1–2. *Hint: Recall that 1 kg = 1,000 g.*

Substance	Mass	Calories Added	Temperature Change (°C)
Water	14 g		30
Water	27 kg	34,000	
Ice	7 g		7
Ice	87 kg	557,000	
Dry sandy clay	34 g		13
Dry sandy clay	674 kg	250,453	
Dry air	63 g		7
Dry air	0.5 kg	100,000	
Dry quartz sand	85 g		8
Dry quartz sand	127 kg	323,000	

TABLE 1–2

Problem-Solving Module #2: Latent Heat

Recall that when successive calories are added to 1 gram of water, each calorie increases the temperature of the water 1°C. Eventually the water's temperature reaches 100°C. The next calorie added, however, does <u>not</u> increase the temperature of the water to 101°C. Instead, the water's temperature remains 100°C. This calorie, along with 539 more, changes the phase (state) instead of the temperature of the water. When all 540 calories are absorbed by the 100°C gram of water, it vaporizes into a gas. These 540 calories are called the latent heat of vaporization and/or condensation (H_v) for water. **H_v (for water) = 540 calories/gram.**

The formula to calculate the calories required to achieve the latent heat of vaporization and/or condensation (H_v) is:

$$Q = mH_v$$

Q = calories required
m = mass (grams)
H_v = latent heat of vaporization and/or condensation

Example #5: Assume you have 14 grams of water at 100°C. How many calories are required to vaporize this water?
Calories required = 14 × 540
Calories required = 7,560

A similar thought process is applicable when calories are added to ice. Notice from Table 1–1, however, that the specific heat of ice is 0.5 calories. It takes 0.5 calories to heat up 1 gram of ice 1°C. Thus, when successive calories are added to 1 gram of ice, each calorie increases the temperature of the ice 2°C. Eventually the ice's temperature reaches 0°C. The next calorie added, however, does <u>not</u> increase the temperature of the ice to 1°C. Instead, the ice's temperature remains at 0°C. This calorie, along with 79 more, changes the phase (state) instead of the temperature of the ice. When all 80 calories are absorbed by the 0°C gram of ice, it melts into a liquid. These 80 calories are called the latent heat of fusion and/or melting (H_f) for water. **H_f (for water) = 80 calories/gram.**

The formula to calculate the calories required by a substance to achieve the latent heat of fusion and/or melting (H_f) is:

$$Q = mH_f$$

Example #6: Assume you have 14 grams of ice at 0°C. How many calories are required to melt this ice?
Calories required = 14 × 80
Calories required = 1,120

1. Assume you have 50 grams of water at 100°C. How many calories are required to vaporize this water?

　　_____

2. Assume you have 357 grams of water at 100°C. How many calories are required to vaporize this water?

　　_____

3. Assume you have 50 grams of ice at 0°C. How many calories are required to melt this ice?

　　_____

4. Assume you have 357 grams of ice at 0°C. How many calories are required to melt this ice?

_____

5. True/False: More calories are required to change ice into water than to change water into vapor.

Using the formulas, we can now calculate how many calories are required to turn ice into vapor at various temperatures. For example, assume we have 3 grams of ice at –10°C. How many calories are required to turn that ice into 120°C vapor?

Steps	Temperature Range (°C)	Temperature Change (°C)	Formula to Determine Calories	Completed Formula	Calories Added
Heat the ice	–10 to 0	10	$Q = cm\Delta T$	$Q = 0.5 \times 3 \times 10$	15
Melt the ice	0 to 0	0	$Q = mH_f$	$Q = 3 \times 80$	240
Heat the water	0 to 100	100	$Q = cm\Delta T$	$Q = 1 \times 3 \times 100$	300
Vaporize the water	100 to 100	0	$Q = mH_v$	$Q = 3 \times 540$	1,620
Heat the vapor	100 to 120	20	$Q = cm\Delta T$	$Q = 0.5 \times 3 \times 20$	30

	Total Calories Added	2,205

TABLE 2–1

We can now graph our Table 2–1 findings to create a heating curve. The completed heating curve for Table 2–1 is shown in Figure 2–1. Notice that the y-axis marks temperature (°C), and the x-axis marks total calories added.

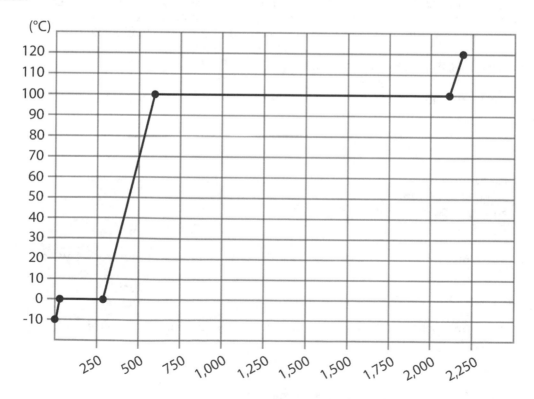

Total Calories Added

FIGURE 2–1

6. Follow the examples in Table 2–1 and Figure 2–1 to complete Table 2–2 and Figure 2–2.
   Assume you have 6.5 grams of ice at –10°C. How many calories are required to turn that ice
   into 110°C vapor?

Steps	Temperature Range (°C)	Temperature Change (°C)	Formula to Determine Calories	Completed Formula	Calories Added

	Total Calories Added	2,205

TABLE 2–2

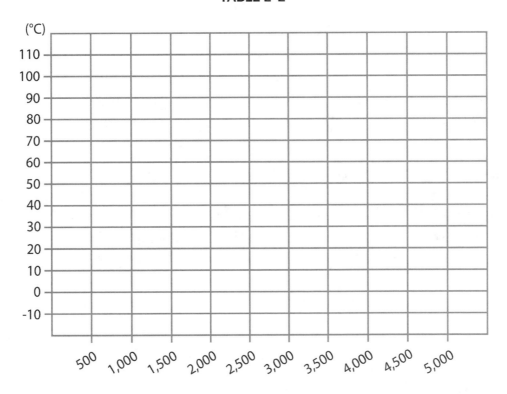

FIGURE 2–2

Problem-Solving Module #3: Relative Humidity

Relative humidity is the amount of water vapor present in the air relative to the amount that would be present if the air was saturated. Relative humidity is expressed as a percentage.

Relative humidity = (water vapor content / water vapor capacity) × 100

Table 3–1 illustrates that air's water vapor capacity is temperature-dependent.

°C	Capacity of Air (g/kg) or How many grams of water vapor it takes to saturate 1 kg of air
−40	0.1
−30	0.3
−20	0.75
−10	2
0	3.5
5	5
10	7
15	10
20	14
25	20
30	26.5
35	35
40	47

TABLE 3–1

1. Raising a kilogram's air temperature from 0°C to 5°C increases its capacity by ___ g/kg.

2. Raising a kilogram's air temperature from 15°C to 20°C increases its capacity by ___ g/kg.

3. Raising a kilogram's air temperature from 35°C to 40°C increases its capacity by ___g/kg.

4. Compose a generalization that compares warm air's water vapor capacity to cold air's water vapor capacity.

   _____

   _____

   _____

5. One kilogram of air contains 5 grams of water vapor. Assume that it can contain 10 grams of water vapor. Write the formula needed to calculate the air's relative humidity in this scenario.

   _____

6. What is the relative humidity of the air in question 5?

   _____

7. One kilogram of air contains 7.5 grams of water vapor. Assume that it can contain 10 grams of water vapor. Write the formula needed to calculate the air's relative humidity in this scenario.

_____

8. What is the relative humidity of the air in question 7?

_____

9. One kilogram of air contains 10 grams of water vapor. Assume that it can contain 10 grams of water vapor. Write the formula needed to calculate the air's relative humidity in this scenario.

_____

10. What is the relative humidity of the air in question 9?

_____

11. Assuming that 1 kilogram of air contains 10 grams of water vapor, what happens to the relative humidity as we keep adding water vapor from 5 grams to 7.5 grams, and finally to 10 grams?

_____

12. Questions 5–11 assume that the capacity of 1 kilogram of air is 10 grams of water vapor. According to Table 3–1, what must be the air's temperature?

_____

13. Assume we take the very same kilogram of air described in question 10 and increase its temperature to 25°C. What is the air's new capacity?

_____

14. Complete Table 3–2 by calculating the air's relative humidity.

Temperature of 1 kg of air	Vapor Content: 5 grams	Vapor Content: 7.5 grams	Vapor Content: 10 grams
15°C			
25°C			

TABLE 3–2

15. According to Table 3–2, does air's relative humidity increase or decrease as temperature rises?

_____

16. If the amount of water vapor in 1 kg of air stays constant, how will cooling that kilogram of air influence its relative humidity?

_____

Figure 3–1 illustrates 1 kilogram of air that is sealed against the outside air and heated to 35°C. The same beaker, <u>still sealed</u>, is then cooled to –20°C .

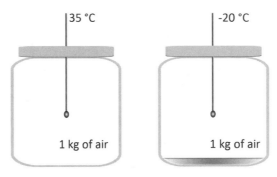

FIGURE 3–1

17. How much water vapor would saturate the air contained in the 35°C jar?

_____

18. How much water vapor would saturate the air contained in the –20°C jar?

_____

19. Since there is a puddle of liquid water at the bottom of the –20°C jar, what can we determine about the relative humidity of the air it contains?

_____

20. What would happen to the puddle of liquid water at the bottom of the –20°C jar if we heated the air inside the jar back up to 35°C?

_____

Problem-Solving Module #4: Sling Psychrometer

Use a sling psychrometer to determine the humidity inside the classroom, as well as outside the building. Remember that there are two thermometers on any sling psychrometer, one with a cotton wick surrounding the bulb—called the wet bulb—and another without a cotton wick surrounding the bulb—called the dry bulb.

Moisten the wet bulb thermometer by dipping it into water. Whirl a psychrometer for several minutes inside the classroom, and a different psychrometer outside the building. Record both the wet and dry bulb values for each psychrometer.

1. Complete Table 4–1 by using your data, as well as the Psychrometric Table for Relative Humidity Determination (Table 4–2) and the Psychrometric Table for Dew Point Temperature Determination (Table 4–3).

Variables	Scenario 1	Scenario 2	Scenario 3	Scenario 4	Inside	Outside
Dry bulb temperature (°C)	20	28	0	36		
Wet bulb temperature (°C)	15	20	−1	26		
Wet bulb depression	5					
Relative humidity (%)	58					
Dew point (°C)	12					

TABLE 4–1

Wet Bulb Depression (°C)

°C	1	2	3	4	5	6	7	8	9	10	11	12	13	14	15	16	17	18	19	20	21	22
-4	77	54	32	11																		
-2	79	58	37	20	1																	
0	81	63	45	28	11																	
2	83	67	51	36	20	6																
4	85	70	56	42	27	14																
6	86	72	59	46	35	22	10	0														
8	87	74	62	51	39	28	17	6														
10	88	76	65	54	43	33	24	13	4													
12	88	78	67	57	48	38	28	19	10	2												
14	89	79	69	60	50	41	33	25	16	8	1											
16	90	80	71	62	54	45	37	29	21	14	7	1										
18	91	81	72	64	56	48	40	33	26	19	12	6	0									
20	91	82	74	66	58	51	44	36	30	23	17	11	5									
22	92	83	75	68	60	53	46	40	33	27	21	15	10	4	0							
24	92	84	76	69	62	55	49	42	36	30	25	20	14	9	4	0						
26	92	85	77	70	64	57	51	45	39	34	28	23	18	13	9	5						
28	93	86	78	71	65	59	53	45	42	36	31	26	21	17	12	8	4					
30	93	86	79	72	66	61	55	49	44	39	34	29	25	20	16	12	8	4				
32	93	86	80	73	68	62	56	51	46	41	36	32	27	22	19	14	11	8	4			
34	93	86	81	74	69	63	58	52	48	43	38	34	30	26	22	18	14	11	8	5		
36	94	87	81	75	69	64	59	54	50	44	40	36	32	28	24	21	17	13	10	7	4	
38	94	87	82	76	70	66	60	55	51	46	42	38	34	30	26	23	20	16	13	10	7	5
40	94	89	82	76	71	67	61	57	52	48	44	40	36	33	29	25	22	19	16	13	10	7

(Dry Bulb Temperature (°C) — left axis label)

TABLE 4–2: Psychrometric Table for Relative Humidity Determination

Wet Bulb Depression (°C)

Dry Bulb Temperature (°C)

°C	1	2	3	4	5	6	7	8	9	10	11	12	13	14	15	16	17	18	19	20	21	22
-4	-7	-22	-17	-29																		
-2	-5	-8	-13	-20																		
0	-3	-6	-9	-15	-24																	
2	-1	-3	-6	-11	-17																	
4	1	-1	-4	-7	-11	-19																
6	4	1	-1	-4	-7	-13	-21															
8	6	3	1	-2	-5	-9	-14															
10	8	6	4	1	-2	-5	-9	-14	-28													
12	10	8	6	4	1	-2	-5	-9	-16													
14	12	11	9	6	4	1	-2	-5	-10	-17												
16	14	13	11	9	7	4	1	-1	-6	-10	-17											
18	16	15	13	11	9	7	4	2	-2	-5	-10	-19										
20	19	17	15	14	12	10	7	4	2	-2	-5	-10	-19									
22	21	19	17	16	14	12	10	8	5	3	-1	-5	-10	-19								
24	23	21	20	18	16	14	12	10	8	6	2	-1	-5	-10	-18							
26	25	23	22	20	18	17	15	13	11	9	6	3	0	-4	-9	-18						
28	27	25	24	22	21	19	17	16	14	11	9	7	4	1	-3	-9	-16					
30	29	27	26	24	23	21	19	18	16	14	12	10	8	5	1	-2	-8	-15				
32	31	29	28	27	25	24	22	21	19	17	15	13	11	8	5	2	-2	-7	-14			
34	33	31	30	29	27	26	24	23	21	20	18	16	14	12	9	6	3	-1	-5	-12	-29	
36	35	33	32	31	29	28	27	25	24	22	20	19	17	15	13	10	7	4	0	-4	-10	
38	37	35	34	33	32	30	29	28	26	25	23	21	19	17	15	13	11	8	5	1	-3	-9
40	39	37	36	35	34	32	31	30	28	27	25	24	22	20	18	16	14	12	9	6	2	-2

TABLE 4–3: Psychrometric Table for Dew Point Temperature Determination

2. Assume you are gathering data using a sling psychrometer. Also assume that the air feels extremely humid. Would you expect a large or small wet bulb depression, and why?

_____

_____

3. Assume you are gathering data using a sling psychrometer. Also assume that the air is extremely dry. Would you expect a large or small wet bulb depression, and why?

_____

_____

Summary of Key Terms and Concepts:
- Condensation is a warming process because it releases latent heat to the environment.
- The dew point temperature is the temperature at which air becomes saturated. A high dew point temperature indicates high atmospheric water vapor content.
- Evaporation is a cooling process because it absorbs heat energy from the environment.
- Humidity refers to the water vapor content of the air.
- Latent heat is energy (often measured in calories) that is either absorbed or released as phase change occurs.
- Relative humidity is the ratio of water vapor content to water vapor capacity of the air. When the relative humidity is 100% the air is saturated.
- Water vapor capacity increases as temperature increases, and it decreases as temperature decreases.
- Water on Earth exists as a solid, liquid, and/or gas. These three states of matter are called phases. Water transitions between its three phases through melting, evaporation, condensation, and freezing.

LAB #8

Station Models, Isobars, and Pressure Gradient Force

Recommended Textbook Reading Prior to Lab:
- Chapter 4, Atmospheric Circulation and Wind Systems
  - 4.1 Measuring and Mapping Wind
  - 4.2 Air Pressure and Wind

Goals: After completing this lab, you will be able to:
- Interpret and assemble station models.
- Calculate sea level pressure from station pressure data at different elevations.
- Create an isobar map illustrating pressure differences across the United States.
- Carry out pressure gradient force calculations and summarize your findings.
- Identify specific weather variables represented on a station model.
- Identify high and low pressure cells by interpreting the direction and motion of air.

Key Terms and Concepts:
- anticyclones
- barometer
- controls on the wind
- cyclones
- isobars
- pressure gradient force
- station pressure
- wind names
- wind streamlines

Required Materials:
- Calculator
- Textbook: *Living Physical Geography,* by Bruce Gervais

85

Problem-Solving Module #1: Station Models

Station models symbolize numerous weather variables at a given location and thereby enable efficient and accurate meteorological data collection and comparison. Figure 1–1 is a simplified station model. At first glance it may seem cryptic, but each symbol and number is one piece of local meteorological data.

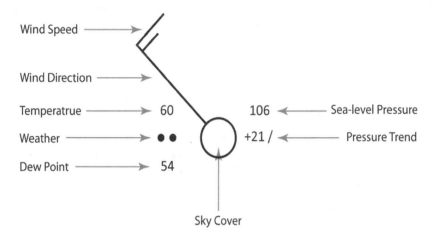

FIGURE 1–1

Wind: Plotted in 5 knot (kt) increments. (1 knot is about 1.15 miles per hour. To visualize 1 knot, imagine yourself on a boat traveling exactly north or south. Your boat moves at 1 knot if it travels 1 minute of latitude in 1 hour.) The wind symbol always points in the direction from which the wind is blowing. Wind speed is determined by adding the flags, lines, and half-lines, each with the following values:

- Flag: 50 kts
- Line: 10 kts
- Half-line: 5 kts

If the station circle is circled and there is no wind symbol present, the wind is calm at that location. Figure 1–1 illustrates wind blowing from the northwest at 15 knots. Figure 1–2 illustrates additional wind directions and velocities.

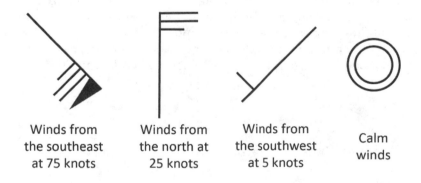

FIGURE 1–2

Temperature: In the United States this is always given in degrees Fahrenheit, °F.

Weather: Plotted to show precipitation or an atmospheric condition that causes reduced visibility. Figure 1–1 illustrates light rain. Figure 1–3 illustrates additional weather symbols.

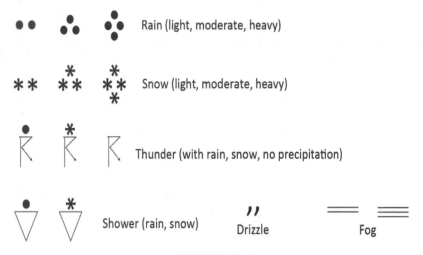

FIGURE 1–3

Dew Point: In the United States this is always given in degrees Fahrenheit,°F.

Sea-level Pressure: Plotted in tenths of millibars (mb) with the leading 10 or 9 omitted. If the first written digit is 6, 7, 8, or 9, a 9 has been omitted. If the first written digit is 0, 1, 2, 3, or 4, a 10 has been omitted. Another way to determine if it's the 10 or 9 that has been omitted is to imagine a 10 or 9 in front of the stated pressure—the one closest to 1,000 (after placing a decimal point between the last two digits) is the real pressure. Figure 1–1 illustrates sea-level pressure as 106. Since 1 is the first written digit, a 10 has been omitted, so the actual pressure is 1010.6 mb. Here are some additional examples.

- 410 = 1041.0 mb
- 103 = 1010.3 mb
- 987 = 998.7 mb
- 872 = 987.2 mb

Pressure Trend: A number and a symbol are needed to illustrate how sea-level pressure changed over the past 3 hours. The number illustrates the 3–hour change in tenths of a millibar and is either positive (meaning increasing pressure over the past 3 hours) or negative (meaning decreasing pressure over the past 3 hours). The symbol to the right of the number graphically illustrates how that change occurred. Figure 1–1 illustrates +21 as the number and "/" as the symbol. Therefore, over the past 3 hours the pressure has continuously risen by 2.1 mb. Figure 1–4 illustrates additional pressure trends.

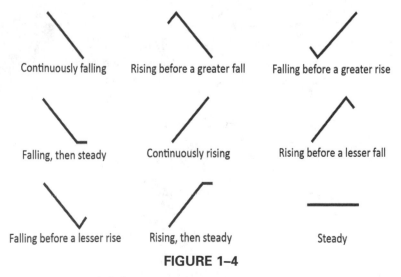

FIGURE 1–4

Sky Cover: The amount of shading within the station model circle illustrates the amount of sky that is covered with clouds. Figure 1–1 illustrates a clear sky. Figure 1–5 illustrates additional sky cover symbols.

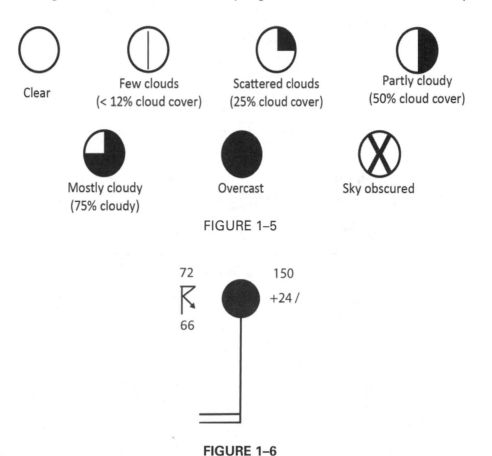

FIGURE 1–5

FIGURE 1–6

1. Decode the station model in Figure 1–6 on Table 1–1.

Wind Speed (kts)	Wind Direction	Temperature (°F)	Weather	Dew Point (°F)	Sea-level Pressure (mb)	Pressure Trend	Sky Cover

TABLE 1–1

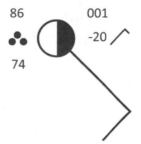

FIGURE 1–7

2. Decode the station model in Figure 1–7 on Table 1–2.

Wind Speed (kts)	Wind Direction	Temperature (°F)	Weather	Dew Point (°F)	Sea-level Pressure (mb)	Pressure Trend	Sky Cover

TABLE 1–2

3. Sketch a station model in Figure 1–8 with the meteorological variables presented in Table 1–3.

Wind Speed (kts)	Wind Direction	Temperature (°F)	Weather	Dew Point (°F)	Sea-level Pressure (mb)	Pressure Trend	Sky Cover
25	North	30	Moderate snow	28	999.6	Down 3.1 mb, steady	Overcast

TABLE 1–3

FIGURE 1–8

4. Sketch a station model in Figure 1–9 with the meteorological variables presented in Table 1–4.

Wind Speed (kts)	Wind Direction	Temperature (°F)	Weather	Dew Point (°F)	Sea-level Pressure (mb)	Pressure Trend	Sky Cover
5	West	78	No precipitation	62	1002.2	Up 1.6, rising then steady	Few clouds

TABLE 1–4

FIGURE 1–9

Problem-Solving Module #2: Station Pressure

Note these critical details about pressure and elevation:
- Average atmospheric pressure at sea level is 1013.25 mb.
- The term "station pressure" refers to a station's air pressure that is unconverted relative to sea level (recall from Lab #4 that air pressure decreases as elevation increases).
- The tem "sea-level pressure" refers to a station's air pressure that has the effect of elevation subtracted from the station pressure—thus, the data are corrected for elevation.
- In the lower troposphere, every 100 meters you go up, air pressure drops by 10 mb.

1. Use the above details to complete Table 2–1.

Station	Elevation (m)	Average Station Pressure (mb)
Lexington, Virginia	324	
Bern, Switzerland	542	
Kathmandu, Nepal	1,400	
Mexico City, Mexico	2,241	
La Paz, Bolivia	3,640	

TABLE 2–1

2. Meteorologists must subtract the effects of _____ when accounting for surface pressure differences between geographic regions.

3. If meteorologists considered only station pressure, mountainous areas would always have the _____ pressure and thus air would always be predicted to move
   (highest/lowest)
   _____ them.
   (toward/away from)

Problem-Solving Module #3: Isobars, Pressure Gradient Force, and Wind

Isobars are lines that connect places of equal barometric pressure (they are graphically akin to contour lines that connect places of equal elevation—seen in Lab #2). Isobars allow map users to quickly assess pressure patterns across large areas. They are created using the following guidelines.

- Isobars never cross each other.
- Isobars are typically spaced 4 millibars apart.
- Drawing isobars requires estimating their placement on a map.
- Widely spaced isobars indicate little barometric pressure difference.
- Widely spaced isobars indicate light winds.
- Narrowly spaced isobars indicate a lot of barometric pressure difference over a short distance.
- Narrowly spaced isobars indicate strong winds.

1. Finish drawing the isobars in Figure 3–1. The 1016 isobars are already drawn for you.

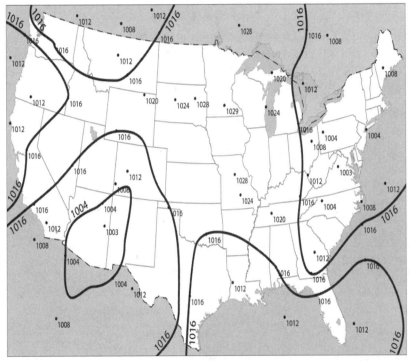

Research from National Atlas/USGS

FIGURE 3–1

2. Based on your completed work in Figure 3–1, does Colorado or Wyoming have stronger winds?

_____

3. Based on your completed work in Figure 3–1, does Georgia or Ohio have stronger winds?

_____

4. Figure 3–1 has three low-pressure centers and one high-pressure center. Place a large letter "L" in each low pressure center and a large letter "H in the single high pressure center.

5. Based on your completed work in Figure 3–1, is the high pressure center over Minnesota or Arizona?

_____

6. Based on your completed work in Figure 3–1, is the pressure center over Virginia and Pennsylvania a cyclone or anticyclone?

_____

7. Based on your completed work in Figure 3–1, are winds blowing "in, toward the center" or "out, from the center" of the pressure center over Virginia and Pennsylvania?

_____

8. Based on your completed work in Figure 3–1, are winds blowing clockwise or counterclockwise in the pressure center over Virginia and Pennsylvania?

_____

9. Draw streamlines on Figure 3–1 indicating the wind direction around the high pressure center.

10. Draw streamlines on Figure 3–1 indicating the wind direction around the pressure center above Arizona and New Mexico.

Pressure gradient force (Pgf) is the horizontal change in atmospheric pressure across a region. Pgf works to equalize pressure differences across areas; it causes high-pressure air to move toward low-pressure air. A high Pgf value indicates a steep gradient and thus strong winds. A low Pgf value indicates a shallow gradient and thus light winds. Pgf values are often reported in units of mb/km.

Calculating the Pgf between two locations requires knowing:
- The air pressure at both locations.
- The distance between both locations.

11. Greenville is 200 kilometers from Franklin. Greenville's barometric pressure is 990 mb, and Franklin's barometric pressure is 1002 mb. What is the Pgf between Greenville and Franklin?

_____

12. Clinton is 200 kilometers from Springfield. Clinton's barometric pressure is 989 mb, and Springfield's barometric pressure is 1009 mb. What is the Pgf between Clinton and Springfield?

_____

13. Is the wind stronger between Greenville and Franklin or between Clinton and Springfield?

_____

Summary of Key Terms and Concepts:
- In the northern hemisphere, an anticyclone rotates clockwise around a high-pressure center.
- A barometer measures atmospheric pressure.
- Controls on the wind include pressure gradient force, Coriolis force, and friction.
- In the northern hemisphere, a cyclone rotates counterclockwise around a low-pressure center.
- Isobars are used to map pressure gradients.
- Pressure gradient force (Pgf) is the horizontal change in atmospheric pressure across a region.
- Station pressure is a station's air pressure that is unconverted relative to sea level.
- Winds are named by the direction they come from.
- Wind streamlines are symbols that are used to portray wind direction on maps.

LAB #9

Winds, Fronts, Midlatitude Cyclones, and Air Masses

Recommended Textbook Reading Prior to Lab:
- Chapter 4, Atmospheric Circulation and Wind Systems
  - 4.3 Global Atmospheric Circulation Patterns
  - 4.4 Wind Systems: Sea Breezes to Gravity Winds
- Chapter 5, The Restless Sky: Storm Systems and El Niño
  - 5.4 Midlatitude Cyclones

Goals: After completing this lab, you will be able to:
- Identify the variables contributing to land and sea breezes.
- Determine the Tibetan Plateau pressure characteristic associated with the summer and winter monsoons of South Asia.
- Deconstruct the anatomy of a midlatitude cyclone and integrate this knowledge with weather predictions.
- Analyze the distinguishing characteristics of cold fronts and warm fronts.
- Predict weather associated with cold fronts and warms fronts using Google Earth and a midlatitude cyclone image overlay.
- Analyze weather forecasts and determine the most likely associated air masses using Google Earth.

Key Terms and Concepts:
- air masses
- Asian monsoon
- breezes
- cold fronts
- midlatitude cyclone
- warm fronts
- weather associated with fronts

Required Materials:
- Calculator
- High-speed Internet connection (for Modules 4 and 5) and Google Earth (free download at http://www.google.com/earth/download/ge/agree.html)
- Textbook: *Living Physical Geography,* by Bruce Gervais

Problem-Solving Module #1: Sea Breezes (Onshore Winds) and Land Breezes (Offshore Winds)

	6 a.m.	8 a.m.	10 a.m.	12 p.m.	2 p.m.	4 p.m.	6 p.m.	8 p.m.	10 p.m.	12 a.m.	2 a.m.	4 a.m.
Coastal City's Boardwalk	30.14	30.13	30.13	30.11	30.11	30.09	30.09	30.10	30.12	30.13	30.13	30.15
Research Buoy #101 at Sea	30.10	30.11	30.12	30.13	30.13	30.13	30.12	30.12	30.11	30.11	30.10	30.10

TABLE 1–1: Air Pressure (inHg)

1. Coastal City's boardwalk is located 150 km from Research Buoy #101, which is deployed at sea. Table 1–1 illustrates the typical air pressure recorded at each site throughout a typical 24-hour period. Using a solid line for Coastal City, and a dashed line for Research Buoy #101, plot each location's air pressure on Figure 1–1.

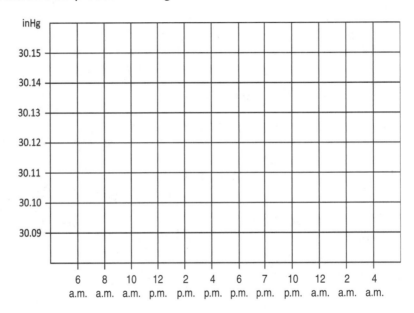

FIGURE 1–1

	6 a.m.	8 a.m.	10 a.m.	12 p.m.	2 p.m.	4 p.m.	6 p.m.	8 p.m.	10 p.m.	12 a.m.	2 a.m.	4 a.m.
Coastal City's Boardwalk	25.5	26	27	27.5	28	28.5	27.5	27	26.5	26	25.5	24.5
Research Buoy #101 at Sea	26	26	26	26.5	27	27	27	26.5	26	26	25.5	25.5

TABLE 1–2: Temperature (°C)

2. Table 1–2 illustrates the typical air temperature recorded at each site throughout a typical 24–hour period. Using a solid line for Coastal City, and a dashed line for Research Buoy #101, plot each location's air temperature on Figure 1–2.

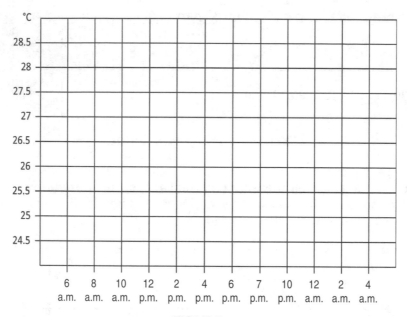

FIGURE 1–2

3. Coastal City has the lowest pressure when its temperature is the _____.

    (highest/lowest)

4. Coastal City has the highest pressure when its temperature is the _____.

    (highest/lowest)

5. Air always flows from _____ pressure areas to _____ pressure areas.

    (high/low)   (high/low)

6. Looking at Figure 1–1, at **4 p.m.** air would flow from _____

    (Research Buoy #1 / Coastal City's Boardwalk)

    to _____.

    (Research Buoy #1 / Coastal City's Boardwalk)

7. Based on your previous answer, the **4 p.m.** air flow is called a _____ breeze, or

    a(n) _____ wind.

8. Looking at Figure 1, at **4 a.m.**, air would flow from _____ to

    (Research Buoy #1 / Coastal City's Boardwalk)

    _____.

    (Research Buoy #1 / Coastal City's Boardwalk)

9. Based on your previous answer, the **4 p.m.** air flow is called a _____ breeze, or

    a(n) _____ wind.

10. True/False: The above two breezes are synoptic scale events.

Problem-Solving Module #2: South Asia Monsoon

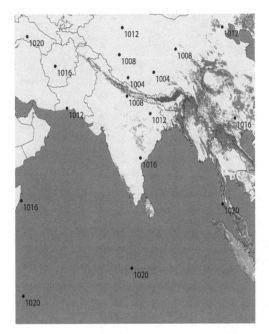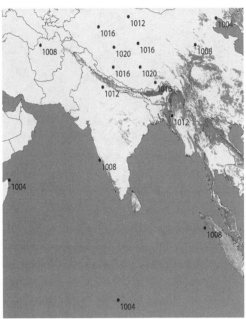

Research from NASA

June–September
Summer Monsoon

June–September
Summer Monsoon

FIGURE 2–1

1. Complete the following on Figure 2–1. (*Hint: A similar exercise is found in Lab #8.*)
   - Draw isobars.
   - Place a letter "L" in the low-pressure center and a letter "H" in the high-pressure center.
   - Draw streamlines indicating the wind direction for both monsoon seasons.

2. Why would South Asians expect rainy weather from June through September, the summer monsoon?

   _____

   _____

   _____

3. Why would South Asians expect dry weather from October through May, the winter monsoon?

   _____

   _____

   _____

4. True/False: The South Asian monsoon is a synoptic scale event.

Problem-Solving Module #3: Cold Fronts and Warm Fronts

1. Complete Table 3–1.

Front	Temperature Expected to...	Duration of Precipitation	Frontal Slope	Cloud Progression	Associated Weather
Cold			Steep		
	Rise				Gentle showers

TABLE 3–1

2. What does the frontal slope of a cold air mass do to the warm air it is moving toward?

_____

3. How are cold fronts symbolized on a weather map?

_____

4. What does the frontal slope of a warm air mass do to the cold air it is moving toward?

_____

5. How are warm fronts symbolized on a weather map?

_____

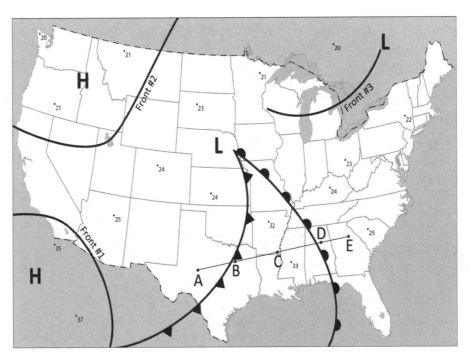

Research from National Atlas/USGS

FIGURE 3–1: Fronts, Midlatitude Cyclone, and Temperatures (°C)

For questions 6–14, assume observers are standing at locations A through E on Figure 3–1.

6. The observer at location _____ is seeing cumulonimbus clouds and severe thunderstorms.

7. The observer at location _____ is experiencing overcast skies and continuous, moderate rain.

8. The observer at location _____ experienced the passage of a front and is now enjoying cool, dry air.

9. The observer at location _____ is looking west and seeing cirrus clouds high overhead.

10. The observer at location _____ is experiencing warm, tropical air with scattered cumulus clouds.

11. The observer at location _____ is standing closest to the warm front.

12. The observer at location _____ is standing closest to the cold front.

13. The observer at location _____ is most likely to experience a tornado.

14. The observer at location _____ is situated in the middle of the warm sector.

15. Front #1 on Figure 3–1 is most likely a _____ front. Explain your reasoning.
         (cold/warm)

_____

_____

_____

16. Front #2 on Figure 3–1 is most likely a _____ front. Explain your reasoning.
         (cold/warm)

_____

_____

_____

17. Front #3 on Figure 3–1 is most likely a _____ front. Explain your reasoning.
         (cold/warm)

_____

_____

_____

18. How does the pressure associated with front #3 explain its movement to the southeast?
    (Hint: Imagine streamlines.)

_____

_____

_____

Problem-Solving Module #4: Midlatitude Cyclone

Download the following file from the book companion site and open it within Google Earth:
  • Mid-Latitude Cyclone.kmz

Use the file to answer the following questions. For questions 1–5, indicate whether the answer is A, B, C, D, or E.

1. Placemark ___ is associated with the following weather forecast: Expect continued overcast skies with moderate, continuous rain from overhead nimbostratus clouds. Over the next 12 hours, expect temperatures to grow warmer and winds to begin blowing from the southwest.

2. Placemark ___ is associated with the following weather forecast: Expect continued clear skies, dry air, and no precipitation. Temperatures will remain cool with winds continuing to blow from the northwest.

3. Placemark ___ is associated with the following weather forecast: Expect the current cirrus clouds in the western skies to lower and thicken over the next 12 hours. Overcast skies are expected, with moderate precipitation lasting about two days.

4. Placemark ___ is associated with the following weather forecast: Expect severe weather, with cumulonimbus clouds, thunderstorms, hail, and possibly tornadoes. Over the next several hours temperatures will quickly fall and winds will begin to blow from the northwest.

5. Placemark ___ is associated with the following weather forecast: Expect continued warm and humid conditions due to the maritime tropical air mass we are currently under. Expect moderate, cumulus cloud cover overhead and no precipitation over the next 6 hours.

6. True/False: Illinois is beneath the low-pressure center of the midlatitude cyclone and is likely experiencing overcast skies with continuously rainy conditions.

7. True/False: Southeastern Illinois and northwestern Indiana are probably experiencing severe weather and may even be issued a tornado watch by the National Weather Service.

8. True/False: Oklahoma is probably experiencing severe weather and possibly even tornadoes.

9. True/False: Ohio is probably experiencing clear skies, cool temperatures, dry air, and an occasional cumulus cloud overhead.

Problem-Solving Module #5: Air Masses

1. Complete Table 5–1.

Air Mass	Abbreviation	Source Region	Characteristics
Continental polar		The polar high	
Maritime polar		The polar high and subpolar low	
Continental tropical		The subtropical high	
Maritime tropical		The ITCZ and the subtropical high	

TABLE 5–1

Download the following file from the book companion site and open it within Google Earth:

• Air Masses.kmz

2. What two characteristics of a cP air mass would make its arrival especially welcome during a typical late summer afternoon in the midwestern United States?

_____

3. What two characteristics of an mT air mass would make its arrival especially unwelcome during a typical late summer afternoon in the midwestern United States?

_____

4. What kind of air mass would bring heavy wet snow into Oregon and northern California during January, and where would this air mass originate?

_____

5. Assume you are in southern California. What kind of air mass would bring heavy rains, potential flooding, and snow melt at higher elevations? Where would this air mass originate?

_____

6. Assume you are in Alabama in July. What type of air mass would bring hot, humid weather, and where would this air mass originate?

_____

7. Assume you are in Iowa during early February. What type of air mass would bring cold, clear, and dry weather, and where would this air mass originate?

_____

8. Assume you are in New England during October. What type of air mass would likely bring cold temperatures and heavy rains, and where would this air mass originate?

_____

9. Assume you are in New Mexico during August. What type of air mass would likely bring high temperatures and clear dry conditions, and where would this air mass originate?

_____

Summary of Key Terms and Concepts:

- Air masses extend over thousands of kilometers, extend upward several kilometers from Earth's surface, and are physically homogeneous (the same throughout).
- The Asian monsoon brings summer rainfall and winter dryness.
- Breezes along the coast and in the mountains are the result of differences of heating and cooling of Earth's surface.
- Cold fronts occur when cold air masses move into warm air masses.
- Midlatitude cyclones are composed of warm and cold fronts and rotate counterclockwise around a central low-pressure region in the northern hemisphere.
- Warm fronts occur when warm air masses move into cooler air masses.
- Severe weather squall lines sometimes occur on cold fronts, while warm fronts often bring gentle precipitation for extended periods of time.

LAB #10 — Hurricanes

Recommended Textbook Reading Prior to Lab:
- Chapter 5, The Restless Sky: Storm Systems and El Niño
  - 5.3 Nature's Deadliest Storm: Hurricanes

Goals: After completing this lab, you will be able to:
- Classify and analyze hurricanes based on the Saffir-Simpson Hurricane Wind Scale.
- Determine and reflect upon the logarithmic scale of economic damages based on increasing hurricane wind speed.
- Recognize the 2012 Hurricane Season Summary Table from NOAA.
- Analyze potential coastal hazards based on the landfall position of historically significant hurricanes.
- Analyze and interpret tropical cyclone advisories from recent hurricanes.
- Create a quadraphonic wind chart using a tropical cyclone advisory.
- Judge potential storm surge and flooding impact at various coastal locations using the NOAA Storm Surge Risk interactive map.
- Carry out probabilistic hurricane storm surge summaries using the NOAA Probabilistic Hurricane Storm Surge interactive map and archive data.

Key Terms and Concepts:
- dangers associated with hurricanes
- eye
- eye wall
- hurricane
- hurricane strength
- rainbands
- Saffir-Simpson Hurricane Wind Scale
- stages of growth to a hurricane
- storm surge
- world hurricane activity

Required Materials:
- Calculator
- High-speed Internet connection (for Module 3) and Google Earth (free download at http://www.google.com/earth/download/ge/agree.html)
- Textbook: *Living Physical Geography,* by Bruce Gervais

Problem-Solving Module #1: Hurricanes, Wind, and Economic Damage

Hurricane-force winds are often reported in miles per hour (mph), knots (kts), and kilometers per hour (km/h). Knowing how these measurements compare is an important first step to understanding hurricane forecasts, classification, and modeling. Table 1–1 provides conversion units among these common units of speed.

Unit of Speed	mph	kts	km/h
1 mph	1	0.868	1.609
1 kt	1.15	1	1.852
1 km/h	0.621	0.539	1

TABLE 1–1

1. Use the values in Table 1–1 to complete the Saffir-Simpson Hurricane Wind Scale presented in Table 1–2.

Category	mph	kts	km/h	Likely Damage to a Typical Home
1	74–95			Damage to roof, shingles, vinyl siding, and gutters
2		83–95		Major roof and siding damage
3			178–208	Major damage or removal of roof decking and gables
4		113–136		Severe damage with loss of most of roof structure and/or some exterior walls
5	≥157			Homes will be destroyed, with total roof failure and wall collapse

TABLE 1–2: The Saffir-Simpson Hurricane Wind Scale

Table 1–2 illustrates that wind speed is the determining variable used to classify hurricanes, and that faster winds create more damage to structures (and thus higher reconstruction costs). Coastal cities, with their dense housing and infrastructure, are especially susceptible to expensive reconstruction costs following a hurricane.

Fast winds are just one of several threats that hurricanes produce. Heavy rains create flooding, and small tornadoes are not uncommon. The deadliest and most destructive element, however, is the storm surge. Where a storm surge makes landfall—whether in a rural or urban environment—makes all the difference between an especially damaging storm and one that yields relatively little destruction. Scientists have found that economic damage resulting from the combined threats of a hurricane rises logarithmically with increasing wind speed. Thus, small increases in hurricane wind speed create very large differences in costs. Table 1–3 illustrates how much more a hurricane will cost in damages as wind speed increases. Note that the cost multiplier is in reference to the economic cost associated with a category 1 hurricane with maximum sustained winds of 75 mph.

Category	One					Two			Three		
Wind speed (mph)	75	80	85	90	95	100	105	110	115	120	125
Cost multiplier	1x	1.6x	2.9x	4.3x	6.6x	10x	15x	21x	30x	43x	60x

Category	Four					
Wind speed (mph)	130	135	140	145	150	155
Cost multiplier	82x	110x	147x	195x	256x	333x

Category	Five						
Wind speed (mph)	160	165	170	175	180	185	190
Cost multiplier	429x	549x	697x	879x	1101x	1371x	1696x

TABLE 1–3

2. Graph the data in Table 1–3 on Figure 1–1.

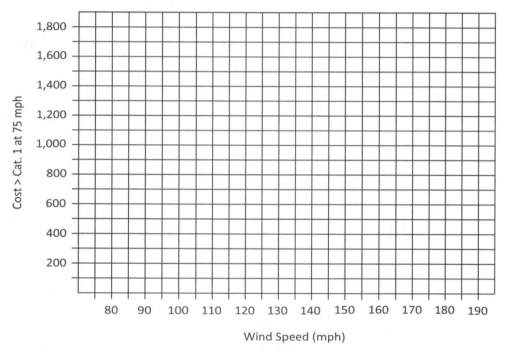

FIGURE 1–1

Consider the data in Table 1–3 and Figure 1–1 to answer questions 3–10.

3. A category 1 hurricane with maximum sustained winds of 95 mph causes _____times more economic damage than a category 1 hurricane with maximum sustained winds of 75 mph.

4. A category 2 hurricane with maximum sustained winds of 110 mph causes _____ times more economic damage than a category 1 hurricane with maximum sustained winds of 75 mph.

5. A category 3 hurricane with maximum sustained winds of 125 mph causes _____times more economic damage than a category 1 hurricane with maximum sustained winds of 75 mph.

6. A category 3 hurricane with maximum sustained winds of 125 mph causes _____ times more economic damage than a category 3 hurricane with maximum sustained winds of 115 mph, and this is because there is a _____ mph increase in wind speed.

7. A category 4 hurricane with maximum sustained winds of 140 mph causes _____ times more economic damage than a category 4 hurricane with maximum sustained winds of 130 mph, and this is because there is a _____ mph increase in wind speed.

8. A category 5 hurricane with maximum sustained winds of 170 mph causes _____ times more economic damage than a category 5 hurricane with maximum sustained winds of 160 mph, and this is because there is a _____ mph increase in wind speed.

9. A category 5 hurricane with maximum sustained winds of 190 mph causes _____ times more economic damage than a category 5 hurricane with maximum sustained winds of 180 mph, and this is because there is a _____ mph increase in wind speed.

10. Small increases in hurricane wind speed create very _____ differences in economic damage.   (small/large)

2012 Tropical Cyclone	Max Wind (mph)	Economic Damage to United States
Debby (tropical storm)	65	$250 million
Isaac (category 1 hurricane)	80	$2.35 billion
Sandy (category 3 hurricane)	115	$50 billion

TABLE 1–4

11. Use the information in Figure 1–1 and Table 1–4 to explain the relationship between wind speed and economic damage. Be sure to explain how logarithmic changes result with changing wind speed.

_____

_____

_____

Problem-Solving Module #2: Hurricane Forecast Advisories and Quadraphonic Wind Charts

Figure 2–1 presents a portion of the Tropical Cyclone Forecast/Advisory for Hurricane Sandy as it approached the New Jersey coastline on October 29, 2012.

The National Hurricane Center issues a Tropical Cyclone Forecast/Advisory (Figure 2–1) to inform people about tropical cyclones. Data on an advisory include (A) the title and office of origination, (B) the time and date of the advisory, (C) any watches and/or warnings, (D) the location of the storm's center, (E) the direction and speed of the storm's motion, and (F) an estimate of the storm's lowest pressure, the diameter of the storm's eye (if known), the maximum sustained wind speed (divided into three speeds: ≥ 64 kt, ≥ 50kt, and ≥ 34 kt), and the radii of maximum wind in the storm's four quadrants, defined as NE (0°–90°), SE (90°–180°), SW (180°–270°), and NW (270°–360°).

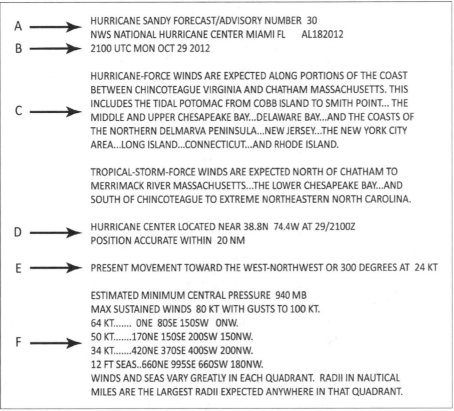

Research from NOAA

FIGURE 2–1

Communities use the information on tropical cyclone advisories to warn people about potential danger and prepare for a storm's landfall. Advisories also allow scientists to illustrate wind fields around a storm's center—which are quite variable—using a quadraphonic wind chart. Figure 2–2 is a quadraphonic wind chart created with Hurricane Sandy data presented in Figure 2–1.

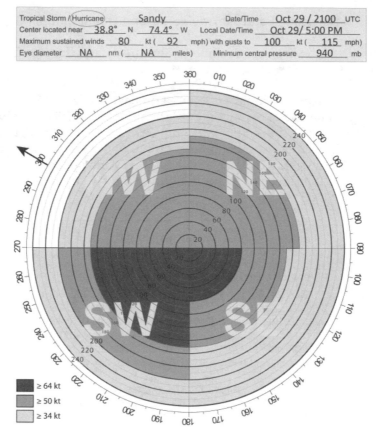

Tropical Storm / Hurricane	Sandy	Date/Time	Oct 29 / 2100 UTC
Center located near 38.8° N 74.4° W		Local Date/Time	Oct 29/ 5:00 PM
Maximum sustained winds 80 kt (92 mph) with gusts to 100 kt (115 mph)			
Eye diameter NA nm (NA miles)		Minimum central pressure	940 mb

≥ 64 kt
≥ 50 kt
≥ 34 kt

Research from NOAA

FIGURE 2–2

The perspective of the quadraphonic wind chart is from above the storm, looking down, with the center of the chart being the eye. The numbers radiating out from the chart's center are nautical miles, from 0 to 250. The arrow at 300° is the forward direction of the hurricane. Data for shading in the chart are taken from the Tropical Cyclone Forecast/Advisory (Figure 2–2), letter F, reporting maximum winds in the storm's four quadrants.

A scientist can thus visualize the following data about Hurricane Sandy at 5:00 p.m. on October 29, 2012:
- The NW and NE quadrants had no wind ≥ 64 knots.
- The SE quadrant had ≥ 64 kt winds extending 80 nautical miles (nm) from the storm's center.
- The SW quadrant had ≥ 64 kt winds extending 150 nautical miles (nm) from the storm's center.

1. Complete Table 2–1 using information from Figure 2–1 and Figure 2–2.

Wind Speed (kt)	NE	SE	SW	NW
> 64	0 nm	80 nm	150 nm	0 nm
≥ 50	_____nm	_____nm	_____nm	_____nm
≥ 34	_____nm	_____nm	_____nm	_____nm

**TABLE 2–1: Extent of Various Winds from Storm's Center,
Hurricane Sandy, 5:00 p.m. October 29, 2012**

2. Figure 2–3 is a portion of the Tropical Cyclone Forecast/Advisory for Hurricane Isaac as it approaches Louisiana on August 28, 2012. Use this figure to create a quadraphonic wind chart in Figure 2–4.

© 2014 W. H. Freeman and Company

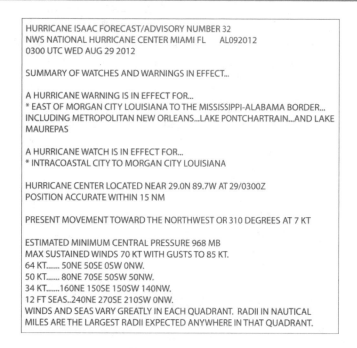

HURRICANE ISAAC FORECAST/ADVISORY NUMBER 32
NWS NATIONAL HURRICANE CENTER MIAMI FL   AL092012
0300 UTC WED AUG 29 2012

SUMMARY OF WATCHES AND WARNINGS IN EFFECT...

A HURRICANE WARNING IS IN EFFECT FOR...
* EAST OF MORGAN CITY LOUISIANA TO THE MISSISSIPPI-ALABAMA BORDER...
INCLUDING METROPOLITAN NEW ORLEANS...LAKE PONTCHARTRAIN...AND LAKE
MAUREPAS

A HURRICANE WATCH IS IN EFFECT FOR...
* INTRACOASTAL CITY TO MORGAN CITY LOUISIANA

HURRICANE CENTER LOCATED NEAR 29.0N 89.7W AT 29/0300Z
POSITION ACCURATE WITHIN 15 NM

PRESENT MOVEMENT TOWARD THE NORTHWEST OR 310 DEGREES AT 7 KT

ESTIMATED MINIMUM CENTRAL PRESSURE 968 MB
MAX SUSTAINED WINDS 70 KT WITH GUSTS TO 85 KT.
64 KT....... 50NE 50SE 0SW 0NW.
50 KT....... 80NE 70SE 50SW 50NW.
34 KT.......160NE 150SE 150SW 140NW.
12 FT SEAS..240NE 270SE 210SW 0NW.
WINDS AND SEAS VARY GREATLY IN EACH QUADRANT. RADII IN NAUTICAL
MILES ARE THE LARGEST RADII EXPECTED ANYWHERE IN THAT QUADRANT.

Research from NOAA

FIGURE 2–3

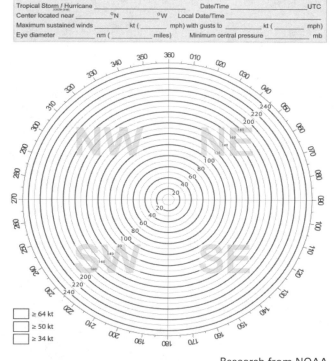

Research from NOAA

FIGURE 2–4: Quadraphonic Wind Chart

3. Complete Table 2–2 using information from Figures 2–3 and 2–4.

Wind Speed (kt)	NE	SE	SW	NW
≥ 64	_____nm	_____nm	_____nm	_____nm
≥ 50	_____nm	_____nm	_____nm	_____nm
≥ 34	_____nm	_____nm	_____nm	_____nm

TABLE 2–2: Extent of Various Winds from Storm's Center, Hurricane Isaac, 7:00 p.m. August 28, 2012

Problem-Solving Module #3: Storm Surges

To answer questions 1–6, navigate to the following NOAA Website: http://www.nhc.noaa.gov/surge/

1. A storm _____ is an abnormal rise of water generated by a storm that is higher than any predicted astronomical tides.

2. A storm tide is a combination of what two variables?

   _____

3. What two forces create a storm surge, and what are their respective percentage contributions to any storm surge?

   _____

   _____

4. Why might a category 4 storm hitting the Louisiana coastline create a 20-foot storm surge, while the same hurricane hitting Miami Beach in Florida create only a 9-foot storm surge?

   _____

   _____

5. Water weighs approximately _____ pounds per cubic _____.

6. What two areas are especially susceptible to salt water intrusion from a storm surge?

   _____

Scroll down to the Galveston 1900 bullet and click on the SLOSH Historical Run link. Click the ">" button in the upper-left corner to reset the Galveston SLOSH loop. The date beneath the NOAA icon should state 09/08/1900, and the time should read 16:00:00 UTC. Use this animation to answer questions 7–11.

7. To the left of the NOAA icon is the map's key. What color is used to represent a storm tide that is 12 to 15 feet above normal?

   _____

8. Use the ">" button to advance the SLOSH simulation to 09/09/1900 at 00:00:00 UTC. Describe the effect the barrier islands are having with respect to Galveston Bay.

   _____

   _____

9. Use the ">" button to advance the SLOSH simulation to 09/09/1900 at 02:30:00 UTC. Notice that the hurricane center has just made landfall on the southern tip of the Galveston barrier island. The city of Galveston, on the northern tip of the island, is now experiencing a storm tide of how many feet? (*Hint: Ignore the dark blue pixels beneath the Galveston star and concentrate on the water off the island.*)

   _____

10. On 09/09/1900 at 02:30:00 UTC, what quadrant of the Galveston Hurricane had the highest storm tide?

   _____

11. Describe the storm tide in the SW quadrant of the Galveston Hurricane on 09/09/1900 at 02:30:00 UTC.

   _____

   _____

Summary of Key Terms and Concepts:

- Dangers associated with hurricanes include coastal flooding and sustained high winds.
- The eye of a hurricane is the center of the cyclone. It is characterized by relatively clearer skies and warmer temperature due to slowly subsiding air undergoing adiabatic warming that forms a temperature inversion above the ocean's surface.
- The eye wall of a hurricane surrounds the eye. It is characterized by the highest sustained winds within the hurricane and strong updrafts.
- A hurricane is a cyclone of tropical origin that has sustained wind speeds of at least 119 km/h (74 mph) or greater.
- Hurricanes derive their strength from a latent heat positive feedback.
- Rainbands are elongated and curved cloud configurations that form concentric, spiraling patterns on the periphery a hurricane. They are characterized by heavy rainfall, squalls (sudden, intense winds), and occasionally tornadoes.
- The Saffir-Simpson Hurricane Wind Scale ranks hurricanes on a scale of 1 through 5 based on sustained wind speed. Category 5 hurricanes have the fastest sustained winds of 157 mph (137 kt, 252 km/h) and higher.
- Hurricanes go through a series of formation stages based on sustained wind speed. These stages are tropical disturbance, tropical depression, tropical storm, and hurricane.
- A storm surge is an unusual increase in coastal water levels (exceeding any normal tides) that is caused by a storm's winds and low pressure.
- World hurricane activity is restricted to tropical oceans and does not occur within about 5° latitude of the equator due to a lack of Coriolis force.

LAB #11 Climate, Weather, Carbon, and Greenhouse Gases

Recommended Textbook Reading Prior to Lab:
- Chapter 6, The Changing Climate
  - 6.1 The Climate System
  - 6.3 Carbon and Climate

Goals: After completing this lab, you will be able to:
- Identify selected atmospheric conditions as weather or climate phenomena.
- Provide examples of positive and negative climate feedbacks.
- Calculate CO_2 emissions from selected fuel sources.
- Clarify the difference between Global Warming Potential (GWP) and carbon dioxide equivalency (CO_2Eq) while calculating the CO_2Eq of selected greenhouse gases (GHG).
- Predict the CO_2 levels from fresh air versus air from an auto exhaust pipe, and generate a hypothesis about your prediction.
- Carry out CO_2 data collection using lab equipment and determine the CO_2 levels from fresh air versus air from an auto exhaust pipe.
- Judge your CO_2 hypothesis.

Key Terms and Concepts:
- carbon dioxide
- carbon dioxide equivalency (CO_2Eq)
- climate
- climate change
- climate feedback
- climate forcings
- Global Warming Potential (GWP)
- greenhouse gas (GHG)
- weather

Required Materials:
- Calculator
- For Module 4 only:
  - Pasco CO_2 Gas Sensor (Pasco: PS–2110)
  - Pasco Xplorer Datalogger (Pasco: PS–2000)
  - Two 250-ml sample bottles
- Textbook: *Living Physical Geography*, by Bruce Gervais

Problem-Solving Module #1: Weather versus Climate

1. In Table 1–1, place an X beneath either Weather or Climate, thereby classifying each phenomenon.

Phenomenon	Weather	Climate
Thunderstorm		
Karoo (360–260 Ma) Ice Age		
Averaged precipitation data from the past three decades		
Sea breeze		
Pliocene (5.3–2.5 Ma) warming		
An F-3 tornado		

TABLE 1–1

2. To represent the climate of a given region, what are the four weather observations that are averaged together over a 30-year period?

_____

3. How much has the average temperature of Earth's lower atmosphere increased since 1880?

_____

4. Can atmospheric scientists definitively state that extreme weather events, such as a large hurricane or a severe drought, are caused by global warming? Why or why not, and how does the temporal scale of extreme weather events contrast with the temporal scale of studies examining global warming?

_____

_____

_____

_____

_____

_____

_____

_____

5. In your own words, explain how climate *forcings* are different from climate *feedbacks*, and provide examples of each.

_____

_____

_____

_____

_____

_____

_____

_____

6. Explain why a period of increased volcanism in Earth's history is an example of a climate forcing instead of a climate feedback.

_____

_____

_____

_____

7. Climate feedbacks _____ or _____ climate change that has already been set in motion.

8. Do positive feedbacks stabilize or destabilize systems?

_____

9. Do negative feedbacks stabilize or destabilize systems?

_____

10. In Table 1–2, place an X beneath either Positive Feedback or Negative Feedback, thereby classifying each phenomenon.

Phenomenon	Positive Feedback	Negative Feedback
Increased CO_2 in Earth's atmosphere warms the climate, which increases plant growth rates. Increased plant growth rates then pull the increased CO_2 levels out of the atmosphere.		
A warming climate increases the amount of water vapor in the atmosphere, thereby causing further warming.		
A warming ocean destabilizes methane hydrates (frozen methane on the seafloor). This releases methane as gas to the atmosphere, further increasing atmospheric and ocean temperatures.		
A warming climate melts Earth's ice caps, thereby decreasing Earth's albedo and inducing further warming.		

TABLE 1–2

Problem-Solving Module #2: Carbon Dioxide (CO_2) Emissions

When fossil-fuel energy resources such as coal, petroleum, and natural gas are burned, carbon dioxide (CO_2) is an unavoidable byproduct. Ever-increasing amounts of CO_2 have been emitted into Earth's atmosphere since the Industrial Revolution, when large-scale consumption of fossil fuels began. Table 2–1 presents how much carbon dioxide is emitted when we consume selected fuels. Note: All values were obtained from the United States Energy Information Administration (EIA): http://www.eia.gov/environment/emissions/co2_vol_mass.cfm

Fuel	Pounds of CO_2 per Unit	Kilograms of CO_2 per Unit
Coal (average of all types)	4,631.5/short ton	1,911.7/metric ton
Methane (CH_4)	117.1/thousand cubic feet	1.5 kg/thousand cubic meters
Gasoline	19.6/gallon	2.3 kg/liter
Jet fuel	21.1/gallon	2.5 kg/liter
Propane (C_3H_8)	12.7/gallon	1.5 kg/liter

TABLE 2–1

Use Table 2–1 to answer questions 1–10.

1. About 1,870 kWh are generated per short ton (2,000 pounds) of coal. In 2011, the average American home annually consumed 11,280 kWh of electricity. Assume you lived in a home in 2011 that consumed the average amount of electricity and got all of its electricity from coal. How many short tons of coal were burned in 2011 to satisfy your home's electricity demand? Be sure to show your work.

   _____

   _____

   _____

2. Based on your answer in question 1, how many pounds of CO_2 were emitted into the atmosphere to satisfy your home's electricity demand in 2011? Be sure to show your work.

   _____

   _____

   _____

3. Based on your answer in question 1, how many metric tons of coal were burned in 2011 to satisfy your home's electricity demand (1 short ton = 0.91 metric ton)? Be sure to show your work.

   _____

   _____

   _____

4. Based on your answer in question 3, how many kilograms of CO_2 were emitted into the atmosphere to satisfy your home's electricity demand in 2011? Be sure to show your work.

   _____

   _____

   _____

5. About 125 kWh are generated per thousand cubic feet of natural gas (methane). In 2011, the average American home annually consumed 11,280 kWh of electricity. Assume you lived in a home in 2011 that consumed the average amount of electricity and got all of its electricity from natural gas. How many thousand cubic feet of natural gas (methane) were burned in 2011 to satisfy your home's electricity demand? Be sure to show your work.

_____

_____

_____

6. Based on your answer in question 5, how many pounds of CO_2 were emitted into the atmosphere to satisfy your home's electricity demand in 2011? Be sure to show your work.

_____

_____

_____

7. Based on your answer in question 6, how many kilograms of CO_2 were emitted into the atmosphere to satisfy your home's electricity demand in 2011 (1 pound = 0.45 kg)? Be sure to show your work.

_____

_____

_____

8. Assume you drive a car that averages 32 miles per gallon (or 13.5 km per liter). Your commute to work is 26 miles (42 km) one way. You work 5 days a week for an entire year (52 weeks), take no holidays or breaks, and never drive the car for anything other than commuting to and from work. How many pounds of CO_2 and how many kilograms of CO_2 are emitted into the air by your car because of your commute to and from work over the course of a year? Be sure to show your work.

_____

_____

_____

_____

_____

9. A Boeing 747-400 flying 3,500 miles (5,632 km) consumes an average of 5 gallons of fuel per mile (11.8 liters of fuel per kilometer). Assume you are on an international vacation and take a Boeing 747-400 from Panama City, Panama to Mar dal Plata, Argentina (3,500 miles). How many pounds of CO_2 and how many kilograms of CO_2 are emitted into the air because of your flight? Be sure to show your work.

_____

_____

_____

_____

_____

10. A typical propane tank for a backyard barbeque holds 4.7 gallons (17.8 liters) of propane. Assume you use an entire tank of propane over several weeks. How many pounds of CO_2 and how many kilograms of CO_2 are emitted into the air because of your barbeque? Be sure to show your work.

_____

_____

_____

_____

Figure 2–1 illustrates carbon CO_2 emissions by region for 1990 and 2007, as well as projected emission within these regions for 2025 and 2035. OECD stands for the Organization for Economic Cooperation and Development. Its members are economically powerful and include the United States and much of Western Europe, as well as Korea, Japan, Australia, and New Zealand. Non-OECD member economies include developing countries and the fast-growing economies of Brazil, China, India, Indonesia, and South Africa.

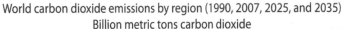

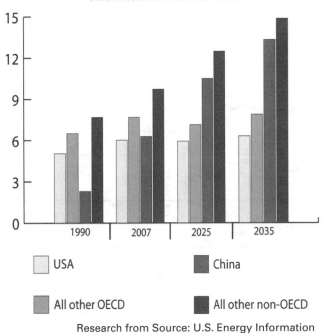

Research from Source: U.S. Energy Information Administration (Mar 2011)

FIGURE 2–1

11. In 1990, how did the United States compare to China in terms of CO_2 emissions?

_____

_____

12. In 2035, how is the United States expected to compare to China in terms of CO_2 emissions?

_____

_____

13. Based on your analysis of Figure 2–1, compose a statement summarizing CO_2 emissions in the United States and China, both in the past and into the future.

_____

_____

_____

_____

14. Of the four regions represented on Figure 2–1, which two regions are expected to produce the greatest volume of CO_2 by 2035?

_____

_____

15. Consider what you have discovered about carbon dioxide emissions by both OECD member and non-member countries. Why do you think the United States and some other OECD member countries are reluctant to curb their carbon dioxide emissions, and what arguments might they use to defend their position? How might non-OECD member countries respond?

_____

_____

_____

_____

_____

_____

_____

_____

_____

_____

Problem-Solving Module #3: Greenhouse Gases (GHGs), Global Warming Potential (GWP), and Carbon Dioxide Equivalent (CO$_2$Eq)

Greenhouse gases (GHGs) are transparent to incoming short-wave radiation from the Sun, but they are opaque to outgoing long-wave radiation from Earth. GHGs thus prevent heat from leaving Earth's atmosphere, thereby warming the planet.

Greenhouse Gas	Chemical Formula	Global Warming Potential (GWP) (100-Year Time Interval)
Carbon dioxide	CO_2	1
Methane	CH_4	25
Nitrous oxide	N_2O	298
Perfluoromethane	CF_4	7,390
Trifluoromethane	CHF_3	14,800
Sulfur hexafluoride	SF_6	22,800

TABLE 3–1: Selected Greenhouse Gases and Their 100-Year Global Warming Potential (GWP)

Table 3–1 presents several GHGs and their global warming potential (GWP). A GWP value is a ratio that compares the warming from a selected mass of a GHG to the warming from the same mass of carbon dioxide over a set period of time. Thus, over 100 years, 1 kilogram of methane traps 25 times more heat energy than 1 kilogram of carbon dioxide. Or, over 100 years, 1 ton of nitrous oxide traps 298 times more heat energy than 1 ton of carbon dioxide.

Carbon dioxide equivalent (CO$_2$Eq) is the quantity of CO_2 that has the same radiative forcing as another GHG over a set period of time. CO$_2$Eq allows scientists to compare GHG emissions based on GWP, which is benchmarked to CO_2. The value of CO$_2$Eq is often stated in *million metric tons of* carbon dioxide equivalents (MMTCO$_2$Eq), and it is calculated by multiplying the tons of the GHG by its GWP.

MMTCO$_2$Eq = million metric tons of the GHG x the GWP of the GHG

Notice that the first three rows in Table 3–2 are finished, and we can thus state the following narrations:
- 2 MMT of CH_2F_2 (difluoromethane) has the same radiative forcing as 1,350 MMT of CO_2.
- 4.6 MMT of CHF_2CHF_2 (tetrafluoroethane) has the same radiative forcing as 5,060 MMT of CO_2.
- 1 MMT of C_3F_8 (perfluoropropane) has the same radiative forcing as 8,830 MMT of CO_2.

1. Complete Table 3–2 using the information in Table 3–1 as well as the MMTCO$_2$Eq equation.

GHG Name	GHG Chemical Formula	Volume (million metric tons)	GWP	MMTCO$_2$Eq
Difluoromethane	CH_2F_2	2	675	1,350
Tetrafluoroethane	CHF_2CHF_2	4.6	1,100	5,060
Perfluoropropane	C_3F_8	1	8,830	8,830
Carbon dioxide	CO_2	1		
Methane	CH_4	7.4		
Nitrous oxide	N_2O	7		
Perfluoromethane	CF_4	1.2		
Trifluoromethane	CHF_3	14		
Sulfur hexafluoride	SF_6	4.6		

TABLE 3–2

For questions 2–4, complete the following narrations of the data that you calculated in Table 3–2.

2. 7.4 MMT of CH_4 has the same radiative forcing as _____ MMT of CO_2.

3. 7 MMT of N_2O has the same radiative forcing as _____ MMT of CO_2.

4. 1.2 MMT of CF_4 has the same radiative forcing as _____ MMT of CO_2.

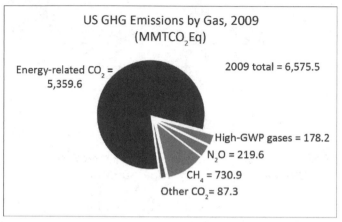

US GHG Emissions by Gas, 2009
(MMTCO$_2$Eq)

Energy-related CO_2 = 5,359.6

2009 total = 6,575.5

High-GWP gases = 178.2
N_2O = 219.6
CH_4 = 730.9
Other CO_2 = 87.3

Research from Source: U.S. Energy Information Administration (Mar 2011)

FIGURE 3–1

Use Figure 3–1 to answer questions 5–7.

5. What percent of U.S. GHG emissions in 2009 were energy related? _____

6. What percent of U.S. GHG emissions in 2009 were from methane? _____

7. What percent of U.S. GHG emissions in 2009 were from nitrous oxide? _____

Problem-Solving Module #4: Emission Data Collection and Analysis

Assume you come across a Website that claims there is no difference between the CO_2 content of fresh air compared to the CO_2 content of air sampled from an exhaust pipe of a gasoline-powered automobile with its engine running. Given what you know about the byproducts of fossil-fuel combustion, you find this claim suspect. You decide to test this claim using the scientific method.

1. State your hypothesis about the CO_2 content of fresh air compared to the CO_2 content of air sampled from an exhaust pipe of a gasoline-powered automobile with its engine running.

   _____

   _____

   _____

2. To test your hypothesis, what data do you need to collect?

   _____

   _____

   _____

   _____

3. Test your hypothesis by collecting data with the Pasco Xplorer Datalogger and CO_2 Gas Sensor. Is your hypothesis supported or not supported by the data?

   _____

   _____

   _____

   _____

4. In your own words, compose a sentence or two that corresponds with Step #6 of the scientific method as it relates to the above scenario. Recall that this step is about further inquiry and includes speculation about new questions, new ideas, and more/different data collecting.

   _____

   _____

   _____

   _____

Summary of Key Terms and Concepts:
  - Carbon dioxide is a greenhouse gas that is produced during combustion of carbon-rich fuels.
  - Carbon dioxide equivalency (CO_2Eq) is the quantity of CO_2 that has the same radiative forcing as a GHG over a set time.
  - Climate is the long-term average and the frequency of extreme events.
  - Climate change occurs when the long-term trend of weather changes.
  - Climate feedbacks operate from within the climate system and either keep the system stable or enhance change.
  - Climate forcings are change variables that originate outside of and independent of the climate system.
  - Global Warming Potential (GWP) is the ratio of warming from 1 kg of a GHG compared to 1 kg of CO_2 over a set time.
  - A greenhouse gas (GHG) is a gas that absorbs heat energy that is reradiated from Earth's land and water bodies.
  - Weather is the daily variation in the atmosphere.

LAB #12

Atmospheric Carbon, Temperature, and the Intergovernmental Panel on Climate Change (IPCC)

Recommended Textbook Reading Prior to Lab:
- Chapter 6, The Changing Climate
  - 6.4 Climate at the Crossroads
  - 6.5 Geographic Perspectives: Stabilizing Climate

Goals: After completing this lab, you will be able to:
- Summarize the Keeling curve and generate several descriptive narratives from the curve graphic.
- Clarify selected atmospheric CO_2 reports from the Intergovernmental Panel on Climate Change (IPCC) and generate several narratives that communicate IPCC data.
- Correlate atmospheric CO_2 concentration and global average temperatures over the past 800,000 years.
- Interpret atmospheric temperature, sea level, and northern hemisphere snow cover relative to 1961–1990 averages from the latest IPCC report.
- Analyze warming scenarios for Earth relative to the year 2000 for several population, economic, and technological development trajectories.
- Identify and discuss the potential impacts on water, ecosystems, food, coasts, and health of projected increases in global average surface temperatures through the twenty-first century.

Key Terms and Concepts:
- carbon dioxide and temperature
- carbon dioxide increase
- climate warming scenarios
- Keeling curve
- projected impacts of rising average surface temperatures

Required Materials:
- Calculator
- Ruler (or straight edge)
- Textbook: *Living Physical Geography*, by Bruce Gervais

Problem-Solving Module #1: The Keeling Curve and Earth's Warming Trend

Scientists report atmospheric CO_2 content in parts per million (ppm). If, for example, CO_2 content is reported as 372 ppm, this literally means that in every million molecules of dry air there are on average 372 CO_2 molecules. Table 1–1 illustrates a selection of 1 million molecules of dry air and the number of molecules of respective gases that it contains.

Gas	Number of Molecules
Nitrogen	780,900
Oxygen	209,400
Argon	9,300
Carbon dioxide	372
Neon	18
Helium	5
Methane	2
Krypton	1
Trace others	1

TABLE 1–1

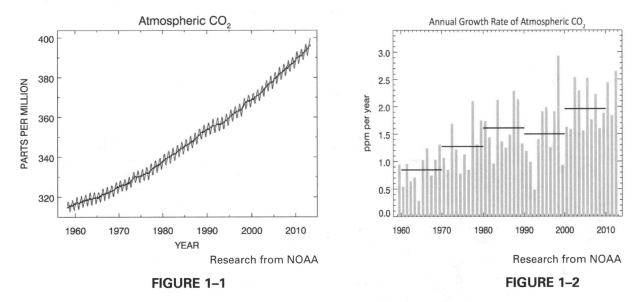

FIGURE 1–1

FIGURE 1–2

Figure 1–1 is a record of atmospheric CO_2. Figure 1–2 is an analysis of the growth rate of atmospheric CO_2, with the black bars indicating decade-specific growth rates. Use Table 1–1 and Figures 1–1 and 1–2 to answer questions 1–11.

1. True or False? The atmospheric CO_2 level reported in Table 1–1 occurred in the year 2011.

2. Consider the "Number of Molecules" column in Table 1–1. What would happen to the number of other molecules if the carbon dioxide value read 400?

3. Consider Figure 1–1. What is the fluctuating line within the graph?

4. Consider Figure 1–1. Why do CO_2 levels drop in the summer?

5. Consider Figure 1–1. Why do CO_2 levels rise in the winter?

_____

6. Consider Figure 1–1. What is the nonfluctuating line within the graph?

_____

7. Consider Figure 1–1. When was the last time that atmospheric CO_2 was 320 ppm?

_____

8. Consider Figure 1–2. In the decade between 1960 and 1970, how much more CO_2 was added annually to the atmosphere?

_____

9. Consider Figure 1–2. In the decade between 1970 and 1980, how much more CO_2 was added annually to the atmosphere?

_____

10. Consider Figure 1–2. In the decade between 1980 and 1990, how much more CO_2 was added annually to the atmosphere?

_____

11. Consider Figure 1–2. In your own words, generally describe the annual CO_2 growth rate trend over the last 50 years.

_____

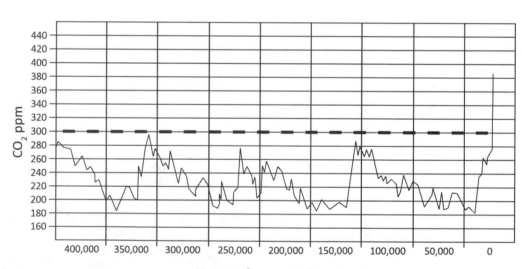

Research from NOAA/NASA

FIGURE 1–3

12. Figure 1–3 illustrates atmospheric CO_2 concentration over the past 400,000 years. Since atmospheric scientists were not around for most of this time span, how do we know this information?

_____

_____

13. Figure 1–3 illustrates that over the 400,000-year period of record shown in the graph, atmospheric CO_2 levels never exceeded 300 ppm until _____.

14. Figure 1–3 illustrates that CO_2 concentration naturally cycles about every 100,000 years, from a low of about _____ ppm to a high of about _____ ppm. This CO_2 pattern is correlated with Earth's cooling (glacial) and warming (interglacial) periods, and it is due to three changes in Earth's orbital relationship to the Sun, which are called _____cycles.

15. What happened during the Industrial Revolution that resulted in higher atmospheric CO_2 concentrations due to anthropogenic forcing?

_____

_____

16. On Figure 1–4, label the temporal scale (*x*-axis) in units of 50,000 years by identifying the halfway point between the existing *x*-axis values, and then identifying the halfway point again.

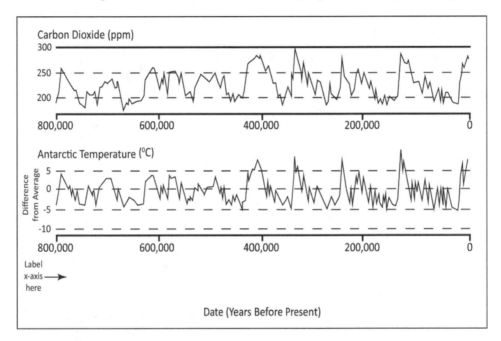

FIGURE 1–4

17. Use Figure 1–4 to complete Table 1–2.

Years Before Present	CO₂ Level (ppm)	Temp Relative to 800,000-Year Average (°C)
130,000		
330,000		
450,000		
665,000		
790,000		

TABLE 1–2

18. Use Figure 1–4 to complete Table 1–3.

Years Before Present	CO₂ Level Relatively High or Low?	Antarctic Temperatures Relatively High or Low?
130,000		
330,000		
450,000		
665,000		
790,000		

TABLE 1–3

19. Figure 1–4 and Tables 1–2 and 1–3 illustrate that _____ and _____ increase
    and decrease together.

20. Given the information in Figures 1–1 through 1–4, what is a reasonable hypothesis about
    Earth's atmospheric temperature in the coming decades?

    _____

    _____

    _____

    _____

Problem-Solving Module #2: The Intergovernmental Panel on Climate Change (IPCC)

The Intergovernmental Panel on Climate Change (IPCC) is the world's leading organization for assessing climate change. It is charged with reviewing and evaluating scientific, technical, and socioeconomic studies, as well as providing information about the potential environmental and socioeconomic impacts of climate change. IPCC reports are policy-neutral. They are used by governments around the world to draft local, regional, and global climate policy initiatives.

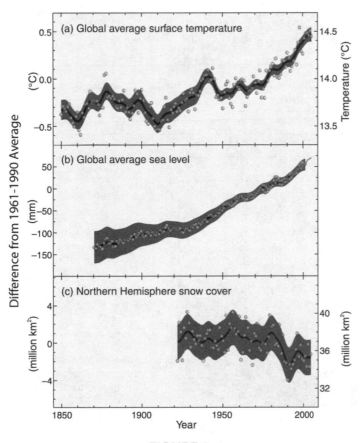

Climate Change 2007: Synthesis Report. Contribution of Working Groups I, II, and III to the Fourth Assessment Report of the Intergovernmental Panel on Climate Change, Figure 1.1; Figure 3.2 (left panel); Figure 3.6. IPCC, Geneva, Switzerland.

FIGURE 2–1

Figure 2–1 is taken from the IPCC's Assessment Report Number 4 (AR4). It illustrates the observed changes in temperature, sea level, and northern hemisphere snow cover relative to 1961–1990 averages. Solid black lines are decade averages, circles show yearly values, and wide shaded areas are uncertainty intervals.

Use Figure 2–1 to answer questions 1–7.

1. In 2000, the global average surface temperature was _____°C, which was _____°C higher than the 1961–1990 average.

2. In 2000, the global average sea level was ____ mm (or __ cm) higher than the 1961–1990 average.

3. In 2000, northern hemisphere snow cover was ____ million km^2, which was ____ million km^2 less than the 1961–1990 average.

4. What has happened to the degree of uncertainty regarding global average surface temperature in 2000 compared to 1850?

5. What has happened to the degree of uncertainty regarding global average sea level in 2000 compared to 1870?

_____

6. What has happened to the degree of uncertainty regarding northern hemisphere snow cover level in 2000 compared to 1920?

_____

7. In your own words, generally summarize all three graphs in Figure 2–1.

_____

_____

_____

_____

_____

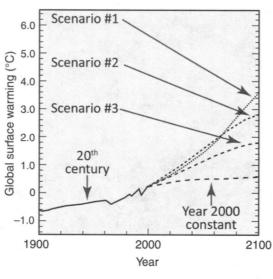

Climate Change 2007: Synthesis Report. Contribution of Working Groups I, II, and III to the Fourth Assessment Report of the Intergovernmental Panel on Climate Change, Figure 1.1; Figure 3.2 (left panel); Figure 3.6. IPCC, Geneva, Switzerland.

FIGURE 2–2

Figure 2–2 is adapted from the IPCC's Assessment Report Number 4 (AR4). It illustrates three warming scenarios as continuations of the twentieth century. The year 2000 constant line illustrates the expected global warming if GHG emissions remained constant at year 2000 levels.

- Scenario #1: a world with high population growth, slow economic development, and slow technological change.
- Scenario #2: a world of very rapid economic growth, a global population that peaks in mid-century, rapid introduction of new and more efficient technologies, and a balance across all energy sources.
- Scenario #3: a world with the same global population as Scenario #1 but with more rapid changes in economic structures toward a service and information economy.

Use Figure 2–2 to answer questions 8–12.

8. How much global surface warming is expected by 2100 if population grows quickly and there is rapid growth in service and information economies?

_____

9. How much global surface warming is expected by 2100 if human population grows quickly but economies and technology develop slowly?

_____

10. How much global surface warming can be avoided by 2100 if population grows quickly and there is rapid growth in service and information economies?

_____

11. Scenario #2 describes a "balance across all energy sources." Explain what you think this phrase means.

_____

_____

12. What scenario do you think is most likely by 2100, and why?

_____

_____

_____

_____

_____

_____

Figure 2–3 is adapted from the IPCC's Assessment Report Number 4 (AR4). It illustrates examples of impacts with different amounts of increase in global average surface temperature through the twenty-first century. Solid back lines link various impacts, and broken-line arrows indicate impacts that continue growing as temperature increases. The left-hand side of any impact text indicates the level of warming associated with its onset.

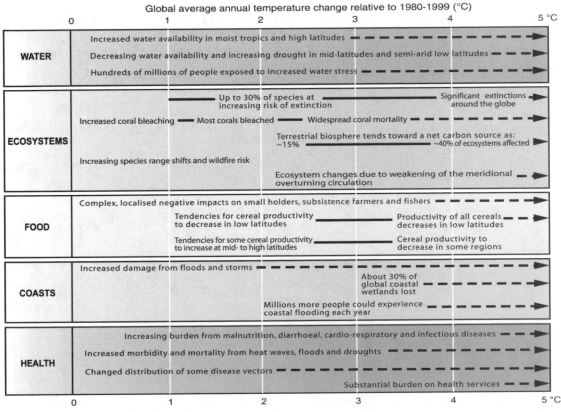

Climate Change 2007: Synthesis Report. Contribution of Working Groups I, II, and III to the Fourth Assessment Report of the Intergovernmental Panel on Climate Change, Figure 1.1; Figure 3.2 (left panel); Figure 3.6. IPCC, Geneva, Switzerland.

FIGURE 2–3

© 2014 W. H. Freeman and Company

13. Use Figure 2–3 to complete Table 2–1.

Impact	Onset Temperature (°C)
About 30% of global coastal wetlands lost	
Substantial burden on health services	2.8
Cereal productivity decreases in low latitudes	
Increased coral bleaching	
Hundreds of millions of people exposed to increased water stress	0.2
Significant extinctions around the globe	
Increased water in moist tropics and high latitudes	
Millions more people experience coastal flooding each year	

TABLE 2–1

Summary of Key Terms and Concepts:

- Carbon dioxide and temperature are very closely coupled together. Both increase and/or decrease at approximately the same time.
- Human activity is increasing carbon dioxide in the atmosphere by about 3% per year. The current carbon dioxide level in the atmosphere exceeds the highest levels during the last 800,000 years.
- Climate warming scenarios vary depending on projections of future population, economic development, and technological development variables.
- The Keeling curve is a graph showing atmospheric carbon dioxide measurements since 1958.
- Potential impacts of rising average surface temperatures on water, ecosystems, food, coasts, and health vary depending on projections of future global average surface temperatures.

Biogeography

Recommended Textbook Reading Prior to Lab:
- Chapter 7, Patterns of Life: Biogeography
  - 7.1 Biogeographic Patterns
  - 7.3 Moving Around: Dispersal
  - 7.4 Starting Anew: Disturbance and Succession

Goals: After completing this lab, you will be able to:
- Describe the spatial pattern of zebra mussel invasion in the United States.
- Recommend zebra mussel mitigation strategies for recreational boaters.
- Identify habitat ranges of selected tree species using USGS tree species coverage maps.
- Summarize key parts of the Endangered Species Act (ESA).
- Differentiate between endangered and threatened species.
- Discuss how disturbances influence succession of ecological communities and describe the spatial pattern of succession.
- Use Google Earth and data from the Predictive Services of the National Interagency Coordination Center (NICC) to examine fire weather, fire danger, and fire reports.

Key Terms and Concepts:
- biogeography
- Endangered Species Act
- fire
- fire suppression
- invasion
- plant succession

Required Materials:
- Atlas
- Calculator
- High-speed Internet connection (for Module 5) and Google Earth (free download)
- Textbook: *Living Physical Geography*, by Bruce Gervais

Problem-Solving Module #1: Invasive Species: Zebra Mussels

The zebra mussel is a small shellfish indigenous to the Black, Caspian, and Azov Seas in Eastern Europe. It was found in the 1980s in Lake St. Clair, east of Detroit, Michigan. The species likely arrived in the ballast water from ocean-going vessels that had previously docked in Europe. Zebra mussels crowd out and kill native mussels, consume algae (a food source for native microscopic organisms), block municipal water and power plant intake pipes, and are a likely source of avian botulism that has killed tens of thousands of birds in the Great Lakes region since 1998.

The black dots on the maps in Figure 1–1 are records of zebra mussel infestations. Notice that the 1986 map has only two data points.

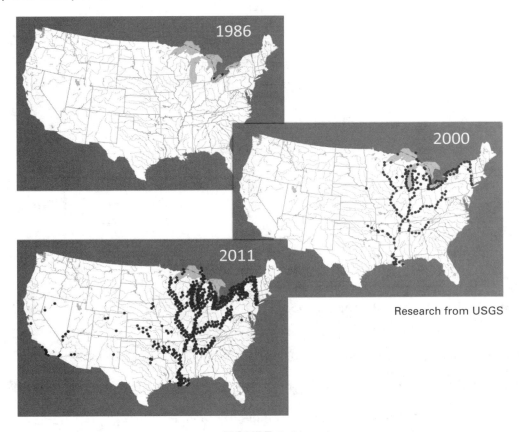

Research from USGS

FIGURE 1–1

1. In _____(how many?) years, the zebra mussel spread from the Great Lakes, south to the Gulf of _____, and west to southern _____and Arizona.

2. How does Figure 1–1 illustrate that zebra mussels have a hydrochore dispersal strategy?

   _____

3. Is the zebra mussel population an example of colonization or invasion, and why?

   _____

Recreational boats often transport zebra mussels from infested waters because juvenile mussels attach to aquatic weeds, engine drive units, propellers, boat trailers, hulls, and anchor chains. Microscopic larvae are also transported because they live in water that is carried in bait buckets or live-fish wells. Many state governments have education campaigns to instruct boaters about how to prevent the mussels' spread. Table 1–1 is an example of the instructional information distributed to boaters.

All Vessels = ●		Vessel in Water < 2 days = ●●	Vessel in Water > 2 days = ●●●

	Hull	Drive Unit	Propeller	Trolling Tab	Anchor Rope/Chain	Bilge	Live Well	Bait Bucket	Trailer	Engine
Inspect for Mussels	●	●	●	●	●	●	●		●	●
Drain Water		●				●	●	●		
Remove Plants		●	●	●	●				●	
Cold Wash	●●	●●	●●	●●	●	●●	●●	●	●●	●●
Hot Wash	●●●	●●●	●●●	●●●		●●●	●●●		●●●	●●●

TABLE 1–1

Use Table 1–1 to answer questions 4–12 with a "yes" or "no."

4. If your boat is in the water for 3 hours, do you need to inspect the anchor chain for mussels? _____

5. If your boat is in the water for 3 hours, do you need to drain the water from the live well? _____

6. If your boat is in the water for 10 hours, do you need to remove plants from the propeller? _____

7. If your boat is in the water for 10 hours, do you need to hot wash the propeller? _____

8. If your boat is in the water for 10 hours, do you need to cold wash the engine? _____

9. If your boat is in the water for 40 hours, do you need to cold wash the hull? _____

10. If your boat is in the water for 40 hours, do you need to cold wash the anchor chain? _____

11. If your boat is in the water for 72 hours, do you need to drain the water from the bilge? _____

12. If your boat is in the water for 72 hours, do you need to hot wash the anchor chain? _____

Problem-Solving Module #2: Range Maps for Selected Tree Species

Forestiera acuminata

Taxus canadensis

Quercus macrocarpa

Pseudotsuga menziesii

Prosopis juliflora

Rhizophora mangle

Ulmus rubra

Larrea divaricata

Acer negundo

Research from USGS

FIGURE 2–1

1. Figure 2–1 illustrates the range maps of nine tree species. Complete Table 2–1.

Description of Species Range	Scientific Name	Common Name
Concentrated in the Midwest, with a significant range lobe extending through eastern Texas to the coast; no significant presence west of North Dakota or south of Tennessee.		bur oak
	Prosopis juliflora	mesquite
Range extends as far west as eastern Nebraska, Kansas, Oklahoma, and Texas, and as far east as the Atlantic coast; some presence in Ontario and Quebec.		slippery elm
	Rhizophora mangle	mangrove

TABLE 2–1

Description of Species Range	Scientific Name	Common Name
Concentrated along the coast in the northwestern states and British Colombia.		Douglas fir
	Taxus Canadensis	Canada yew
Similar but smaller range as the mesquite, with no presence in the Yucatan Peninsula.		creosote bush
	Forestiera acuminate	swamp privet
Range extends as far west as eastern Wyoming and into southern Alberta and Saskatchewan; significant presence in the Midwest, with range extending south through eastern Texas to the Gulf coast.		Boxelder

TABLE 2–1 (continued)

Problem-Solving Module #3: Endangered Species

Table 3–1 is a summary table of the number of United States' species and foreign species that are listed under the Endangered Species Act (ESA) as of June, 2013.

	United States	Foreign	Total				
Group	Endangered	Threatened	Total	Endangered	Threatened	Total	U.S. and Foreign
Sponges	0	0	0	0	0	0	0
Birds	78	15	93	208	16	224	317
Reptiles	14	22	36	70	20	90	126
Amphibians	16	10	26	8	1	9	35
Fishes	83	70	153	11	1	12	165
Clams	72	12	84	2	0	2	86
Snails	30	13	43	1	0	1	44
Insects	57	10	67	4	0	4	71
Arachnids	12	0	12	0	0	0	12
Crustaceans	19	3	22	0	0	0	22
Corals	0	2	2	0	0	0	2
Annelid Worms	0	0	0	0	0	0	0
Flatworms and Roundworms	0	0	0	0	0	0	0
Hydroids	0	0	0	0	0	0	0
Mammals	69	16	85	256	20	276	361
Millipedes	0	0	0	0	0	0	0
ANIMALS TOTAL	450	173	623	560	58	618	1241
Flowering Plants	670	148	818	1	0	1	819
Conifers and Cycads	2	1	3	0	2	2	5
Ferns and Allies	28	2	30	0	0	0	30
Lichens	2	0	2	0	0	0	2
PLANTS TOTAL	702	151	853	1	2	3	856
Grand Totals	1152	324	1476	561	60	621	2097

TABLE 3–1

Highlights of the ESA of 1973:
- Species: any subspecies of fish or wildlife or plants, and any distinct population segment of any species of vertebrate fish or wildlife that interbreeds when mature.
- Threatened species: any species that is likely to become an endangered species within the foreseeable future throughout all or a significant portion of its range.

- Endangered species: any species that is in danger of extinction throughout all or a significant portion of its range other than a species of the Class Insecta determined by the Secretary to constitute a pest whose protection under the provisions of this Act would present an overwhelming and overriding risk to man.
- A Species is Threatened or Endangered due to any of the following factors:
  - ☐ The present or threatened destruction, modification, or curtailment of its habitat or range.
  - ☐ Overutilization for commercial, recreational, scientific, or educational purposes.
  - ☐ Disease or predation.
  - ☐ The inadequacy of existing regulatory mechanisms.
  - ☐ Other natural or manmade factors affecting its continued existence.

Use Table 3–1 and the highlights of the ESA to answer questions 1–9.

1. The ESA includes _____, _____, and _____ within the definition of a species.

2. If a species is being considered under the ESA, does "threatened" status or "endangered" status come first?

   _____

3. How is range an important variable in determining the status of a species under the ESA?

   _____

   _____

4. Assume that a disease-spreading insect's population and range was rapidly shrinking. What argument, using ESA language, would disqualify that insect from protection under the ESA?

   _____

   _____

5. Is an anthropogenic reason required for a species to be threatened or endangered under the ESA?

   _____

   _____

6. What group of animals in the United States has the largest number of endangered species?

   _____

7. What group of foreign animals has the largest number of endangered species?

   _____

8. What group of plants in the United States has the largest number of endangered species?

   _____

9. Compare the number of endangered flowering plants in the United States to those in foreign places. Given that the United States is a relatively small part of the entire planet, what could be a likely explanation for the extreme difference between these two numbers?

   _____

   _____

   _____

   _____

   _____

   _____

Problem-Solving Module #4: Fire and Ecological Disturbance

1. Fire is a widespread, common, and important _____ event in most vegetated regions.

2. State four adaptations that plants have in order to survive fire.

   _____

3. Forest managers use _____ burning and mechanical thinning to reduce fuel buildup in overgrown forests.

4. _____ is the process of vegetation reestablishment following disturbance.

5. How does disturbance result in a "mosaic patchwork" spatial pattern of succession across a region?

   _____

   _____

   _____

   _____

Table 4–1 presents fire data from the southwest United States on Wednesday, June 26, 2013 at 5:30 a.m. Mountain Time. The data were acquired from the Incident Management Situation Report of the National Interagency Coordination Center (NICC). NICC coordinates the mobilization of resources for wildland fires; it also provides incident information and predictive services.

Fire Name	State	Burnt Area (acres)	24-hr Burnt Size Change (acres)	% Contained	Total Personnel	24-hr Personnel Change
Silver	NM	85,000	5,000	20	691	86
Jaroso	NM	7,902	2,302	0	90	80
Doce	AZ	6,767	0	80	228	−253
Creek	AZ	11,400	3,150	N/A	214	−5
Sycamore	AZ	780	211	60	172	21
Rock Creek	AZ	795	0	67	291	−26
Thompson Ridge	NM	23,965	28	90	158	−3
Tres Lagunas	NM	10,219	0	90	165	0
Whites Peak	NM	1,275	0	100	5	−21

TABLE 4–1: Large Fires (>100 acres) in the Southwest United States, June 26, 2013 at 5:30 a.m.

Use Table 4–1 to answer questions 6–10.

6. One square mile is 640 acres. How many square miles had the Silver fire burned?

   _____

7. Which fire burned the most area in the past 24 hours? _____

8. How much of the Thompson Ridge fire was contained? _____

9. Why does it make sense that 253 people stopped fighting the Doce fire during the last 24 hours?

   _____

10. Why does it make sense that the Silver fire had the largest number of people assigned to it?

   _____

Problem-Solving Module #5: Large U.S. Fires in 2013

Download the following file from the textbook companion site and open it in Google Earth:
- June 2013 Large Fires.kmz

The June 2013 Large Fires.kmz file is a snapshot of fire conditions in the United States at one point in time. Click on a fire icon to bring up information about a particular fire incident.

1. The _____ Fire was located in the Prescott National Forest. *Hint: Hover the mouse over the graphics that look like little green pine trees.*

2. In what national forest was the Thompson Ridge fire located?

   _____

3. Which fire was located in the Gila National Forest?

   _____

4. What transportation asset was located in the town of Whiteriver that would enable both firefighting equipment and personnel to quickly arrive on the scene?

   _____

5. What caused the Doce fire? _____

6. How much has the Doce fire cost to date? _____

7. Whom should people contact to report suspicious activity related to the Doce fire?

   _____

8. What caused the Jaroso fire? _____

9. What did residents living in the upper Pecos Canyon see from the Jaroso fire in the evening?

   _____

10. What vegetation was the Jaroso fire burning through?

    _____

    _____

11. What caused the Rock Creek fire? _____

12. How many structures were threatened by the Rock Creek fire? _____

13. How much has the Rock Creek fire cost to date? _____

14. What caused the Silver fire? _____

15. What was the fuel's potential for ignition in the Silver fire? _____

16. What happened to the communities of Kingston and Hillsboro as a result of the Silver fire?

    _____

17. What caused the Thompson Ridge fire?

_____

18. What kinds of fuels were burning in the Thompson Ridge fire?

_____

19. Are the communities around the Santa Fe National Forest open and accessible? _____

20. On what date did the Tres Lagunas fire start? _____

21. What caused the Tres Lagunas fire? _____

22. What conditions created a fire weather watch at the Tres Lagunas fire location?

_____

_____

Summary of Key Terms and Concepts:
- Biogeography is the study of the geographic patterns of organisms and how they change through space and time.
- The Endangered Species Act is a U.S. law passed in 1973 to protect imperiled species from extinction due to economic growth and development.
- Many ecosystems depend on fire for their health.
- In most regions fires have been intentionally suppressed, resulting in an accumulation of fuel and catastrophic fires.
- An invasion is the successful and unwanted establishment of a species in a new geographic area as a result of human activity.
- After a disturbance event, life returns to an area through plant succession.
- Plant succession takes place in a mosaic patchwork and takes decades to centuries or longer to complete.

LAB #14   Climate and Biomes

Recommended Textbook Reading Prior to Lab:
- Chapter 8, Climate and Life: Biomes
  - 8.1 Climate and Life: Biomes
  - 8.2 Low-Latitude Biomes
  - 8.3 Midlatitude and High-Latitude Biomes
  - 8.4 Biomes Found at All Latitudes
  - 8.5 Geographic Perspectives: The Value of Nature

Goals: After completing this lab, you will be able to:
- Identify and work with the various biome classification categories created by Robert Whittaker.
- Determine temperature and precipitation variables of selected graphically presented biomes.
- Summarize common vegetation and geography of specific biomes.
- Select the best-fit biome for selected plant species.
- Carry out Köppen classifications of selected locations on Google Earth using the Oak Ridge National Laboratory (ORNL) world map of the Köppen-Geiger climate classification.
- Evaluate changes in Congo's historical land use and land cover using spatial analysis and the scientific method.

Key Terms and Concepts:
- biomes
- boreal forests
- deserts
- Köppen climate classification system
- Mediterranean biomes
- montane forests
- precision
- sampling frame
- temperate deciduous forests
- temperate grasslands
- temperate rainforests
- tropical rainforests
- tropical savannas
- tropical seasonal forests
- tundra biomes

Required Materials:
- Calculator
- High-speed Internet connection (for modules 2, 3, and 4) and Google Earth (free download)
- Textbook: *Living Physical Geography*, by Bruce Gervais

Problem-Solving Module #1: Climates and Biomes

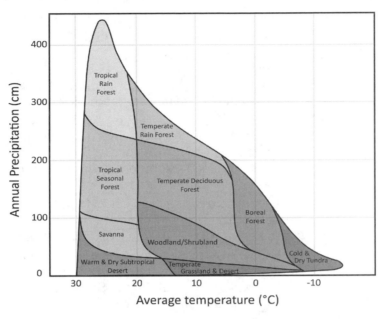

FIGURE 1–1

Figure 1–1 presents a simplified biome classification scheme created by Robert Whittaker in the mid-twentieth century. Whittaker used precipitation and temperature as the two determining variables. His work is one of several biome classification schemes that scientists consider when examining Earth's climates and associated biodiversity.

1. Use Figure 1–1 to complete Table 1–1.

Biome Name	Average Temperature (°C)	Annual Precipitation (cm)
	0	100
	11	150
	–9	25
	25	175
	15	75
	15	250
	25	300
	10	10
	23	50
	25	10

TABLE 1–1

Biome Name	Common Flora and Geography
Tropical rainforest	Vines, palm trees, orchids, and ferns. Seen close to the equator. The Amazon rainforest in South America is the premier example.
Tropical seasonal forest	Deciduous trees such as teak and mountain ebony. Year-round warmth with several dry months. Often adjacent to savannas. Seen in southern Mexico, Peru, Brazil, and central India.
Temperate rain forest	Coniferous or broadleaf flora depending on location. Canopy can cover 70% of sky. Seen on the western coast of Canada, southern Chile, southern China, and New Zealand.
Temperate deciduous forest	Broadleaf trees such as oaks, maples, and beeches. Leaves transition through four distinct seasons. Seen in the eastern United States, Canada, Europe, and China.
Savanna	Primarily grasses but with widely spaced and open canopy trees or shrubs. Seen south of the Amazon basin in Brazil, south of the Sahara Desert in Africa, throughout Southeast Asia and northern Australia.
Woodland/shrubland	Woody shrubs such as sage, rosemary, and thyme. Larger shrubs have many stems and average 4 meters high. Hot, dry summers. Seen on western coasts between 30°– 40° north and south latitude.
Boreal forest	Coniferous-evergreen trees. Long and snowy winters and warm, humid summers. Between four and six frost-free months. Seen in Canada, Europe, and Asia.
Warm and dry subtropical desert	Cacti, small bushes, and short grasses. Perennials survive dormant for years and flourish when water is available. Annuals are ephemerals and complete their life cycle in just weeks. Seen between 15° and 35° latitude, north and south of equator. Examples include the North American Mojave, Sonoran, Chihuahua, and Great Basin; the Sahara in Africa; and the Negev in the Middle East.
Temperate grassland and desert	Grasses such as prairie clover, oats, wheat, barley, and coneflowers. Seen in the prairies of the Great Plains, the South American Pampas, the steppes of central Eurasia, and adjacent to Australian deserts.
Cold and dry tundra	Lichens, mosses, grasses, and shrubs. No trees. Significant permafrost. The coldest biome. Seen in regions south of the Arctic ice cap in North America, Europe, Siberia, and on mountain slopes.

TABLE 1–2

2. Table 1–2 illustrates common plants specific to particular biomes. Use Figure 1–1 and Tables 1–1 and 1–2 to identify the correct biome associated with each plant specimen listed on Table 1–3. Note: Each of the 10 presented biomes in Whittaker's classification scheme will be used only once.

Plant Specimen	Characteristics
Saguaro cactus Lives in a _____biome	• A tree-sized cactus native to the Sonoran Desert in Arizona and Mexico. • Pleats on trunk and arms visibly expand after soaking up rainwater. • Fast growth occurs after infrequent rains.
White spruce Lives in a _____biome	• Evergreen with short, waxy needles. • Waxy coating on the needles helps conserve water during winters when soil water is frozen. • Produces seed cones instead of flowers. • Grows slowly and is easily killed by fire.
Northern red oak Lives in a _____biome	• A deciduous tree, it loses leaves in winter. • Native to northeastern United States. • Lives near streams with well-drained soils. • Leaves turn rich-red or brown in autumn before falling to ground.
Lady Ackland's cattleya Lives in a _____biome	• An epiphyte, it grows on tree trunks and relies on the tree for support. • Requires constant warmth and humidity. • Native to eastern Brazil. • Cannot withstand dry spells or temperature fluctuations.
Crustose lichen Lives in a _____biome	• A symbiosis of a fungus and algae. • Are not plants. • Can survive in barren and severe regions. • Tolerate extreme cold and dry conditions. • Require little rainfall.
Blue grama Lives in a _____biome	• A green, warm-season perennial grass. • Adapted to well-drained soils. • Thrives in warm temperatures with moderate rain. • Drought tolerant. • Goes dormant during winter.
Dalmatian sage Lives in a _____biome	• Prefers well-drained slopes in full sunlight. • Grows well in semi-arid conditions. • Can withstand hot temperatures, but its biome does not normally exceed 20°C. • Creates aromatic oils that keep animals from eating the leaves. • Adapted to summer drought.
Big leaf mahogany Lives in a _____biome	• A deciduous tree that is briefly leafless. • Range has about 1,000–2,000 mm of annual precipitation. • Grows within the warm tropics. • Flowers during the late dry season.
Mulga Lives in a _____biome	• A species of Acacia native to Australia. • Adapted to warm, dry, near-desert conditions. • Leaf structure funnels water toward trunk. • Form loose, open canopies that allow wire grasses to grow.
Sitka spruce Lives in a _____biome	• A large species of conifer evergreen tree. • Stiff, needle-like leaves. • Native to the western coast of North America. • Adapted to extremely wet climates.

TABLE 1–3

Problem-Solving Module #2: Köppen Climate Types and Associated Biomes

A well-recognized climate classification scheme was created by German climatologist and botanist Wladimir Köppen (1846–1940). He divided Earth's climates into six major groups based on temperature and latitude, and then he further divided these groups into smaller units based on precipitation and temperature. The six major groups are listed in Table 2–1.

Climate Group	Köppen Letter Designation	Characteristics
Tropical climates	A	Extends north and south from the equator to about 15° to 25°. Average temperature of all months is > 18°C and annual precipitation is > than 150 cm.
Dry climates	B	Evaporation and transpiration often > precipitation. Extends from 20°–35° north and south of equator and in continental regions of midlatitudes.
Mild midlatitude climates	C	Warm, humid summers with mild winters. Extends from 30° to 50° latitude on eastern and western borders of many continents.
Severe midlatitude climates	D	Warm to cool summers with cold winters. Extends poleward of the "C" climates. Warmest month is > 10°C, coldest month < –30°C. Severe winter storms are common.
Polar climates	E	Year-round cold temperatures with the warmest month < 10°C. Extends over northern coasts of North America, Europe, and Asia.
Highlands	H	Rapid elevation changes in mountainous landscapes yield rapid and varying climate changes.

TABLE 2–1

Köppen again used letters to designate specific precipitation and temperature patterns. Thus, you may see a two-letter or three-letter Köppen climate group, such as Af, BWh, Cfa, or Dwa. There are many, many smaller categories that we'll see in the accompanying Google Earth file that we consider later. For now, however, a condensed version is presented in Table 2–2.

Climate Group	Smaller Climate Unit	Climate Name	Associated Biome
Tropical Climates (A)			
	Af	Tropical wet	Tropical rainforest
	Am	Tropical monsoon	Tropical seasonal forest
	Aw	Tropical savanna	Tropical savanna
Dry Climates (B)			
	BWh	Subtropical desert	Desert
	BWk	Midlatitude desert	Desert
	BSh	Subtropical steppe	Temperate grassland
	BSk	Midlatitude steppe	Temperate grassland
Mild Midlatitude Climates (C)			
	Cfa, Cwa, Cwb	Humid subtropical	Temperate deciduous forest
	Cfb, Cfc	Marine west coast	Temperate rainforest
	Csa, Csb	Mediterranean	Mediterranean
Severe Midlatitude Climates (D)			
	Dfa, Dwa, Dfb, Dwb	Humid continental	Temperate deciduous forest
	Dfc, Dwc, Dfd, Dwd	Subarctic	Boreal forest
Polar Climates (E)			
	ET	Tundra	Northern tundra
	EF	Ice cap	Not vegetated
Highlands (H)			
	H	Cold mountain climates	Montane

TABLE 2–2

Download the following file from the textbook companion site and open it within Google Earth:
- Köppen Climate Zones.kmz

1. How many Köppen classifications are listed in the legend on the left side of the screen? _____

Use Tables 2–1 and 2–2 to answer questions 2–6.

2. Fly to the Saudi Arabia placemark by double-clicking its name in the Places Sidebar. Given the Köppen climate classification system, what can we say about evaporation and transpiration compared to precipitation at this location?

_____

3. Fly to the Greenland placemark. How warm is the warmest month at this location? _____

4. Fly to the Iowa placemark. Are severe winter storms common here? _____

5. Fly to the Indonesia placemark. The average temperature of all months is greater than _____.

6. Fly to the France placemark. What kind of summers should we expect at this location?

_____

7. Complete Table 2–3 by flying to each Google Earth placemark. Use the Köppen legend on the Google Earth screen to obtain the Köppen Climate Classification, and use Table 2–2 to identify the climate name and associated biome. Placemark #1 on Table 2–3 is already done for you as an example.

Placemark	Country	Köppen Climate Classification	Climate Name (see Table 2–2)	Associated Biome (see Table 2–2)
#1	Brazil	Am	Tropical monsoon	Tropical seasonal forest
#2				
#3				
#4				
#5				
#6				
#7				
#8				
#9				
#10				
#11				
#12				
#13				
#14				
#15				
#16				
#17				
#18				
#19				
#20				

TABLE 2–3

8. Type your home or school address into Google Earth's search window, and click the search button. What is the Köppen classification of the address, the climate name, and the associated biome?

   Address: _____

   Climate name: _____

   Associated biome: _____

9. Fly to the Australia Path. How many climate categories does the Australia Path cover? _____

Turn off the Köppen Climate Map image overlay in the Places Sidebar.

10. Fly to placemark #7, zoom in, and describe the vegetation.

   _____

   _____

11. Fly to placemark #8. Zoom in and describe how the vegetation has changed from placemark #7 to placemark #8.

   _____

12. Fly to placemark #9. Zoom in and describe how the vegetation has changed from placemark #8 to placemark #9.

_____

13. Using the Köppen climate categories and relative precipitation amounts, explain why the vegetation changed, in the manner observed, as you progressed from placemark #7 to #9.

_____

_____

_____

_____

Turn on the Köppen Climate Map image overlay in the Places Sidebar.

14. Fly to the Africa Path. How many climate categories does the Africa Path cover? _____

Turn off the Köppen Climate Map image overlay in the Places Sidebar.

15. Fly to placemark #14, zoom in and describe the vegetation.

_____

16. Fly to placemark #15. Zoom in and describe the vegetation.

_____

17. Fly to placemark #16. Zoom in and describe how the vegetation has changed from placemark #15 to the area around placemark #16.

_____

_____

18. Fly to placemark #17. Zoom in and describe how the vegetation has changed from the area around placemark #16 to the area around placemark #17.

_____

_____

_____

19. Fly to placemark #18, zoom in, and describe the vegetation.

_____

_____

_____

_____

20. Using the Köppen climate categories and relative precipitation amounts, explain why the vegetation changed, in the manner observed, as you progressed from placemark #14 to #18.

_____

_____

_____

Problem-Solving Module #3: Congo Historical Land Cover and Use

Download the following file from the textbook companion site and open it within Google Earth:

• Congo Historical Land Cover and Use.kmz

This file opens to a view of the African country of Congo and an image overlay of land cover and use in the year 1700. Notice from the color coding in the legend that at this time in history Congo had "tropical woodland," "tropical forest," and a small amount of "pasture/land used for grazing." In the Places Sidebar, click the "Land Cover and Use in 1990" box to see how Congo's land use changed by 1990. Notice that "Pasture land" expanded considerably by 1990.

Assume the government of Congo is interested in conserving its "tropical woodland" and "tropical forest" biomes. Before conservation planning can begin, however, it needs to know what percentage of these biomes has been lost to pasture since 1700. Various ministry officials look at both maps and make nonscientific and conflicting judgments. Here are three of their statements.

• Between 1700 and 1990, 10% of Congo's tropical woodland and tropical forest was lost to pasture.
• Between 1700 and 1990, 40% of Congo's tropical woodland and tropical forest was lost to pasture.
• Between 1700 and 1990, 60% of Congo's tropical woodland and tropical forest was lost to pasture.

The officials argue about who is correct, but nobody agrees, so they call you in to study the problem using the scientific method.

1. In your own words, compose a hypothesis about the above land-use change scenario in Congo. Compose your hypothesis in the same style as the three ministry officials.

_____

_____

_____

_____

_____

2. What data do you need to collect to test your hypothesis?

_____

_____

_____

To complete Step #5 of the scientific method, click the "Congo's Sample Sites" box in the Places Sidebar. Notice that numerous red dots, organized in a grid, now cover the country. Each dot is a sampling site.

3. In 1700, how many sampling sites were located in tropical woodland and tropical forest? (Count as valid any red dot that is at least 50% within tropical woodland and/or tropical forest.)

_____

4. In 1990, how many sampling sites were located in tropical woodland and tropical forest? (Count as valid any red dot that is at least 50% within tropical woodland and/or tropical forest.)

_____

5. How many fewer tropical woodland and tropical forest sites existed in 1990 compared to 1700? Express your answer as a whole number and as a percentage of total sampled sites.

_____

6. Explain why your hypothesis is supported or not supported by the data.

_____

_____

_____

_____

7. In your own words, compose a sentence or two that corresponds with Step #6 of the scientific method as it relates to the above land-use change scenario in Congo. Recall that this step is about further inquiry and includes speculation about new questions, new ideas, and more/different data collection.

_____

_____

_____

_____

_____

_____

Problem-Solving Module #4: Edmonton, Canada Historical Land Cover and Use

Download the following file from the textbook companion site and open it in Google Earth:
  • Edmonton Historical Land Cover and Use.kmz

This file opens to a view centered on the city of Edmonton, in the Canadian province of Alberta, and an image overlay of land cover and use in the year 1700. Notice from the color coding in the legend that at this time in history the area had substantial forest coverage. In the Places Sidebar, turn on and off the "Land Cover and Use in 1700" layer and the "Land Cover and Use in 1990" layer. Notice how "Cultivated land" replaces a substantial amount of previously forested landscape from 1700 to 1990.

Assume you are a geographer and need to quantify land-use change around Edmonton as part of a larger study commissioned by the provincial government of Alberta. The government is specifically interested in the following question:

How much boreal forest has been lost from 1700 to 1990?

You are assigned a study area—called a sampling frame—that is centered on Edmonton. It is within this sampling frame that specific sites will be examined and classified. Some scientists on your team argue that sampling only nine sites within the sampling frame will produce the best results. Others argue that sampling 25 sites will produce better results, and it is thus worth the extra time, effort, and cost.

1. Complete Table 4–1 by turning on the "9 Sites Sampling Frame" layer (count as valid any red dot that is at least 50% within Boreal forest and/or Cultivated land).

Land Cover	Total Number of Sample Sites	Boreal Forest Sites in 1700	Boreal Forest Sites in 1990	Boreal Forest Change from 1700 to 1990 (%)
Boreal forest	9			

TABLE 4–1: 9 Sites Sampling Frame Data

2. Complete Table 4–2 by turning on the "25 Sites Sampling Frame" layer (count as valid any red dot that is at least 50% within Boreal forest and/or Cultivated land).

Land Cover	Total Number of Sample Sites	Boreal Forest Sites in 1700	Boreal Forest Sites in 1990	Boreal Forest Change from 1700 to 1990 (%)
Boreal forest	25			

TABLE 4–2: 25 Sites Sampling Frame Data

3. Compose a statement comparing the different results of each study.

_____
_____
_____
_____
_____

4. What is the percentage difference between each study? _____

5. Compare the findings seen in Tables 4–1 and 4–2 in terms of precision. *Precision* refers to the sharpest resolution and highest accuracy of values from a measurement.

_____

_____

_____

_____

_____

6. Consider the time it took to examine 9 sites compared to 25 sites. Why might Alberta's provincial government choose to fund a study that examines fewer sites in a sampling frame?

_____

_____

_____

_____

_____

_____

Summary of Key Terms and Concepts:

- Biomes are regions of vegetation with a similar structure. The structure of Earth's vegetation is determined mostly by climate.
- Boreal forests are found only in the northern hemisphere, where there are very cold winters and a short summer growing season.
- Deserts are characterized by extreme moisture deficits in all months and are commonly found centered on 30° north and south latitude, but they also occur due to rain shadows, high elevations, and high latitudes.
- The Köppen climate classification system is used to create categories of world climate.
- Mediterranean biomes are found on the west coasts of continents, have a dry summer and wet winter climate pattern, with sclerophyllous vegetation that is adapted to fire and drought.
- Montane forests are found on mountains with cool temperatures and precipitation 20 cm (8 in.) or more. They have evergreen needleleaf trees in the northern hemisphere, and broadleaf evergreen trees in the southern hemisphere.
- Precision is the sharpest resolution and highest accuracy of values from a measurement.
- A sampling frame is the area in which specific cases are drawn.
- Temperate deciduous forests have strong climatic seasonality and trees that drop their leaves in response to winter cold.
- Temperate grasslands occur at midlatitudes with strong continental seasonality. They are often called prairies, pampas, steppes, or veldts, and have largely been transformed by livestock grazing and agriculture.
- Temperate rainforests are dominated by a moderate maritime climate, receive more precipitation than the temperate deciduous forests, and commonly have mosses, ferns, lichens, epiphytes, and bryophytes.
- Tropical rainforests have no dry or cold season. They have broadleaf evergreen forests with layered structure, high biodiversity, and nutrient-poor soils.
- Tropical savannas have long winter dry seasons and widely spaced trees with a grass understory. Large grazing mammals are common.
- Tropical seasonal forests have dry winters and high levels of biodiversity.
- Tundra biomes have long, very cold winters, brief summer growing seasons, no trees, and many migrating animals during summer.

LAB #15　Soils

Recommended Textbook Reading Prior to Lab:
- Chapter 9, Soil and Water Resources
  - 9.2 The Living Veneer: Soils

Goals: After completing this lab, you will be able to:
- Identify the physical and chemical characteristics of soil horizons.
- Classify soils based on soil taxonomy descriptions and selected map locations.
- Carry out texture classification of selected soil samples and plot the soils within the soil texture classification triangle.
- Conduct soil texture classification exercises using "feel analysis" and its flow chart.
- Carry out pH determination and evaluation exercises.
- Determine what plants are appropriate to grow in selected soils after pH measurements.

Key Terms and Concepts:
- climate as a soil-forming factor
- leaching
- loam
- parent material
- regolith
- soil components
- soil composition
- soil formation
- soil horizons
- soil orders

Required Materials:
- Calculator
- For the "feel analysis" portion of Module 3:
  - Clay (Ward's Natural Science: 45 V 1981)
  - Fine Sand (Ward's Natural Science: 45 V 1983)
  - Silt (Ward's Natural Science: 45 V 1982)
- Textbook: *Living Physical Geography*, by Bruce Gervais

Problem-Solving Module #1: Soil Horizons

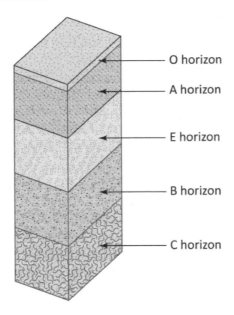

FIGURE 1–1

1. Figure 1–1 is a profile of soil horizons. Complete Table 1–1 by matching the horizon description to its letter.

Soil Profile Description	Figure Letter (Figure 1–1)
This horizon is formed by eluviation (leaching) as rainwater dissolves minerals and carries clay to deeper layers. It is lighter in color than the horizon above it, and it represents a transition zone between horizons.	
This layer is called topsoil and is rich in organic matter. The activities and remains of organisms play an important part in forming this layer. Plant roots are found here.	
Transported clays and dissolved chemicals are deposited (a process of illuviation) in this horizon, which is also called subsoil. It is a zone of accumulated minerals and clay particles. High concentrations of clay, aluminum, and iron are typically found here.	
This layer is composed mostly of both living and dead organic material. Humus is a brownish-black mixture of organic material rich in carbon and nitrogen, essential for plant growth. The best farmlands have well-developed humus.	
This horizon is composed of unconsolidated rock sandwiched between the soil horizons above and the bedrock below. There is little to no organic material here.	

TABLE 1–1

Problem-Solving Module #2: Soil Taxonomy

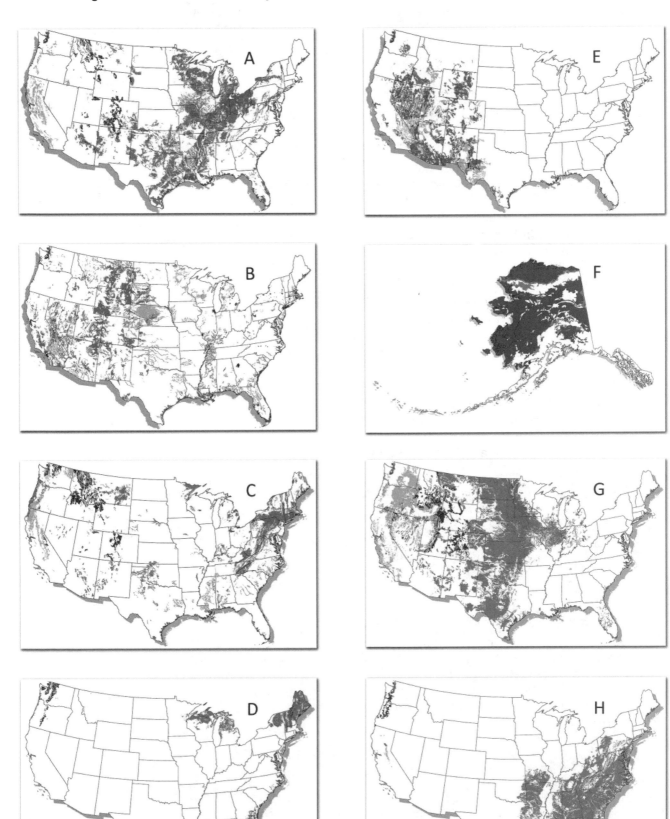

FIGURE 2–1

Research from USDA, NRCS

© 2014 W. H. Freeman and Company

1. Figure 2–1 presents eight maps showing the location of various soil orders in the United States. Complete Table 2–1 by first naming the soil orders by their correct taxonomical classification (see your textbook), and then identifying the map letter (from Figure 2–1) that is associated with the soil order.

Soil Order Description	Taxonomical Name	Map Letter (Figure 2–1)
☐ Desert soils with low organic matter and rapid drainage ☐ Easily leached ☐ Salinization is common as irrigation water evaporates ☐ Common in the southwestern United States		
☐ Have permafrost and evidence of disturbance by frost ☐ Restricted to high-latitude polar areas ☐ Store large quantities of carbon		
☐ Develops in humid climates ☐ Formed under forest or savanna vegetation ☐ B horizon is gray/brown, with clay accumulation ☐ High fertility and thus good for agriculture ☐ Common in the U.S. Midwest, east of the Mississippi River		
☐ Formed under forest vegetation ☐ Old, weathered, heavily leached, and nutrient-poor ☐ Often yellow or reddish, with significant clay ☐ Acidic soils that requires fertilizers and lime for agricultural use ☐ Common in the southeastern United States		
☐ Formed under grass or savanna vegetation ☐ Extensive beneath prairies in the Great Plains ☐ Thick, dark A horizon with a soft texture ☐ High nutrient content and fertility, thus excellent for agriculture		
☐ Young, recently deposited soils ☐ Have little to no evidence of soil horizons ☐ Many are sandy and very shallow. ☐ Often found in new deposits from rivers, glaciers, or sand dunes ☐ Common in western Nebraska, eastern Montana, and Wyoming		
☐ Formed under coniferous forests with cool and snowy climates ☐ E horizon is often bleached ☐ Acidic soils that require lime for agricultural use ☐ Nutrient-poor ☐ Common in Maine and northern Michigan		
☐ Young soils with poorly developed horizons ☐ Common on steep slopes and the northern tundra ☐ Form from resistant parent material ☐ No clay and little organic matter ☐ Common in southern New York, eastern Pennsylvania, and northern California		

TABLE 2–1

Problem-Solving Module #3: Soil Texture

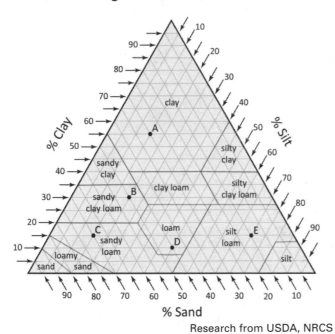

Research from USDA, NRCS

FIGURE 3–1

Texture analysis determines how much clay, silt, and sand are present in soil. This type of analysis is important because nutrient load and water retention vary from one soil texture to another. The soil texture diagram of Figure 3–1 is a ternary graph, where three different variables sum to 100%.

1. Complete Table 3–1 by identifying the soil texture percentages of sample points A–E on Figure 3–1.

Identification Letter (Figure 3–1)	% Clay	% Silt	% Sand
A			
B			
C			
D			
E			

TABLE 3–1

2. Complete Table 3–2 by using the soil texture percentages and names seen on Figure 3–1.

% Clay	% Silt	% Sand	Soil Texture
	40	25	
10		30	
45	45		
	50	15	
40	5		
55		20	
5	5		
	85	10	
	5	85	
20		45	
15		65	
	10	60	

TABLE 3–2

© 2014 W. H. Freeman and Company

If a scientist has a general understanding of a local area's soil composition, a field technique called "feel analysis" is useful in determining the texture classification of a soil sample. This diagnostic field judgment can then be tested in a laboratory when time and resources allow. Figure 3–2 is a feel analysis flow chart.

Follow the flow chart instructions on Figure 3–2 to classify the soil samples provided by your instructor (note that your hands will get quite dirty in this exercise).

3. What is the texture classification of soil sample #1? _____.

4. What is the texture classification of soil sample #2? _____.

5. What is the texture classification of soil sample #3? _____.

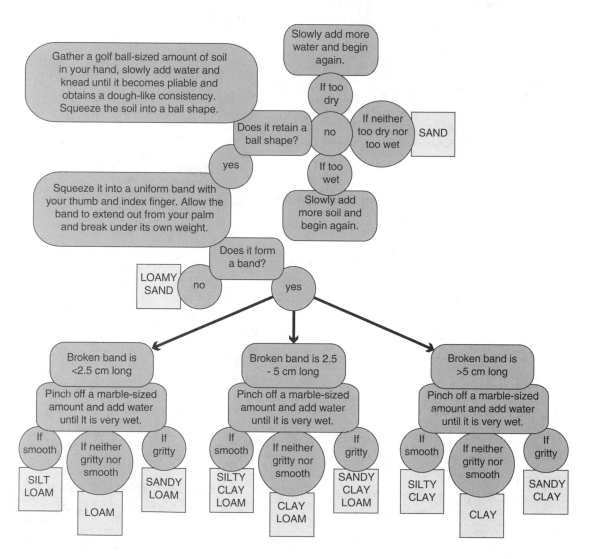

FIGURE 3–2

Problem-Solving Module #4: Soil pH

Depending on the plant, up to 20 chemical elements may be essential for growth. Three elements—carbon, hydrogen, and oxygen—are acquired from the air. All other elements must be obtained from the soil, and all of these must be dissolved in the soil matrix in order to be available to a plant's roots. Slightly acidic soils contain more dissolved nutrients compared to neutral or slightly alkaline soils.

The pH scale—from 0 to 14—is a measure of a solution's acidity or alkalinity. Greater concentrations of hydrogen ions in a solution lower the pH. Soils with pH from 7 to 0 have increasing concentrations of hydrogen ions and are thus increasingly acidic. Soils with pH from 7 to 14 have decreasing concentrations of hydrogen ions and are thus increasingly alkaline.

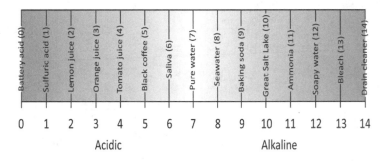

FIGURE 4–1

Crop	Soil pH				
	4.7	**5**	**5.7**	**6.8**	**7.5**
	Relative Yield (100 is best, 0 is worst)				
Corn	34	73	83	100	85
Wheat	68	78	89	100	99
Soybeans	65	79	80	100	93
Oats	77	93	99	98	100
Barley	0	23	80	95	100
Alfalfa	2	9	42	100	100
Timothy grass	31	47	66	100	95

Credit/courtesy of USDA (adapted)

TABLE 4–1

Different plants require different nutrients, and depending upon soil pH, these nutrients may be more or less available. Table 4–1 presents the relative yield of seven crops in soils with different pH. Use Table 4–1 to answer questions 1–4.

1. Which crop produces the best yields in pH 5 soil? _____

2. Soybeans can grow in pH 4.7 soil but will produce best yields in pH _____ soil.

3. If a farmer grows corn in pH 7.5 soil and struggles to meet his financial obligations, what crop change might you recommend and why?

   _____

   _____

   _____

4. Which crop produces the best yields across the widest range of soil pH? _____

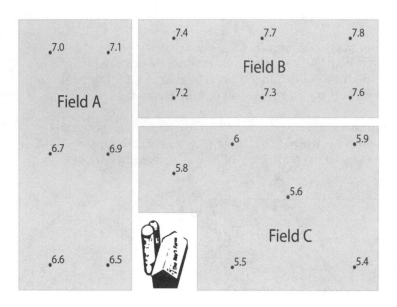

Rather than switching crops to accommodate a soil's pH, many farmers choose to modify their soil to accommodate a crop. Thus, you may see a farmer adding ground limestone (simply called "lime") to an especially acidic soil in order to increase the soil's pH (make it more alkaline). Or, you may see a farmer adding sulfur to an especially alkaline soil in order to decrease the soil's pH (make it more acidic).

FIGURE 4–2

Figure 4–1 is a model of a farm with three agricultural fields. Each field has six pH sample sites. Use the information on Figures 4–1 and 4–2, as well as in Table 4–1, to answer questions 5–11.

5. The average pH of Field A is _____, making it slightly _____.
                                                            (acidic/alkaline)

6. The average pH of Field B is _____, making it slightly _____.
                                                            (acidic/alkaline)

7. The average pH of Field C is _____, making it _____.
                                                    (acidic/alkaline)

8. List the crops that would grow best in Field A.

   _____

   _____

9. Assume the farmer grows corn in Field B. As a soil scientist, what would you advise him to grow instead of corn, and why?

   _____

   _____

10. Assume the farmer grows corn in Field B, and because corn prices are high, he wants to continue growing corn in Field B. As a soil scientist, what would you advise him to do in order to increase his yield in this field, and why?

   _____

   _____

   _____

11. Assume the farmer grows barley in Field C, and because barley prices are high, he wants to continue growing barley in Field C. As a soil scientist, what would you advise him to do in order to increase his yield in this field, and why?

   _____

   _____

   _____

Summary of Key Terms and Concepts:

- Climate is the most important soil-forming factor. Deep soils form where climate is humid and warm.
- Leaching is the process of dissolving and carrying minerals deeper into the soil, often out of reach of plant roots.
- Loam is soil that is somewhat equal parts sand, silt, and clay, and with a high organic content.
- Parent material is composed of both the weathered bedrock beneath the soil and regolith that has been transported and deposited by erosion.
- Regolith is any unconsolidated fragmented rock that covers bedrock.
- Soil components include rock fragments and minerals, water, air, and organic material.
- Soil is composed of rock fragments and living organisms.
- Soil forms from weathering and the actions of organisms over time.
- Soil horizons develop as soils form and rainwater leaches minerals and nutrients deeper down.
- There are 12 soil orders. They are based on soil color, texture, and chemistry.

LAB #16 Groundwater

Problem-Solving Module #1: Groundwater, Wells, and the Water Table

1. What is an aquifer?

_____

2. How is a zone of saturation different from a zone of aeration?

_____

_____

_____

3. What is a water table?

_____

4. List three reasons why water table depth varies over time.

_____

_____

_____

_____

5. How does porosity differ from permeability?

_____

_____

_____

_____

6. Why would unfractured igneous rock make a poor aquifer?

_____

_____

_____

_____

Figure 1–1 is a map with contour lines that graphically present the depth of the water table relative to Earth's surface. (Because U.S. data is measured and recorded in feet, so too is this exercise—most of the rest of the world uses meters, as mentioned in the textbook.) Notice that the map also contains four wells (labeled A–D), a feed lot, and a chemical spill site.

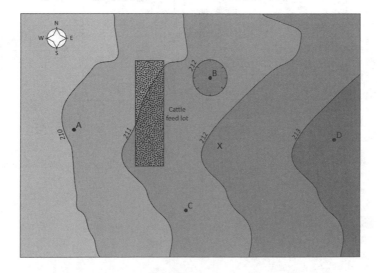

FIGURE 1–1

7. Graph the well data in Table 1–1 to the respective graphs on Figure 1–2.

	Depth to Water Table (feet below Earth's Surface)			
	Well A	**Well B**	**Well C**	**Well D**
Monday	210.80	212.88	211.89	213.72
Tuesday	210.75	212.86	211.85	213.70
Wednesday	210.74	212.86	211.84	213.64
Thursday	210.50	212.70	211.54	213.42
Friday	210.37	212.82	211.60	213.44
Saturday	210.72	212.82	211.75	213.55
Sunday	210.80	212.88	211.85	213.65

TABLE 1–1

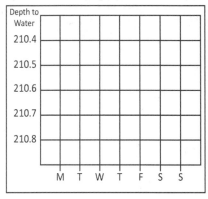

Well A

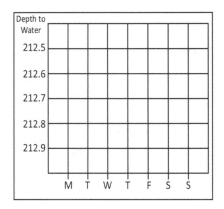

Well B

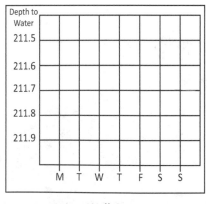

Well C

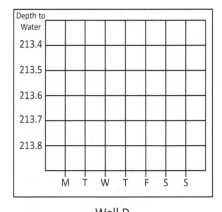

Well D

Credit/courtesy USGS (adapted)

FIGURE 1–2

Use Figures 1–1 and 1–2 to answer questions 8–14.

8. If you walked from west to east across the landscape modeled on Figure 1–1, what would happen to the depth of the water table?

_____

9. What is happening at well B, and what is this phenomenon called?

_____

_____

10. What meteorological phenomenon do you think happened on Wednesday and Thursday?

_____

11. What happened to the water table between Wednesday and Thursday?

_____

12. Did groundwater recharge or discharge happen between Wednesday and Thursday, and why do you think so?

_____

_____

13. Why would the feedlot (a factory farm) on Figure 1–1 be a concern for wells B and D?

_____

_____

_____

14. Assume a liquid, toxic, chemical spill occurred in the map's center, just east of contour line 212. Which well(s) would need testing to ensure water safety? Explain why you selected the well(s) you did.

_____

_____

_____

_____

Problem-Solving Module #2: The Ogallala (High Plains) Aquifer

1. Why is the water that is stored in the Ogallala Aquifer called fossil groundwater?

_____

_____

2. In what portion of the Ogallala Aquifer is groundwater mining occurring, and why?

_____

_____

_____

Download the following file from the textbook companion site and open it in Google Earth:
- Ogallala (High Plains) Aquifer.kmz

This map shows water-level changes in the Ogallala Aquifer from predevelopment to 2011. Predevelopment is defined as the time before 1950, except in the Texas Panhandle, where it is defined as before 2000.

3. What does the color red symbolize on the Ogallala Legend?

_____

4. What does the color grey symbolize on the Ogallala Legend?

_____

5. What does the color blue symbolize on the Ogallala Legend?

_____

Consider this statement, which broadly describes what has happened since predevelopment to the Ogallala Aquifer beneath Kansas.
- Since predevelopment, the Ogallala Aquifer beneath Kansas has generally experienced moderate to severe declines in water level. The southwestern corner of the state is where the steepest water-level declines are observed.

6. In your own words, compose a sentence that broadly describes what has happened to the Ogallala Aquifer beneath Nebraska since predevelopment. Use the Kansas description (above) to model your own sentence.

_____

_____

_____

_____

7. In your own words, compose a sentence that broadly describes what has happened to the Ogallala Aquifer beneath the Texas Panhandle since predevelopment. Use the Kansas description (above) to model your own sentence.

_____

_____

_____

_____

8. Complete Table 2–1 by flying to the listed locations and recording the water-level change since predevelopment.

Location	State	Water-Level Change (Decline, No Change, or Rise)	Water-Level Change (ft)
A			
B			
C			
D			
E			
F			
G			

TABLE 2–1

In the Places Sidebar, turn off (uncheck) the following image overlay: Ogallala (High Plains) Aquifer.

9. Fly to locations B, D, and F. What type of irrigation is visible at these locations?

_____

10. Describe how the irrigation method seen at locations B, D, and F works.

_____

_____

_____

_____

11. Why is the irrigation method seen at locations B, D, and F an example of unsustainable land use?

_____

_____

_____

Fly to the USGS Groundwater Watch Well located in Texas, and click on the accompanying Web link. Use the USGS information to answer questions 12–18.

12. How deep is this well? _____

13. What organization maintains the records for this site?

_____

14. What was the first date that data was collected for this well? _____

15. What was the last date that data was collected for this well? _____

16. How high was the water in this well in 2009? _____

17. How high was the water in this well in 2013? _____

18. How much has the water level dropped between the first and last measurements? _____

Fly to the USGS Groundwater Watch Well located in Kansas, and click on the accompanying Web link. Use the USGS information to answer questions 19–25.

19. How deep is this well? _____

20. What organization maintains the records for this site?

_____

21. What was the first date that data was collected for this well? _____

22. What was the last date that data was collected for this well? _____

23. How high was the water in this well in 1954? _____

24. How high was the water in this well in 2013? _____

25. How much has the water level dropped between the first and last measurements? _____

Fly to the USGS Groundwater Watch Well located in Nebraska, and click on the accompanying Web link. Use the USGS information to answer questions 26–32.

26. How deep is this well? _____

27. What organization maintains the records for this site?

_____

28. What was the first date that data was collected for this well? _____

29. What was the last date that data was collected for this well? _____

30. How high was the water in this well in 1975? _____

31. How high was the water in this well in 2013? _____

32. How much has the water level dropped between the first and last measurements?

_____

33. Compose a summary statement describing the height of the water in the three examined wells.

_____

_____

_____

34. Based on your above work, what recommendations would you make to lawmakers as they consider public and private access to Ogallala Aquifer groundwater resources? Explain your reasoning.

_____

_____

_____

_____

Summary of Key Terms and Concepts:
- An aquifer is solid rock that contains water and allows that water to flow through it.
- Aquifers are contaminated by careless land-use practices, including leaking landfills, gas-station tanks, sewage from factory farms, and agricultural chemical use.
- Water exits aquifers through groundwater discharge.
- Groundwater mining occurs when water in an aquifer is not replaced through natural recharge, such as occurs in arid regions.
- Water enters aquifers through groundwater recharge.
- Permeability is the ease with which water can enter the pore spaces within sediments or rocks.
- Porosity is the volume of air space that water can move into and occupy.
- The water table is the boundary between the zone of aeration and zone of saturation.
- The zone of aeration lies above the water table.
- The zone of saturation lies below the water table.

LAB #17   Seawater

Recommended Textbook Reading Prior to Lab:
- Chapter 10, The Living Hydrosphere: Ocean Ecosystems
  - 10.1 The Physical Oceans

Goals: After completing this lab, you will be able to:
- Evaluate the human impact on Earth's marine ecosystems using spatial analysis and the scientific method.
- Express and convert seawater salinity in parts per hundred (%) and parts per thousand (‰).
- Judge why particular locations have higher or lower sea surface salinity values, using an atlas (or Google Earth) and a global seawater salinity map.
- Hypothesize, graph, and solve the question of which of Earth's hemispheres has a greater seawater surface temperature range using data within Google Earth.

Key terms and concepts:
- human impact on Earth's marine ecosystems
- seawater chemistry
- surface seawater salinity
- surface seawater temperature

Required materials:
- Atlas (or Google Earth)
- Calculator
- High-speed Internet connection (for Module 3) and Google Earth (free download)
- Textbook: *Living Physical Geography*, by Bruce Gervais

Problem-Solving Module #1: Human Impact on Marine Ecosystems

Assume you are a marine scientist and concerned about the health and stability of marine ecosystems. To better understand this issue, you need to know the extent of human impact on Earth's marine ecosystems. You define human impacts to include land-based activities (such as runoff of pollutants and nutrients) and ocean-based activities (such as biological and nonbiological resource extraction). You decide to sample Earth's oceans and rank human impact based on the scale presented in Table 1–1.

Marine Ecosystem Ranking	Impact Extent
1	Very low
2	Low
3	Medium
4	Medium high
5	High
6	Very high

TABLE 1–1

Before you begin your study, other marine scientists use your proposed ranking system to posit their own hypotheses about the extent of human impact on Earth's marine ecosystems. Here are some of their statements:

- Human impact on Earth's marine ecosystems is very low.
- Human impact on Earth's marine ecosystems is high.
- Human impact on Earth's marine ecosystems is very high.

1. Compose a hypothesis about the human impact on Earth's marine ecosystems. Compose your hypothesis in the same style that the three marine scientists used.

   _____

   _____

2. To test your hypothesis, what data do you need to collect?

   _____

   _____

   _____

   _____

Figure 1–1 is a map of Earth with a grid of marine ecosystem sampling points. Each sampling location is assigned a rank based on the scheme presented in Table 1–1.

3. Use Figure 1–1 to collect and process data. Complete Table 1–2.

Total Number of Sampling Sites	Total Value of all Sampled Sites	Average Value of all Samples	Marine Ecosystem Ranking (Table 1)

TABLE 1–2

4. Complete Step #5 of the scientific method. Is your hypothesis supported or not supported by the data?

_____

_____

_____

_____

5. Compose a sentence or two that corresponds with Step #6 of the scientific method as it relates to the human impact on Earth's marine ecosystems. Recall that this step is about further inquiry, and it includes speculation about new questions, new ideas, and more/ different data collection.

_____

_____

_____

_____

6. How do you think your results might have been different if a targeted sampling system correlated to coastal urban centers was used instead of a regular, gridded sampling system covering the entire planet? Explain your reasoning.

_____

_____

_____

_____

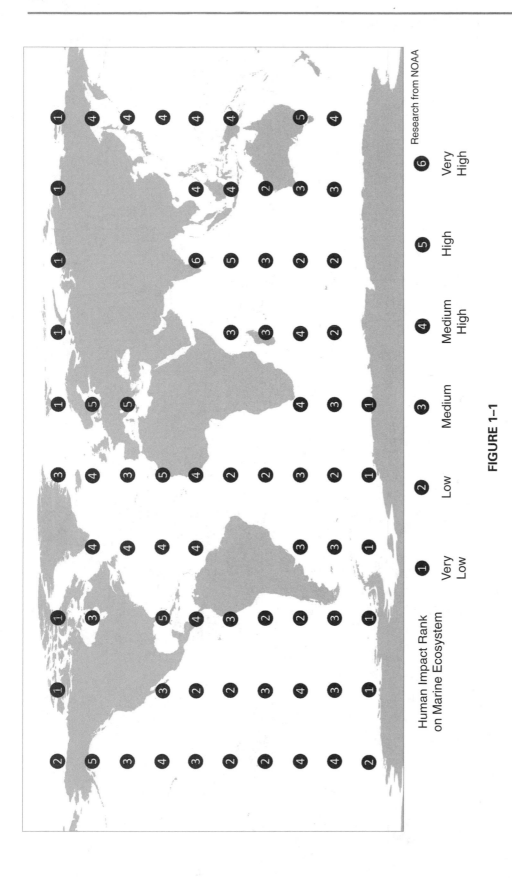

FIGURE 1-1

Problem-Solving Module #2: Seawater Salinity

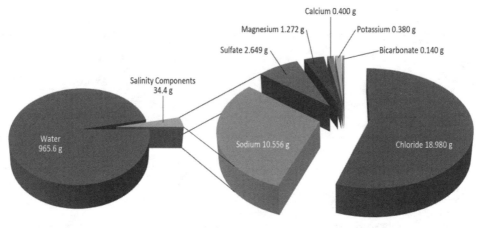

FIGURE 2–1

Average ocean salinity is 3.5%, although it ranges geographically from as little as 1% to as high as 4.1%. Expressing salinity as a percentage (%), or parts per hundred, is a readily-understood method. A more precise way to express salinity is in grams per kilogram, or parts per thousand. Because 1 kilogram is 1,000 grams, when expressing salinity this way the permille (‰) is used. A permille means parts per thousand. One permille is one tenth of one percent, or more simply, one part per thousand.

1. Figure 2–1 expresses the salinity in a random sample of seawater. Complete Table 2–1 using Figure 2–1.

Salinity Component	g/kg (‰)	Percent by Mass (%)
Chloride		1.9
Sodium	10.556	
Sulfate		0.3
Magnesium	1.272	
Calcium		0.04
Potassium	0.380	
Bicarbonate		0.01

Total	34.4‰	

TABLE 2–1

Figure 2–1 is a map of Earth showing ocean surface salinity in grams per kilogram. Salinity values range from a high of 40 g/kg (40‰) to a low of 30 g/kg (30‰). The data were acquired from NASA's Aquarius mission between August 25 and September 11, 2011.

Seawater surface salinity is relatively high where there is a lot of evaporation, such as in the subtropics (30° N and 30° S latitude). The effect of high evaporation in the subtropics is further exacerbated in places where water is relatively restricted from greater ocean circulation, such as in the Mediterranean Sea.

Seawater surface salinity is relatively low where there is little evaporation (such as in cool, high-latitude places), where rivers discharge into the sea, or where heavy rainfall dilutes the sea with freshwater.

2. Complete Table 2–2. Use an atlas (or Google Earth) to identify the likely reason why particular locations on Figure 2–2 have their respective seawater surface salinity value.

Location	Salinity (g/kg) or (‰)	Likely Reason for Salinity Value
Yellow Sea		
1° N, 48° W		
32° N, 45° W		
58° N, 138° W		
Bay of Bengal		
68° N, 169° W		
25° S, 3° W		
35° N, 18° E		
Hudson Bay		

TABLE 2–2

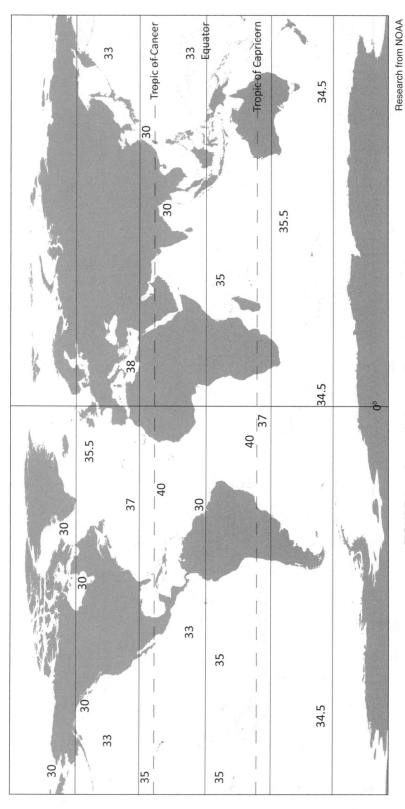

FIGURE 2–2: Ocean Salinity in Parts Per Thousand

Research from NOAA

Problem-Solving Module #3: Seawater Surface Temperature

Download the following file from the textbook companion site and open it in Google Earth:
- Seawater Surface Temperature.kmz

This Google Earth file has two image overlays, each showing average seawater surface temperatures. One image presents temperatures in January, the other in July. The data were acquired using ships, buoys, and satellites. The file also has a north/south oriented "Temperature Recording Path" upon which 14 equally-spaced data-collection sites are located. Seven locations are in the northern hemisphere, and seven are in the southern hemisphere.

Consider the following information:
- Maritime areas have lower annual temperature ranges than continental areas due to the moderating effect of water's specific heat.
- Specific heat is the amount of energy required to raise 1 gram of a substance 1°C.
- It takes less energy to raise the temperature of 1 gram of land 1°C compared to 1 gram of water 1°C.
- The northern hemisphere contains more land than the southern hemisphere.

Assume you are an atmospheric scientist and are investigating the effect of Earth's land and water areas on climate patterns. To begin your work, you need to know if the northern or southern hemisphere has a greater annual temperature range.

1. Using the background information above, compose a hypothesis about which of Earth's hemispheres has a greater annual temperature range.

   _____

   _____

   _____

2. To test your hypothesis, what data do you need to collect?

   _____

   _____

   _____

3. On Figure 3–1, graph the average temperature data for every sample site along the "Temperature Recording Path." Create a solid line for the January data and a dashed line for the July data. Note: If the data are difficult to discern at any particular location, make your best judgment based on the available information. Recall that you can fly to any site by double-clicking its letter in the Places Sidebar. Don't forget to turn the January and July temperature overlays on or off to obtain data for the correct month.

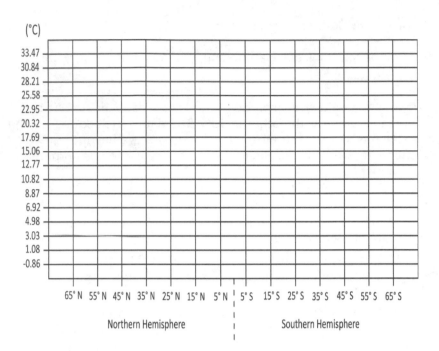

FIGURE 3–1

4. Carefully consider the gap between the January and July temperature lines and how this gap is different in the northern hemisphere compared to the southern hemisphere. Given this information, is your hypothesis supported or not supported by the data? Explain your reasoning by specifically referring to the data at 45° N latitude compared to 45° S latitude.

_____

_____

_____

_____

_____

_____

_____

5. Compose a sentence or two that corresponds with Step #6 of the scientific method as it relates to the human impact on Earth's marine ecosystems. Recall that this step is about further inquiry, and it includes speculation about new questions, new ideas, and more/different data collection. Consider, for example, temperature data from specific oceans, the data collection path location and orientation, and seawater chemistry.

_____

_____

_____

_____

_____

_____

_____

Summary of Key Terms and Concepts:

- Humans have a significant impact on marine ecosystems and profoundly influence the health and stability of marine ecosystems.
- Every element on Earth is dissolved in ocean water in extremely minute trace amounts. By volume, most dissolved material is chlorine and sodium.
- Salinity is the concentration of salt in the oceans that results from rocks dissolving as rivers flow over them. Each year, rivers deposit about 2.5 billion tons of salt into the oceans. The average ocean salinity is 3.5% or 35‰ (35 parts per thousand).
- The temperature at the surface of the oceans varies considerably between the tropics and high latitudes.

LAB #18

Ocean Currents and the Great Pacific Ocean Garbage Patch

Recommended Textbook Reading Prior to Lab:
- Chapter 10, The Living Hydrosphere: Ocean Ecosystems
  - 10.1 The Physical Oceans
  - 10.5 Geographic Perspectives: The Problem with Plastic

Goals: After completing this lab, you will be able to:
- Identify Earth's major surface currents based on descriptions of their characteristics and locations.
- Analyze ocean gyres and discuss their relative motions within the northern and southern hemispheres.
- Judge where upwelling and sinking sites are located along all of Earth's major global thermohaline circulation belts.
- Map research transects in the North Pacific Gyre to study the abundance of neustonic plastic.
- Compose narratives describing the abundance of neustonic plastic in the North Pacific Gyre.
- Constructively critique the research design, methods, and findings of the neustonic plastic study in the North Pacific Gyre.

Key terms and concepts:
- deep ocean currents
- neustonic plastic
- ocean gyres
- pelagic
- surface ocean currents
- thermohaline circulation
- upwelling

Required materials:
- Atlas (or Google Earth)
- Calculator
- Textbook: *Living Physical Geography*, by Bruce Gervais

Problem-Solving Module #1: Surface Currents and Thermohaline Circulation

Figure 1–1 is a map of Earth's major ocean surface currents. Each black arrow represents a specific current, and most of the currents are identified with a letter.

1. Complete Table 1–1 by first reading the description of the current and then using an atlas to determine the correct letter on Figure 1–1 that is associated with that current.

Current Name	Description	Identification Letter on Figure 1–1
North equatorial	Flows parallel to and north of the equator. In the Pacific it carries warm water to the Philippines.	
Benguela	A cold current flowing parallel to the coast of Namibia, thereby creating the Namib Desert.	
South equatorial	Flows parallel to and south of the equator. It carries warm water to Madagascar in the Indian Ocean.	
Gulf Stream	A warm current flowing parallel to the east cost of the United States. It creates a temperate climate in northwest Europe.	
Brazil	A south-flowing current that brings warm water off the coast of Rio de Janeiro.	
California	A south-flowing current that brings cold water off the coast of San Francisco.	
Canary	A south-flowing current moving past the Canary Islands.	
North Pacific	An east-flowing current moving south of the Aleutian Islands.	
Labrador	A south-flowing, cold current flowing through the Davis Strait and into the Labrador Sea.	
Peru	A cold current flowing parallel to the coast of Peru, thereby creating the Atacama Desert.	

TABLE 1–1

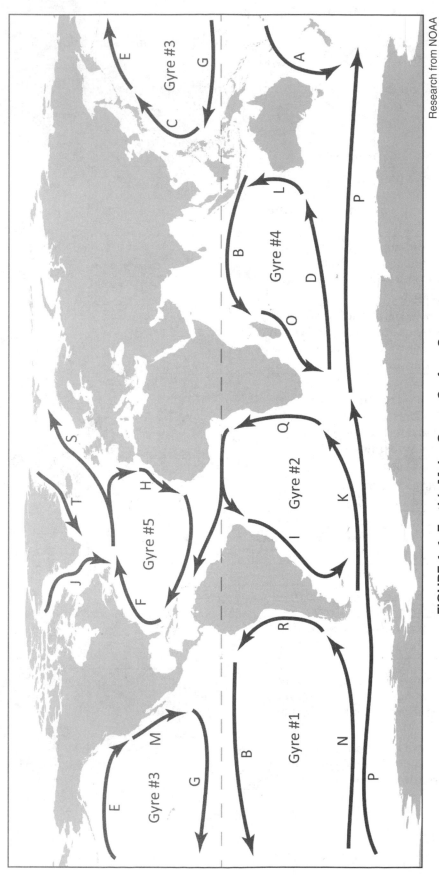

FIGURE 1–1: Earth's Major Ocean Surface Currents

Ocean gyres are circular currents caused by Coriolis force—a deflective force caused by Earth's rotation. The Coriolis force causes wind and water to bend to the right in the northern hemisphere, and to the left in the southern hemisphere.

2. How many major ocean gyres are on Earth? _____

3. Do northern hemisphere gyres flow clockwise or counterclockwise? _____

4. Use Figure 1–1, your work in Table 1–1, and an atlas (or Google Earth) to complete Table 1–2.

Gyre Description	Gyre # on Figure 1–1
Flows counterclockwise; its eastern leg is the Benguela current.	
Flows clockwise; its western leg is the Gulf Stream current.	
Flows counterclockwise; its eastern leg is the Peru current.	
Flows counterclockwise in the Indian Ocean.	
Flows counterclockwise; its northern leg is the North Pacific current.	

TABLE 1–2

Figure 1–2 a map of Earth's thermohaline circulation. This deep-water, global-scale flow is initiated when sea ice forms in the North Atlantic. Dense, high-saline water sinks as a result of surface ice formation. As this water sinks, warm surface water moves north to take its place. Thermohaline circulation is often compared to a conveyor belt moving heat and matter around Earth's oceans.

5. Table 1–3 describes specific legs along the thermohaline conveyor belt and respectively enumerates these legs from 1 to 7. In the blank lines on Figure 1–2, identify these legs at their correct locations.

Leg Description	Respective Leg # on Conveyor Belt
Sea ice forms in the North Atlantic creating dense, salty water that sinks.	1
A deep water current flows south along the western Atlantic basin.	2
A deep water current divides into two forks; one flows north into the Indian Ocean, and the other flows toward southern Australia and the western pacific.	3
A deep water current flows along Antarctica and becomes colder, saltier, and denser.	4
The current warms as it travels north along the east coast of Africa.	5
The current warms as it moves into the western Pacific Ocean and travels north.	6
The warmed current flows around South Africa and then north into the south Atlantic.	7

TABLE 1–3

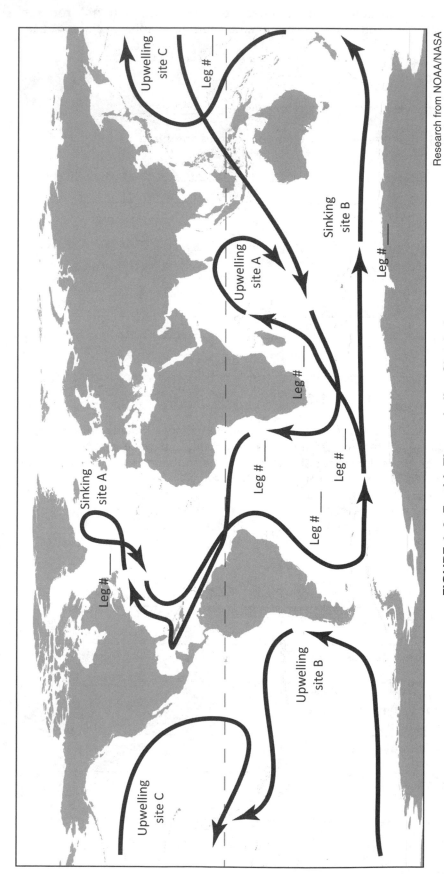

FIGURE 1–2: Earth's Thermohaline Circulation

Research from NOAA/NASA

6. Figure 1–2 identifies several upwelling and sinking sites along the global thermohaline circulation conveyor belt. Table 1–4 describes these specific sites. Use Figure 1–2 and an atlas (or Google Earth) to determine the correct name and letter on Figure 1–2 that is associated with each site.

Site Description	Identification Name and Letter
Dense, salty water sinks off the coast of Antarctica.	Sinking site B
Nutrient-rich water rises off Russia's Kamchatka Krai coast and flows east to North America.	
Dense, salty water sinks off the coast of southern Greenland and Iceland.	
Nutrient-rich water rises off Peru's coast and flows north and west toward the eastern Pacific.	
Nutrient-rich water rises off the coasts of southern India and Sri Lanka.	

TABLE 1–4

Problem-Solving Module #2: The Great Pacific Ocean Garbage Patch

The Great Pacific Ocean Garbage Patch is located in the relatively stable, open-ocean (pelagic) waters inside the North Pacific Gyre. It consists of very small pieces of floating (neuston) plastic debris. The neustonic plastic pieces are too small to be seen from the deck of a boat, and undetectable with satellites, so the complete content and abundance of the garbage patch are unknown.

Assume you are an oceanographer working with the Algalita Marine Research Foundation, a nonprofit research foundation dedicated to the protection of the marine environment. You are part of an ocean expedition studying the abundance of neustonic plastic in the North Pacific Gyre. The expedition samples the ocean along two transects (paths) with an especially fine sieve that is dragged alongside a ship (the mechanism is called a "manta trawl" and it is lined with a 333 µ (micron) mesh net). The ship's transect coordinates are presented in Table 2–1.

	Beginning Coordinates	**Ending Coordinates**
Transect #1	35°45' N, 138° 30' W	36° 4' N, 142° 4' W
Transect #2	36° 4' N, 142° 4' W	34° 40' N, 142° 4' W

TABLE 2–1

1. On Figure 2–1, identify the beginning and ending location of each transect and then draw an arrow showing the direction of motion of the research vessel along each transect.

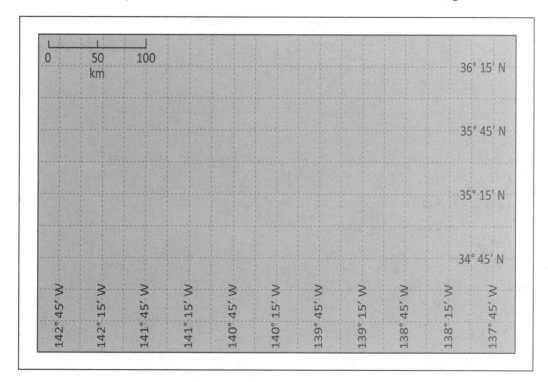

FIGURE 2–1

2. How many kilometers long is Transect #1? _____

3. How many kilometers long is Transect #2? _____

After processing samples from the expedition's two transects, you and your colleagues then calculate the mean (average) abundance of neustonic plastic in the entire North Pacific Gyre. This information is presented in Table 2–2.

Size (mm)	Fragments	Styrofoam	Pellets	Mono-filaments	Thins Plastics	Tar	Misc.	Total
>4.760	1,931	84	36	16,811	5,322	217	350	
4.759–2.80	4,502	121	471	4,839	9,631	97	36	
2.799–1.000	61,187	1,593	12	9,969	40,622	833	72	
0.999–0.710	55,780	591	0	2,933	26,273	378	48	86,003
0.709–0.500	45,196	567	12	1,460	10,572	121	0	
0.499–0.355	26,888	338	0	845	3,222	169	229	
Total	195,484							

Courtesy of Charles J. Moore, PhD (hon)

TABLE 2–2: Mean Abundance (pieces/km2) of Neustonic Plastic and Tar in the North Pacific Gyre

4. Complete Table 2–2 by calculating the total number of neustonic plastic pieces by size and by type.

Consider the following narrative of the data in Table 2–2.
   • In every square kilometer of the North Pacific Gyre there are 195,484 fragments of plastic.

5. Compose a narrative explanation about the pieces of monofilament that are presented on Table 2–2. Use the above narration as a model.

_____

_____

6. Compose a narrative explanation about the data sized between 2.799–1.000 mm that is presented on Table 2–2. Use the above narration as a model.

_____

_____

7. You and your colleagues calculate the average mass of neustonic plastic and tar in the North Pacific Gyre as 5,114 g/km². If the total area of the North Pacific Gyre is 20 million square kilometers, how many kilograms of neustonic plastic and tar are in the North Pacific Gyre? Be sure to show your work.

_____

_____

_____

Good scientists are constructively critical about research designs, methods, and findings. The intent is to achieve the highest possible standards so that the results of scientific inquiry are as close as possible to the truth. Constructive critiques often take the form of helpful statements and/or questions.

8. Research design is the structure of a study that establishes the plan to collect and process data. For the above study of neustonic plastic in the North Pacific Gyre, offer a constructive critique of the <u>research design</u>.

_____

_____

_____

_____

_____

_____

9. Research methods are the manner in which data are collected and processed. Methods include the physical tools by which data are acquired. For the above study of neustonic plastic in the North Pacific Gyre, offer a constructive critique of the <u>research method</u>.

_____

_____

_____

_____

_____

_____

10. Research findings are the conclusions drawn from a study. Conclusions may be specific to the researched area or topic and/or may be generalized beyond the researched area and/or topic. For the above study of neustonic plastic in the North Pacific Gyre, offer a constructive critique of the <u>research findings</u>. *Hint: Consider the total area that was studied (see Figure 2–1) and then consider the entire North Pacific Gyre.*

_____

_____

_____

_____

_____

_____

Summary of Key Terms and Concepts:
- Deep ocean currents are created by changes in water density.
- Neustonic plastic is plastic that floats on or near the surface of the water.
- Ocean gyres are circular currents caused by Coriolis Effect.
- The pelagic ocean is the open sea far from an adjacent landmass.
- Surface ocean currents are driven by wind.
- Thermohaline circulation is deepwater-ocean circulation due to water density differences. It is initiated in the North Atlantic from the formation of sea ice.
- Upwelling of deep ocean currents carries nutrient-rich water to ocean surfaces.

LAB #19

Relative and Absolute Dating and the Geological Time Scale

Recommended Textbook Reading Prior to Lab:
- Chapter 11, Earth History, Earth Interior
  - 11.2 Deep History: Geologic Time

Goals: After completing this lab, you will be able to:
- Carry out relative dating investigations using the established principles of the discipline.
- Clarify the difference between relative and absolute dating, as well as their associated methods.
- Provide examples of commonly used radionuclides and their half-lives.
- Identify specific divisions on the geologic time scale and discuss their geological and paleontological characteristics.

Key Terms and Concepts:
- absolute dating
- daughter product
- geologic time scale
- half-life
- isotopes
- parent product
- principle of cross-cutting relationships
- principle of faunal succession
- principle of inclusions
- principle of lateral continuity
- principle of original horizontality
- principle of superposition
- principle of uniformitarianism
- radionuclides
- relative dating
- stratigraphy

Required Materials:
- Atlas
- Calculator
- Textbook: *Living Physical Geography*, by Bruce Gervais

Problem-Solving Module #1: Relative Dating

Relative dating is a technique used by physical geographers to express the relative ages of rock formations. For example: "This rock layer formed *before* that rock layer." Relative dating is one tool used in a discipline called *stratigraphy,* in which scientists investigate questions about the sequences of layered deposits.

The relative dating technique is anchored on several principles:

- Principle of uniformitarianism: Geological processes that modify Earth today worked the same way in the past.
- Principle of superposition: In sedimentary rock layers, a layer formed after the one below it but before the one above it.
- Principle of original horizontality: Sediment is deposited in horizontal beds.
- Principle of inclusions: If inclusions (chunks of rock) are found within a rock formation, the inclusion formed before the formation.
- Principle of cross-cutting relationships: Faults and intrusions (rocks that solidify within existing rocks) formed after the rocks they cut through or disturb.
- Principle of lateral continuity: Rocks that are otherwise similar but are separated by an erosional feature were at one time continuous.
- Principle of faunal succession: Rock formations containing plant and animal fossils can be relatively dated using these fossils.

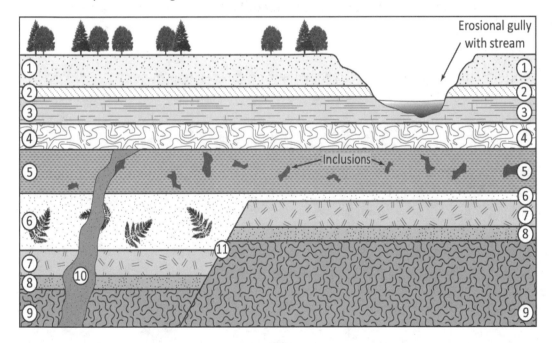

FIGURE 1–1

Figure 1–1 is a profile view of a section of Earth. Use the relative dating techniques explained above, and Figure 1–1, to answer questions 1–9.

1. Which relative dating principle tells us that layer 2 formed after layer 3 but before layer 1?

_____

2. Which formed first, layer 5 or the inclusions within layer 5, and which dating principle applies?

_____

3. Which relative dating principle tells us that the geologic processes that formed the rock strata are the same processes operating on Earth today?

_____

4. Which relative dating principle tells us that we ought to expect all the rock layers to be deposited horizontally?

_____

5. Consider layers 1 and 2. By what relative dating principle do we know that these layers were at one time continuous?

_____

6. Consider layer 6. If we ignore the intrusion identified by number 10, what principle allows us to relatively date layer 6?

_____

7. Which relative dating principle tells us that the fault identified by number 11 occurred after layers 7 and 8 formed?

_____

8. Which relative dating principle tells us that the intrusion identified by number 10 occurred after layers 5–9 formed?

_____

9. If we know how long ago the plants in layer 6 lived, what else can we determine?

_____

_____

Problem-Solving Module #2: Absolute Dating

Absolute dating is a technique used by physical geographers to express the absolute age of rock formations. For example: "This rock is 1.7 million years old." Absolute dating requires measuring the parent/daughter ratio of radioactive elements within a rock sample. A parent product is the original element, and daughter products are the elements left over following radioactive decay.

Radioactive elements (called *radionuclides*) are those that spontaneously emit particles and/or electromagnetic radiation, and thereby decay into different elements. The constant probability of a parent product's decay rate is called its half-life. A *half-life* is the time it takes for half of the parent product's atoms to decay into some other element. Depending on the parent product, half-lives range from fractions of seconds to billions of years.

For example, a form of uranium (forms of elements are called *isotopes*) called U-238 has a half-life of 4.5 billion years. Imagine picking up a rock and counting 1,000,000 atoms of U-238 within this rock. Now imagine 4.5 billion years passing and then recounting the U-238 atoms. You'll find only 500,000 because half of the original U-238 atoms have decayed into daughter products. Thus, 1 half-life has elapsed.

For another example, consider an isotope of cesium, Cs-134, with its half-life of 2 years. Imagine sweeping up a pile of dust and counting 1,657,994,000 atoms of Cs-134 within this dust. Now imagine 2 years passing and then recounting the Cs-134 atoms. You'll find only 828,997,000 because half of the original Cs-134 atoms have decayed into daughter products. Thus, 1 half-life has elapsed.

After 7 half-lives, less than 1% of the original radionuclides remain in any sample.

1. Complete Table 2–1.

Half Lives	% of Original Radionuclide Remaining	% of Daughter Product Accumulated
0	100%	
1		
2		75%
3		
4		
5	3.13%	
6		
7		99.22%

TABLE 2–1

2. Create a line graph on Figure 2–1. Use a solid line and the left *y*-axis to show the relationship between half-life and the percent of the original radionuclide in any sample. Use a dashed line and the right *y*-axis to show the relationship between half-life and the percent of the accumulated daughter product in any sample.

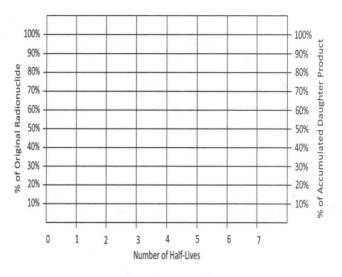

FIGURE 2–1

Parent Radionuclide	Half-Life (years)	Stable Daughter Isotope
Carbon-14	5.73×10^3	Nitrogen-14
Lutetium-176	3.8×10^{10}	Hafnium-176
Potassium-40	1.3×10^9	Argon-40
Rhenium-187	4.2×10^{10}	Osmium-187
Rubidium-87	4.88×10^{10}	Strontium-87
Samarium-147	1.06×10^{11}	Neodymium-143
Thorium-232	1.40×10^{10}	Lead-208
Uranium-238	4.5×10^9	Lead-206
Uranium-235	7.04×10^8	Lead-207

TABLE 2–2

Table 2–2 lists the parent and daughter isotopes used to determine the age of Earth. Use the above information to answer questions 3–6. *Hint: Earth's oldest rocks are about 4 billion (4 x 10^9) years old.*

3. An analysis of a mineral in Rock Sample A-123 reveals that 75% of its potassium-40 atoms have decayed into a stable daughter isotope.

   A) What is this stable daughter isotope? _____

   B) How many half-lives have elapsed in Rock Sample A-123? _____

   C) How old is Rock Sample A-123? Be sure to show your work. _____

   _____

   _____

4. An analysis of a mineral in Rock Sample B-273 reveals that only 6.25% of the original parent radionuclide carbon-14 remains.

   A) What is the stable daughter isotope we would also find? _____

   B) How many half-lives have elapsed in Rock Sample B-273? _____

   C) How old is Rock Sample B-273? Be sure to show your work. _____

   _____

   _____

5. An analysis of a mineral in Rock Sample C-451 reveals that 75% of the original parent radionuclide uranium-238 remains.

   A) What is the stable daughter isotope we would also find? _____

   B) How many half-lives have elapsed in Rock Sample C-451? _____

   C) How old is Rock Sample C-451? Be sure to show your work. _____

   _____

   _____

6. Why is it improbable that scientists will discover a terrestrial rock containing minerals with an original parent isotope of rubidium-87 where 2 half-lives have elapsed?

   _____

   _____

   _____

Problem-Solving #3: The Geologic Time Scale

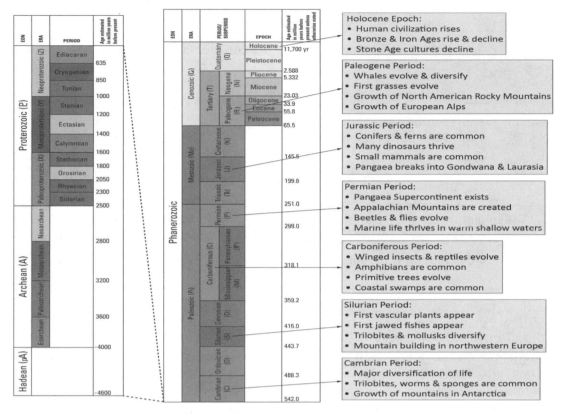

Research from USGS

FIGURE 3–1

Figure 3–1 is a condensed version of the geologic time scale (GTS). The GTS is a guide to Earth's immense history and correlates stratigraphic records to time. It encompasses the time span from Earth's formation, 4.6 billion years ago, to the present. Divisions in the scale are based on 1) significant geologic events, such as increased volcanism or the growth of supercontinents, and/or 2) significant paleontological events, such as an explosion of life or a mass extinction.

Notice on Figure 3–1 that, except for the Holocene Epoch, age is estimated in millions of years before the present. Thus, the Pleistocene Epoch began 2.588 million years ago and ended 11,700 years ago. Finally, recall that "millions of years ago" is abbreviated "Ma," and billions of years ago is abbreviated "Ga."

Use Figure 3–1 to answer questions 1–15.

1. What is the longest time division on the GTS called? _____

2. An era is divided into _____, which are then divided into _____.

3. The _____ Period begin 542.0 Ma and ended _____ Ma.

4. The Pangaea Supercontinent existed during the _____ Period, but it broke up during the _____ Period.

5. The Rocky Mountains experienced significant growth during the _____ Period, which began _____ Ma and ended _____ Ma.

6. Primitive trees evolved during the _____ Period, which began _____ Ma and ended _____ Ma.

7. Trilobites and mollusks diversified during the _____ Period, which began _____ Ma and ended _____ Ma.

8. Both the Bronze and Iron Ages rose and declined during the _____ Epoch, which is one of two divisions of the _____ Period.

9. The _____ Period, which began 65.5 Ma and ended _____ Ma, has five epochs.

10. The _____ Era, which began _____ Ma and ended 65.5 Ma, has three periods.

11. The _____ Era, which began 542 Ma and ended _____ Ma, has six periods.

12. The Tonian and Stenian Periods are both within the _____ Eon, but the Stenian is in the _____ Era while the Tonian is in the _____ Era.

13. The date between the Tonian and Stenian Periods is _____ Ma. Since dates on the GTS are estimated in Ma, _____ zeroes must to be added to this date, which makes it 1 _____ years ago.

14. The date of the beginning of the Hadean Eon is _____ Ma. Since the dates on the GTS are estimated in Ma, _____ zeroes must to be added to this date, which makes it _____ years ago.

15. What percent of Earth's history has seen human civilization rise? Be sure to show your work.

_____

_____

Summary of Key Terms and Concepts:
- Absolute dating is a technique used by physical geographers to express the absolute age of rock formations.
- A daughter product is the element left over following radioactive decay.
- The geologic time scale is a guide to Earth's immense history and correlates stratigraphic records to time.
- A half-life is the time it takes for half of the parent product's atoms to decay into some other element.
- Isotopes are different forms of the same element, differing by the number of neutrons within their atomic nucleus.
- A parent product is the original radionuclide.
- The principle of cross-cutting relationships tells us that faults and intrusions (rocks that solidify within existing rocks) formed after the rocks they cut through or disturb.
- The principle of faunal succession tells us that rock formations containing plant and animal fossils can be relatively dated using these fossils.
- The principle of inclusions tells us that if inclusions (chunks of rock) are found within a rock formation, the inclusion formed before the formation.
- The principle of lateral continuity tells us that rocks that are otherwise similar but are separated by an erosional feature were at one time continuous.
- The principle of original horizontality tells us that sediment is deposited in horizontal beds.
- The principle of superposition tells us that in sedimentary rock layers, a layer formed after the one below it, but before the one above it.
- The principle of uniformitarianism tells us that geological processes that modify Earth today worked the same way in the past.
- Radionuclides are radioactive elements. The elements spontaneously emit particles and/ or electromagnetic radiation, and thereby decay into different elements.
- Relative dating is a technique used by physical geographers to express the relative ages of rock formations.
- Stratigraphy investigates questions about the sequences of layered deposits.

LAB #20　Earth's Internal Structure

Recommended Textbook Reading Prior to Lab:
- Chapter 11, Earth History, Earth Interior
  - 11.3 Anatomy of a Planet: Earth's Internal Structure

Goals: After completing this lab, you will be able to:
- Identify Earth's internal layers and describe their state and chemical composition.
- Use the scientific method to test a hypothesis about the thickness of Earth's crust.
- Determine, graph, and analyze the depth of the Mohorovičić discontinuity beneath several cross sections spanning South America.
- Summarize P-wave and S-wave characteristics.
- Interpret profile and cross section models of Earth's internal structure based on P-wave and S-wave propagation.

Key Terms and Concepts
- asthenosphere
- continental crust
- inner core
- lithosphere
- mantle
- Mohorovičić discontinuity
- oceanic crust
- outer core
- P waves (primary)
- S waves (secondary)
- seismic waves

Required Materials:
- Atlas (or Google Earth)
- Calculator
- Textbook: *Living Physical Geography*, by Bruce Gervais

Problem-Solving Module #1: Earth's Layers

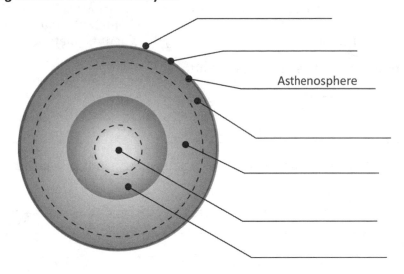

Asthenosphere

FIGURE 1–1

1. Label Figure 1–1 using the information from your textbook and Table 1–1.

Name	Approximate Beginning Depth (km)	Approximate Ending Depth (km)
Crust	0	35
Lithosphere	0	100
Asthenosphere	100	200
Mantle	35	2,900
Outer core	2,900	5,155
Inner core	5,155	6,371

TABLE 1–1

2. Complete Table 1–2. See the textbook to research the state and composition of each of Earth's layers. Use the terms "solid," "liquid," or "plastic" in the State column. Use rock and mineral descriptions from your textbook in the Composition column.

Name	State	Composition
Continental crust		
Oceanic crust		
Lithosphere		Granite and basalt
Mantle		
Outer core		
Inner core		

TABLE 1–2

Assume you are part of a physical geography team that is studying Earth's crust in order to catalog its thickness for seismological research. Some scientists think that Earth's crust is the same thickness all over the planet, while others argue that it is relatively thick where there are continents and relatively thin where there are oceans. You volunteer to investigate this question using the scientific method.

3. Compose a hypothesis about the relative thickness of Earth's crust.

_____

_____

_____

4. To test your hypothesis, what data do you need to collect, and what spatial extent should the data encompass?

_____

_____

_____

_____

5. Test your hypothesis by using an atlas and Figure 1–2 to determine the thickness and type of Earth's crust at the locations specified on Table 1–3.

Coordinates	Location	Crustal Thickness (km)	Ocean Crust or Continental Crust
73° 45' N, 40° 30' W			
28° 30' N, 89° 30' E			
25° 15" N, 48° 15" W			
25° 30" N, 151° 30" E			
19° 30" N, 17° 30" E			
38° 30" S, 131° 30" W			
20° 15' S, 67° 30' W			

TABLE 1–3

6. Is your hypothesis supported or not supported by the data? Give a specific example of how the data support or do not support your hypothesis.

_____

_____

_____

_____

_____

7. Compose a sentence or two that corresponds with Step #6 of the scientific method as it relates to the relative thickness of Earth's crust. Recall that this step is about further inquiry, and it includes speculation about new questions, new ideas, and more/different data collection.

_____

_____

_____

_____

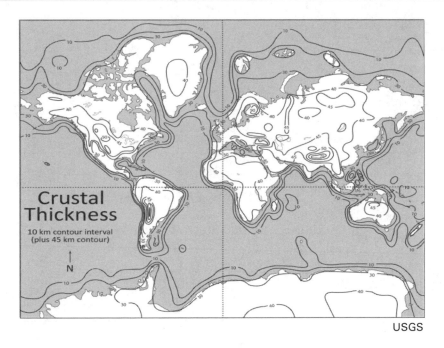

USGS

FIGURE 1–2

The information in Figure 1–2 was determined in part by examining seismic waves released by earthquakes. Seismic wave velocity increases when passing through the boundary between Earth's crust and upper mantle—the Mohorovičić discontinuity discontinuity (Moho)—because there is a significant increase in rock density. By timing seismic waves around an earthquake, it is possible to map the Moho's depth along any cross section of Earth. Figure 1–3 presents three such cross sections.

Figure 1–3 presents several transects that cross South America. Each transect contains sample sites where the Moho's depth is recorded. Illustrate each transect as a cross section on Figure 1–4.

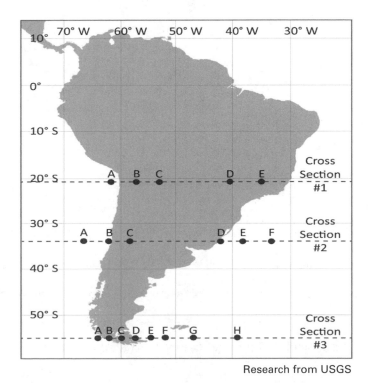

Research from USGS

FIGURE 1–3: Transects for Measuring Moho's Depth

Table 1–4 presents the Moho's depth at the sample sites illustrated in Figure 1–3.

Cross Section	Moho depth (km)							
	A	**B**	**C**	**D**	**E**	**F**	**G**	**H**
#1	31	58	42	42	38	---	---	---
#2	12	42	41	23	13	10	---	---
#3	20	35	30	28	27	17	12	11

TABLE 1–4: Moho's Depth at Each Sample Site

8. On Figure 1–4, map the Moho for each cross section illustrated in Figure 1–3.

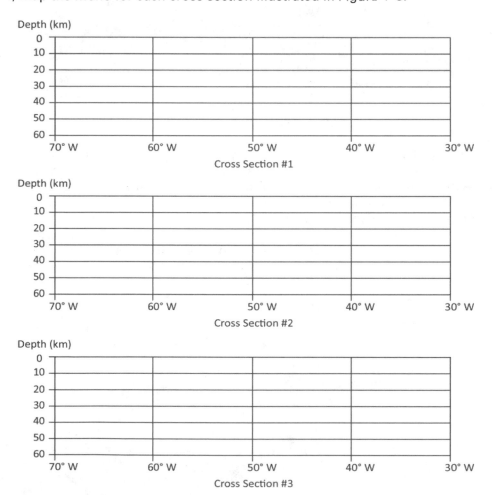

FIGURE 1–4: Cross Sections of Figure 1–3 Transects

Use an atlas (or Google Earth), Figures 1–3 and 1–4, and Table 1–4 to answer questions 9–19.

9. On Cross Section #1, what physical geographic feature is located at position A?

_____

10. On Cross Section #1, what physical geographic feature is located at position B?

_____

11. On Cross Section #1, the Moho at position B is _____ kilometers deeper than the Moho at position A.

12. On Cross Section #2, explain why the depths at positions A and F are so similar.

_____

13. On Cross Section #2, the Moho at position B is ___ kilometers deeper than the Moho at position A.

14. The Moho depths at positions ___ and ___ on Cross Section #2 are most similar to Moho depths at positions G and H on Cross Section #3 because all of these positions are on _____ crust.

15. The Moho depths at position B on all three cross sections are similar because all of these positions are on or near _____ crust beneath the _____ Mountains.

16. Imagine walking south from position B on Cross Sections #1 to position B on Cross Section #2 and finally to position B on Cross Section #3. What happens to the depth of the Moho as you walk south?

_____

17. Imagine walking east along Cross Section #2. What happens to the depth of the Moho as you walk from position C to position D?

_____

18. On Cross Section #___, the deepest part of the Moho is east of 60° W longitude, while on Cross Section #3 the deepest part of the Moho is _____ of 60° W longitude.

19. Use an atlas (or Google Earth) to describe the landscape and relief where the Moho depth is greatest.

_____

_____

_____

Problem-Solving Module #2: Studying Earth's Internal Structure

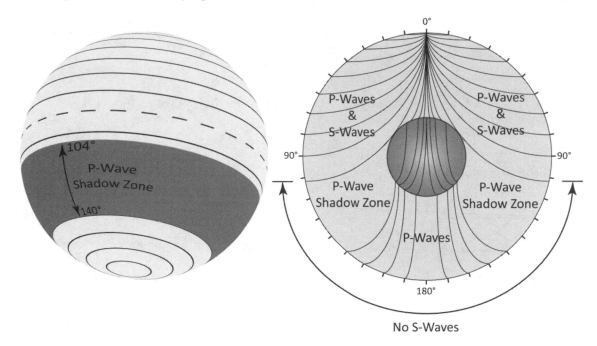

FIGURE 2–1

Earthquakes generate both P waves (primary) and S waves (secondary)—these are called *seismic waves*. Table 2–1 illustrates their relative motions as well as the mediums through which they travel. Scientists use these wave characteristics to infer Earth's internal structure.

	Motion	**Travels Through**
P waves	Compression and dilation	Solids, liquids, and gases
S waves	Shearing	Solids

TABLE 2–1

Figure 2–1 illustrates Earth from two perspectives. When an earthquake occurs, seismic waves radiate away from the earthquake's focus in concentric waves of increasing diameter, in all directions. As these waves travel, their signal is detected and recorded by instruments called seismometers. Notice that any earthquake's focus is 0°, and the point on Earth opposite to that focus is 180°.

Also notice these important points about Figure 2–1:
- The dashed line is 90° from any earthquake's focus.
- A shadow zone exists where no seismic waves are detected.
- Only one type of seismic wave reaches the point on Earth opposite to an earthquake's focus.

Use Figure 2–1 and Table 2–1 to answer questions 1–12.

1. When an earthquake occurs, both P waves and S waves are detected by seismometers up to _____ from the earthquake's focus.

2. How many degrees wide is the P-wave shadow zone? _____

3. When an earthquake occurs, only ___ waves are detected from _____° to _____° from the earthquake's focus.

4. When an earthquake occurs, S waves completely disappear _____° from the earthquake's focus.

5. What seismic waves would be detected and recorded by a seismometer located 163° from an earthquake's focus?

   _____

6. What seismic waves would be detected and recorded by a seismometer located 54° from an earthquake's focus?

   _____

7. What seismic waves would be detected and recorded by a seismometer located 132° from an earthquake's focus?

   _____

8. P waves are _____ when they reach Earth's outer core.

9. Because _____ waves have a compression and dilation motion, they can travel through solids, _____ , and gases.

10. Because S waves have a _____ motion, they can travel through solids but not through _____ or _____.

11. What do scientists infer about the state of Earth's outer core due to the fact that S waves completely disappear when they reach it?

   _____

12. If the diameter of Earth's inner core was larger, what would happen to the width of the P-wave shadow zone?

   _____

Summary of Key Terms and Concepts:

- The asthenosphere is the layer of mantle found between 100 and 200 km deep. The asthenosphere deforms and flows as a result of mantle convection below it.
- Continental crust makes up the continents. It is composed mainly of granite, a silica-rich rock composed of coarse grains.
- The inner core is found at Earth's center and is composed of solid iron and nickel alloy.
- The lithosphere is the rigid outer layer of Earth, including the crust and the top of the mantle.
- The mantle is the layer of heated and slowly deforming solid rock between the base of the crust and the outer core.
- The Mohorovičić discontinuity is the boundary that separates the crust from the upper mantle where rock density rapidly increases.
- Oceanic crust makes up the ocean floor and is composed mainly of basalt, a dark, heavy volcanic rock with fine grains that cools from lava on the crust's surface. It is composed mostly of silica compounds high in iron and magnesium.
- The outer core is found at Earth's center and is composed of liquid iron and nickel alloy. Its motion generates Earth's magnetic field.
- P waves (primary) are seismic waves that propagate via compression and dilation and travel through solids, liquids and gases.
- S waves (secondary) are seismic waves that propagate via shearing and travel only through solids.
- Seismic waves are energy-waves that propagate along and/or through Earth following an earthquake.

LAB #21   Plate Tectonics

Recommended Textbook Reading Prior to Lab:
- Chapter 12, Drifting Continents: Plate Tectonics
  - 12.1 Continental Drift: Wegener's Theory
  - 12.2 Plate Tectonics: An Ocean of Evidence
  - 12.3 Plate Boundary Landforms

Goals: After completing this lab, you will be able to:
- Identify Earth's 14 major and minor tectonic plates.
- Complete vector illustrations of selected tectonic plates, thereby illustrating direction and velocity of plate movement.
- Complete a vector illustration of the North Anatolian Fault (NAF) in Turkey and determine the geomorphology along the fault.
- Use the scientific method to study the age of Earth's seafloor.
- Use Google Earth to test a seafloor age hypothesis.
- Evaluate the age and depth of ocean floor sites at selected distances from the Mid-Atlantic Ridge in the North Atlantic and the South Atlantic oceans.
- Use Google Earth to graph ocean floor profiles in the North Atlantic and South Atlantic.

Key Terms and Concepts:
- azimuth
- divergent plate boundary
- mid-ocean ridge
- North Anatolian Fault (NAF)
- plate boundary
- plate tectonics
- seafloor age
- transform plate boundary
- vectors

Required Materials:
- Calculator
- High-speed Internet connection (for Module 2) and Google Earth (free download at http://www.google.com/earth/download/ge/agree.html)
- Ruler
- Textbook: *Living Physical Geography*, by Bruce Gervais

Problem-Solving Module #1: Plate Motion

1. Use your textbook to identify the names of the plates illustrated in Figure 1–2 on page 239.

Plate	Name
1	
2	
3	
4	
5	
6	
7	
8	
9	
10	
11	
12	
13	
14	

TABLE 1–1

Recall that azimuth is the angular distance along the horizon, where geographic north is 0° or 360°, east is 90°, south is 180°, and west is 270°. Figure 1–1 illustrates an azimuth circle. To determine an azimuth angle, imagine standing in the center of the circle looking out to the horizon. The direction you are looking always has a numeric value between 0° and 360°.

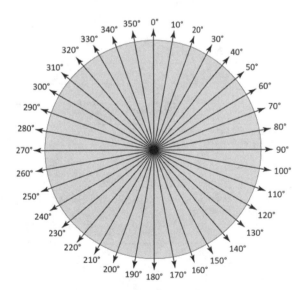

FIGURE 1–1

A vector is an arrow showing azimuth and magnitude. For example, consider a divergent plate boundary where one plate is moving northeast, away from another plate, at 1 cm per year. To illustrate this movement we can draw a 1 cm arrow pointing 45° on a map. If, at a different boundary, a plate is moving northeast at 2 cm per year, we can illustrate this movement by drawing a 2 cm arrow, again pointing 45°. The different vector lengths communicate that one plate is moving faster than the other.

2. Use Figure 1–1 and Table 1–2 to draw vectors directly on Figure 1–2. For vector magnitude lengths, use 1 mm vector length = 1 cm relative plate movement per year. Because they are small, the North American plate vectors are already done for you.

Importantly, these vectors illustrate *relative* plate velocity—how fast a plate is moving *in relation to another plate*. The vectors do not illustrate *absolute* plate velocity—how fast a plate is moving *in relation to a fixed object* such as the center of Earth.

Hint: Some vectors are very short, so keep your pencil sharp and be patient!

Plate	Vector Letter	Relative Velocity (cm/year)	Azimuth
North American	A	1	310
	B	1.2	310
	C	1.4	290
	D	1.4	290
	E	1.3	280
Antarctic	A	3.7	220°
	B	3.7	210°
	C	3.7	200°
	D	3.7	190°
	E	3.7	180°
Pacific	A	7.7	275°
	B	7.8	275°
	C	8	275°
	D	4.7	280°
	E	4.4	290°
South American	A	1.9	260
	B	1.9	260
	C	2	260
	D	2	270
	E	2	270

TABLE 1–2

3. Considering Figure 1–2 and the material in your textbook, are the four tectonic boundaries in Table 1–2 divergent, convergent, or transform?

_____

4. Which for the four boundaries in Table 1–2 (and illustrated on Figure 1–2) is spreading fastest?

_____

5. Would you find a ridge or valley at the four boundaries listed in Table 1–2 and illustrated on Figure 1–2? Describe the process that creates the seafloor feature you selected.

_____

_____

_____

_____

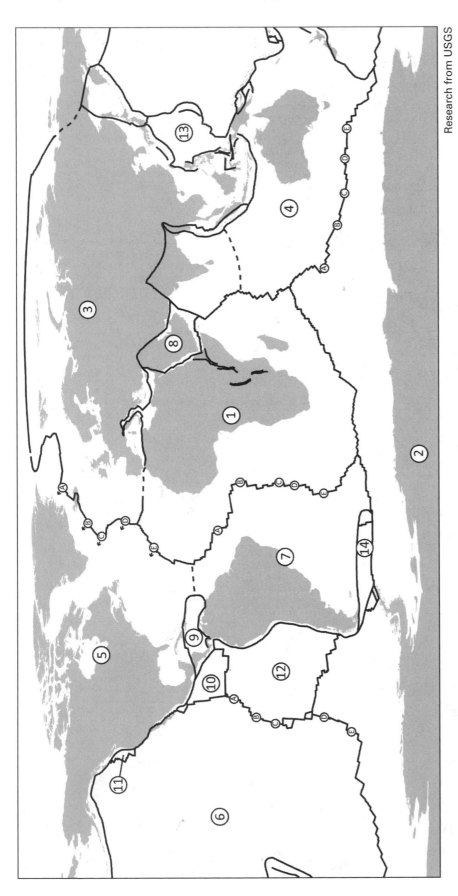

FIGURE 1–2: Major Tectonic Plates and Boundaries

Figure 1–3 is an illustration of the North Anatolian Fault (NAF), a transform tectonic boundary between the Eurasian Plate and the Anatolian Plate in Turkey. The region south of the fault moves at an azimuth angle of 270° relative to the region north of the fault at an average rate of 1.5 cm/year.

6. Draw a vector from the Ankara location marker that illustrates the relative movement of the region south of the fault. For vector magnitude length, use 1 cm vector length = 1 cm plate movement per year.

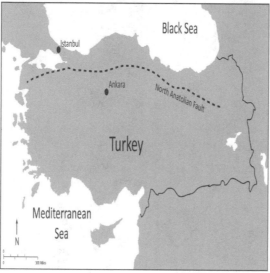

Research from Central Intelligence Agency
World Factbook

FIGURE 1–3

7. Is new crust being formed along the North Anatolian Fault? Describe the tectonic process that determined your answer.

_____

_____

_____

_____

_____

_____

8. Is old crust being recycled back into the mantle along the North Anatolian Fault? _____

9. Ankara is 315 km away from Istanbul's longitudinal coordinates. Calculate how many years it will take Ankara to reach Istanbul's longitudinal coordinates. Be sure to show your work.

_____

_____

_____

_____

_____

_____

Problem-Solving Module #2: Seafloor Age

Download the following file from the textbook companion site and open it within Google Earth:
- Seafloor Age.kmz

Assume two different groups are arguing over the age of Earth's seafloor. One group contends that the age of Earth's seafloor is the same all over the planet. The second group argues that the age of Earth's seafloor is not the same age all over the planet. You are called in to study the problem using the scientific method.

1. In your own words, compose a hypothesis about the age of Earth's seafloor. Use one of the two arguments presented above to formulate a concise hypothesis.

   _____

   _____

   _____

2. To complete Step #3 of the scientific method, what kind of data do you need to collect, where on Earth should it be collected, and how do you think it might be collected and be processed?

   _____

   _____

   _____

   _____

   _____

   _____

Collect the data by double-clicking the "Pacific Path" folder in the Places Sidebar. Notice that there are four placemarks along the path. Also, notice that colors correspond to the map's legend.

3. Complete Table 2–1 by flying to each of the four placemarks along the Pacific Path.

Placemark	Age of Seafloor (Ma)
A	
B	
C	
D	

TABLE 2–1

Now double-click the "Antarctic Path" folder in the Places Sidebar. Notice that there are four placemarks along the path. Also, notice that colors correspond to the legend on the left side of the screen.

4. Complete Table 2–2 by flying to each of the four placemarks along the Antarctic Path.

Placemark	Age of Seafloor (Ma)
A	
B	
C	
D	

TABLE 2–2

5. Is your hypothesis supported or not supported by the data?

   _____

   _____

6. Compose a sentence or two that corresponds with Step #6 of the scientific method as it relates to the seafloor age scenario. Recall that this step is about further inquiry, and it should include speculation about new questions, new ideas, and more/different data collection.

_____

_____

_____

_____

Double-click the "North Atlantic Path" folder in the Places Sidebar. Notice that there are four placemarks on the west side of the Mid-Atlantic Ridge and four on the east side of the Mid-Atlantic Ridge.

7. Complete Table 2–3 by flying to each placemark along the North Atlantic Path.

Placemark	Age of Seafloor (Ma) <u>West</u> of Mid-Atlantic Ridge	Age of Seafloor (Ma) <u>East</u> of Mid-Atlantic Ridge
A		
B		
C		
D		

TABLE 2–3

In the Places Sidebar, right-click the "North Atlantic Path" and select "Show Elevation Profile."

8. True or False? The mid-ocean ridge (where placemark A is located) is located in relatively deep water compared to placemarks B and C.

9. True or False? The mid-ocean ridge is older than the ocean floor at placemarks B, C, and D.

10. Compose a sentence or two about the age, depth, and symmetry of the North Atlantic Ocean floor.

_____

_____

11. Graph the North Atlantic Path elevation profile on Figure 2–1.

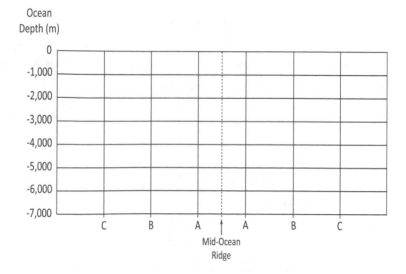

FIGURE 2–1

12. Complete Table 2–4 by flying to each placemark along the South Atlantic Path.

Placemark	Age of Seafloor (Ma) <u>West</u> of Mid-Atlantic Ridge	Age of Seafloor (Ma) <u>East</u> of Mid-Atlantic Ridge
A		
B		
C		

TABLE 2–4

In the Places Sidebar, right-click the "South Atlantic Path" and select "Show Elevation Profile."

13. True or False? The mid-ocean ridge (where placemark A is located) is located in relatively shallow water compared to placemarks B and C.

14. True or False? The mid-ocean ridge is younger than the ocean floor at placemarks B, C, and D.

15. Compose a sentence or two about the age, depth, and symmetry of the South Atlantic Ocean floor.

_____

_____

16. Graph the South Atlantic Path elevation profile on Figure 2–2.

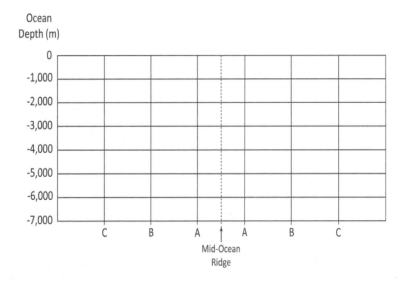

FIGURE 2–2

Summary of Key Terms and Concepts:
- Azimuth is the angular distance along the horizon, where geographic north is 0° or 360°, east is 90°, south is 180°, and west is 270°.
- A divergent plate boundary is a tectonic plate boundary where two separate plates diverge. If divergence occurs in an ocean, a mid-ocean ridge is created. If divergence occurs on a continent, a rift valley is created.
- A mid-ocean ridge is a divergent plate boundary where new ocean floor forms.
- The North Anatolian Fault (NAF) is a transform tectonic boundary between the Eurasian Plate and the Anatolian Plate in Turkey.

- Plate tectonics is a theory describing the origin, movement, and destruction of lithospheric plates, and the resulting landforms.
- Seafloor age varies around the planet and is relatively young at mid-ocean ridges and relatively old with increasing distance away from the ridge.
- A transform plate boundary is a plate boundary where one lithospheric plate slips laterally past another.
- A vector is an arrow showing azimuth and magnitude.

LAB #22 Rocks and Earth's Crust

Recommended Textbook Reading Prior to Lab:
- Chapter 13, Building the Crust with Rocks
  - 13.1 Minerals and Rocks: Building Earth's Crust
  - 13.2 Cooling the Inferno: Igneous Rocks
  - 13.3 Layers of Time: Sedimentary Rocks
  - 13.4 Pressure and Heat: Metamorphic Rocks

Goals: After completing this lab, you will be able to:
- Identify the transformational processes associated with the rock cycle.
- Summarize rock-cycle steps and rock interrelationships.
- Categorize selected igneous rocks based on their compositions and textures.
- Summarize the processes associated with igneous rock formation within Earth's crust.
- Organize selected sedimentary rocks based on their descriptions and classifications.
- Summarize the processes associated with sedimentary rock formation on Earth's crust.
- Classify selected metamorphic rocks based on protolith and texture.
- Summarize the processes associated with metamorphic rock formation within Earth's crust.

Key Terms and Concepts:
- chemical sedimentary rock
- clastic sedimentary rock
- contact metamorphism
- evaporite
- extrusive igneous rock
- igneous rock
- intrusive igneous rock
- lithification
- metamorphic rock
- organic sedimentary rock
- regional metamorphism
- rock cycle
- sediment
- sedimentary rock

Required Materials:
- Classes with no samples should complete those portions of this lab that do not require rocks.
- Rock samples: 10 igneous rocks
  - andesite
  - basalt
  - diorite
  - gabbro
  - granite
  - obsidian
  - pumice
  - rhyolite
  - scoria
  - volcanic breccia
- Rock samples: 10 sedimentary rocks
  - banded agate
  - bituminous coal
  - chalk
  - conglomerate
  - coquina
  - fossiliferous limestone
  - quartz sandstone
  - rock gypsum
  - rock salt
  - shale
- Rock samples: 6 metamorphic rocks
  - anthracite
  - gneiss
  - marble
  - mica schist
  - quartzite
  - slate

- Textbook: *Living Physical Geography*, by Bruce Gervais

245

Problem-Solving Module #1: The Rock Cycle

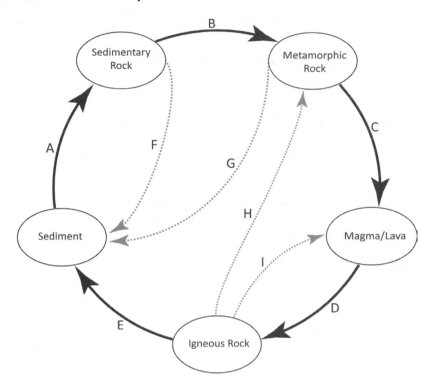

FIGURE 1–1

1. Use Figure 1–1 and your textbook to complete Table 1–1 using the provided vocabulary terms. Some terms may be used more than once.
   - Melting
   - Cooling and crystallization
   - Weathering, transportation, and deposition
   - Lithification
   - Heat and pressure

Letter	Action
A	
B	
C	
D	
E	
F	
G	
H	
I	

TABLE 1–1

Indicate whether each of the following statements is true or false.

2. Sedimentary rocks are formed through cementation and compression of sediments.

3. Metamorphic rocks are formed when magma or lava crystallizes.

4. Igneous rocks are formed when heat and pressure are applied to pre-existing rocks.

5. All rocks can be transformed from one type to another.

6. Cementation is the process by which minerals fill the spaces between particles and bind them together to form sedimentary rock.

7. Wind is the most common manner in which rock fragments are transported downhill.

8. Lithification is the process of reducing a pre-existing rock into fragments of varying size.

9. Any rock can be transformed into a new metamorphic rock through weathering and erosion.

Problem-Solving Module #2: Igneous Rocks

1. Identify and classify each of the 10 igneous rock samples by physically placing each one within its appropriate location on Figure 2–1. Use Table 2–1 as a guide for each rock's composition and texture. Use the information on Figure 2–1 to clarify compositional and textural terms. When finished, call your instructor over to check your work.

Rock	Composition	Texture
Andesite	Intermediate	Aphanitic
Basalt	Mafic	Aphanitic
Diorite	Intermediate	Phaneritic
Gabbro	Mafic	Phaneritic
Granite	Felsic	Phaneritic
Obsidian	Felsic or intermediate or mafic	Glassy
Pumice	Felsic or intermediate	Vesicular
Rhyolite	Felsic	Aphanitic
Scoria	Mafic	Vesicular
Volcanic Breccia	Felsic or intermediate or mafic	Pyroclastic

TABLE 2–1

Indicate whether each of the following statements is true or false.

2. Rock that has cooled from lava on the crust's surface is called *extrusive igneous rock*.

3. A laccolith is an extrusive igneous rock.

4. A dike is an intrusion that forms parallel to pre-existing rock layers.

5. A batholith is a large, homogenous mass of extrusive igneous rock.

6. Felsic igneous rocks are composed of about 70% silica.

7. Mafic igneous rocks are relatively low in minerals such as magnesium, iron, and olivine.

8. Aphanitic igneous rocks cooled slowly and formed deep within the crust.

9. Coarse-grained rocks cooled quickly and formed on the crust.

10. Rocks with high silica content tend to be lighter in color than rocks with less silica content.

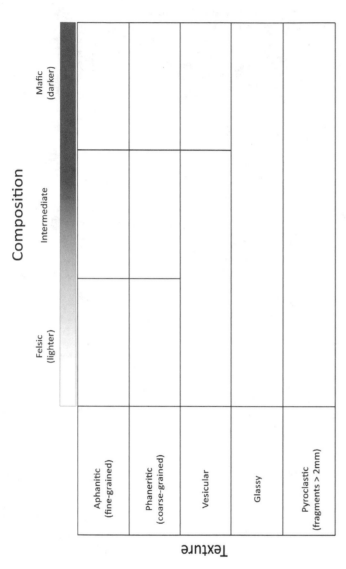

FIGURE 2-1

Problem-Solving Module #3: Sedimentary Rocks

1. Identify and classify each of the 10 sedimentary rock samples by physically placing each one within its appropriate location on Figure 3–1. Use Table 3–1 as a guide for each rock's description and classification. Use the information on Figure 3–1 to clarify classification terms. When finished, call your instructor over to check your work.

Rock	Description	Classification
Banded agate	Microcrystalline, parallel bands of varying color	Chemical
Bituminous coal	Brittle, black, lightweight, and combustible	Organic
Chalk	Microscopic shells, soft, often white, effervesces in hydrochloric acid	Organic
Conglomerate	Well-cemented, rounded rock fragments	Clastic
Coquina	Poorly cemented shell fragments, effervesces in hydrochloric acid	Organic
Fossiliferous limestone	Well-cemented, visible fossils, effervesces in hydrochloric acid	Organic
Quartz sandstone	Visible sand grains, well-cemented	Clastic
Rock gypsum	Often white, coarsely crystalline, and soft	Chemical
Rock salt	Tastes salty, often coarsely crystalline	Chemical
Shale	Fine clay grains, well-cemented	Clastic

TABLE 3–1

Indicate whether each of the following statements is true or false.

2. Clastic sedimentary rocks are composed mostly of organic material derived from ancient plants.

3. Chemical sedimentary rocks are composed mostly of broken pieces of other rocks.

4. Organic sedimentary rocks are composed mostly of minerals that have precipitated out of water.

5. River sediments often lithify into sandstone, siltstone, and shale.

6. Shells from microscopic marine organisms often lithify into chalk and limestone.

7. Most of the rocks covering Earth's crust are sedimentary rocks.

8. When peat is compacted and heated from deep burial, it can lithify into coal.

Chemical Sedimentary Rocks
(precipitate out from evaporating water solutions)

Banded Agate	
Rock Gypsum	
Rock Salt	

Clastic Sedimentary Rocks
(contain fragments or particles of rocks)

Conglomerate	
Quartz Sandstone	
Shale	

Organic Sedimentary Rocks
(fossils or evidence of once-living material)

Bituminous Coal	
Chalk	
Coquina	
Fossiliferous Limestone	

FIGURE 3–1

Indicate whether each of the following statements is true or false.

9. Coal produces abundant and inexpensive energy, but it also creates a relatively heavy toll on the environment when it is mined and burned.

10. Petroleum oil is only rarely found in sedimentary rocks.

11. Evaporites form when ancient plant matter is preserved and compacted, instead of decomposing.

12. Fossils are the remains or impressions of plants or animals preserved in sedimentary rocks.

13. If an undisturbed sedimentary rock bed contains fossils, the youngest fossils will be at the bottom of the bed and the oldest fossils will be at the top.

14. Index fossils provide stratigraphic markers that allow scientists to determine the age of a sedimentary rock at a glance.

Problem-Solving Module #4: Metamorphic Rocks

1. Identify and classify each of the six metamorphic rock samples by physically placing each one within its appropriate location on Figure 4–1. Use Table 4–1 as a guide for each rock's description and classification. Use the information on Figure 4–1 to clarify texture terms. When finished, call your instructor over to check your work.

Rock	Parent Rock	Texture
Anthracite	Bituminous coal	Nonfoliated
Gneiss	Shale, schist, or granite	Foliated
Marble	Limestone	Nonfoliated
Mica Schist	Shale	Foliated
Quartzite	Quartz sandstone	Nonfoliated
Slate	Shale	Foliated

TABLE 4–1

Indicate whether each of the following statements is true or false.

2. Metamorphic rocks can be metamorphosed more than once.

3. Metamorphism occurs while a rock is in a liquid state.

4. The thermal range for metamorphism is roughly between 1,000°C and 1,500°C.

5. Metamorphic rocks are the most common of the three rock families exposed on the crust's surface.

6. Contact metamorphism occurs after rock has come in contact with, and has been heated by, magma.

7. Metamorphism can occur at tectonic plate subduction zones.

8. A foliated texture in a metamorphic rock is due to sedimentation.

9. The protolith of slate is shale.

10. The protolith of marble is limestone.

11. The protolith of sandstone is quartzite.

12. Anthracite coal is originally derived from plant matter.

13. For metamorphism to occur, gneiss requires higher temperatures than slate.

Foliated Metamorphic rocks
(flat or wavy banding patterns)

Slate	
Mica Schist	
Gneiss	

Nonfoliated Metamorphic rocks
(no structured grain pattern or mineral arrangement)

Quartzite	
Marble	
Anthracite	

FIGURE 4–1

Summary of Key Terms and Concepts:

- Chemical sedimentary rocks form when dissolved minerals precipitate out of water.
- Clastic sedimentary rocks are composed of broken pieces of other rocks.
- Contact metamorphism occurs after a rock has come in contact with, and has been heated by, magma.
- Evaporites are salt and mineral deposits that result from the repeated evaporation of water from a basin.
- Extrusive igneous rock cooled from lava on the crust's surface.
- Igneous rocks form from cooled magma or lava.
- Intrusive igneous rock cooled from magma deep underground.
- Lithification is the process of forming sedimentary rocks through compaction and cementation of sediment.
- Metamorphic rocks form when heat and pressure are applied to a pre-existing rock.
- Organic sedimentary rocks are composed mostly of carbon and are derived from ancient organisms.
- Regional metamorphism occurs at convergent tectonic plates and subduction zones where there is great heat and pressure.
- The rock cycle is a model demonstrating how rocks form, are transformed from one type to another, and are recycled back into the mantle.
- Sediment is an accumulation of small fragments of rock and organic material that is not cemented together.
- Sedimentary rocks form from cemented and compressed sediment.

Recommended Textbook Reading Prior to Lab:
- Chapter 14, Geohazards: Volcanoes and Earthquakes
  - 14.1 About Volcanoes
  - 14.2 Pele's Power: Volcanic Hazards

Goals: After completing this lab, you will be able to:
- Classify stratovolcanoes and shield volcanoes using physical characteristics such as eruptive type, lava temperature and viscosity, and geohazard caliber.
- Use a drawing compass to identify geohazard risk radii around selected volcanoes.
- Carry out predictions of volcanic eruption effects using the Volcanic Explosivity Index (VEI).
- Locate the ruins of Pompeii and consider the geohazard risk to the population currently living in the metropolitan area around Mount Vesuvius.
- Provide examples of how lahars are different from pyroclastic flows.
- Calculate the time it takes for specified lahars and pyroclastic flows to reach selected locations.
- Judge an eruption's characteristics using volcanic blast evidence.
- Identify the defining geohazard characteristics of significant historical eruptions using Google Earth and data from NOAA's National Geophysical Data Center.

Key Terms and Concepts:
- effusive eruption
- explosive eruption
- felsic lava
- geohazard
- lahar
- mafic lava
- pyroclastics
- pyroclastic flow
- shield volcano
- stratovolcano
- viscosity
- volcanic ash
- volcanic explosivity index (VEI)

Required Materials:
- Calculator
- Drawing compass
- High-speed Internet connection (for Module 4) and Google Earth (free download at http://www.google.com/earth/download/ge/agree.html)
- Ruler
- Textbook: *Living Physical Geography*, by Bruce Gervais

Problem-Solving Module #1: Stratovolcanoes and Shield Volcanoes

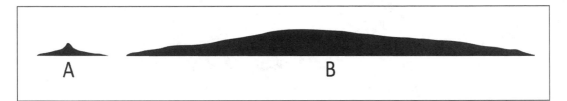

FIGURE 1–1

1. Complete Table 1–1 by identifying the correct volcano profile with its listed characteristic.

Volcano Characteristic	Volcano A or B (Figure 1–1)
Composed of sheets of solidified lava flows	
Explosive eruptions	
Lower viscosity lava	
Lava is about 600°C to 800°C.	
Lava does not easily flow.	
Lava falls may occur.	
Called a stratovolcano	
Lava is about 1,800°C to 2,200°C.	
Lava easily flows.	
Silica content ≤ 50% (mafic lava)	
Called a shield volcano	
Composed of alternating layers of lava and pyroclastics	
Significant geohazard	
Example: Mauna Loa	
Magma migrates through basaltic crust.	
Plug domes may occur.	
Lava is more mafic.	
Silica content ≥70% (felsic lava)	
Effusive eruptions	
Higher viscosity lava	
Not a significant geohazard	
Example: Mt. Fuji	
Lava is more felsic.	
Magma migrates through granitic crust.	

TABLE 1–1

Problem-Solving Module #2: Volcanic Explosivity Index (VEI)

VEI	Example	Rate on Earth (approximate)	Bulk Volume of Erupted Products
8	Yellowstone Caldera, 640,000 years ago	2 per 10,000 years	> 1,000 km³
7	Crater Lake, Oregon, 7,600 years ago	3 per 1,000 years	> 100 km³
6	Pinatubo, Philippines, 1991	3 per 100 years	> 10 km³
5	Mount St. Helens, USA, May 18, 1980	1 per 10 years	> 1 km³
4	Mont Pelée, Martinique, 1902	1 per year	> 0.1 km³
3	Mount St. Helens, USA, May 25 and June 12, 1980	3 per year	> 10,000,000 m³
2	Mount St. Helens, USA, December 7, 1989	50 per year	> 1,000,000 m³
1	Mount St. Helens, USA, October 1, 2004	Daily	> 10,000 m³

TABLE 2–1: Volcanic Explosivity Index (VEI) and Occurrence Rate

VEI	Eruption Column Height Above Vent	Approximate Ash Thickness (varies due to eruption and wind conditions)		
		At 16 km	At 160 km	At 480 km
8	> 50 km	6 meters	1 meter	8 cm
7	> 40 km	6 meters	1 meter	8 cm
6	> 30 km	3 meters	30 cm	2.5 cm
5	20–35 km	61 cm	8 cm	1 cm
4	10–25 km	30 cm	2.5 cm	0.5 cm
3	3–15 km	8 cm	1.5 cm	Dusting
2	1–5 km	1.5 cm	Dusting	Nil
1	100–1000 m	Dusting	Nil	Nil

TABLE 2–2: Volcanic Explosivity Index (VEI) and Eruption Column

On Figure 2–1, use your drawing compass to draw a 160 km radius ring around Mount St. Helens. On Figure 2–2, use your drawing compass to draw a 16 km radius ring around Mount Vesuvius. Use Tables 2–1 and 2–2, and Figures 2–1 and 2–2, to answer questions 1–13.

1. Under appropriate eruption and wind conditions, how much ash could theoretically fall on Seattle if Mount St. Helens experienced a VEI 5 eruption?

_____

2. How high above the vent would be the eruption column of Mount St. Helens during a VEI 5 eruption?

_____

3. Under appropriate eruption and wind conditions, how much ash could theoretically fall on Seattle if Mount St. Helens experienced a VEI 7 eruption?

_____

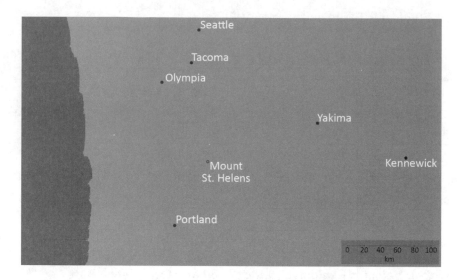

FIGURE 2–1

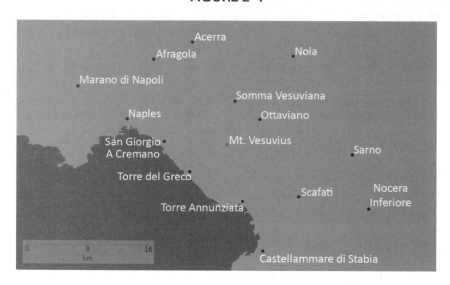

FIGURE 2–2

4. How high above the vent would be the eruption column of Mount St. Helens during a VEI 7 eruption?

_____

5. The cruising altitude of jets is approximately 11,000 meters. Why is this important when considering a flight from Portland to Seattle during a VEI 5 or VEI 7 eruption from Mount St. Helens?

_____

_____

_____

_____

6. How does the bulk volume of erupted products compare during a VEI 5 eruption from Mount St. Helens versus a VEI 7 eruption?

_____

_____

7. Under appropriate eruption and wind conditions, how many Italian cities could theoretically have 3 meters of ash falling on them if Mount Vesuvius experienced a VEI 6 eruption?

_____

8. Ruins of the ancient city of Pompeii are located between the modern cities of Torre Annunziata and Scafati. According to your textbook, how much ash buried Pompeii in the year 79?

_____

_____

_____

9. The eruption column height of the Vesuvius eruption in the year 79 was a minimum of 25 km high. Given this well-documented observation, the VEI rating of this eruption is often pegged at about 5. According to Table 2–1, a VEI 5 eruption deposits ash 61 cm deep at 16 km. How is it possible, then, that Pompeii was buried in ash many times deeper than 61 cm? _Hint: Consider other ways volcanic ash and debris may be deposited._

_____

_____

_____

_____

10. The metropolitan area around Naples numbers about 4 million people, and Mount Vesuvius has not erupted since 1944. Given these facts, what do you think might happen during an evacuation if volcanologists warned of an impending, large eruption?

_____

_____

_____

_____

_____

11. How often should we generally expect to see a VEI 4 eruption on Earth?

_____

12. How often should we generally expect to see an eruption such as the one that occurred from Mount Pinatubo in 1991?

_____

13. How often should we generally expect to see an eruption such as the one that occurred from the Yellowstone Caldera 640,000 years ago?

_____

Problem-Solving Module #3: Lahars and Pyroclastic Flows

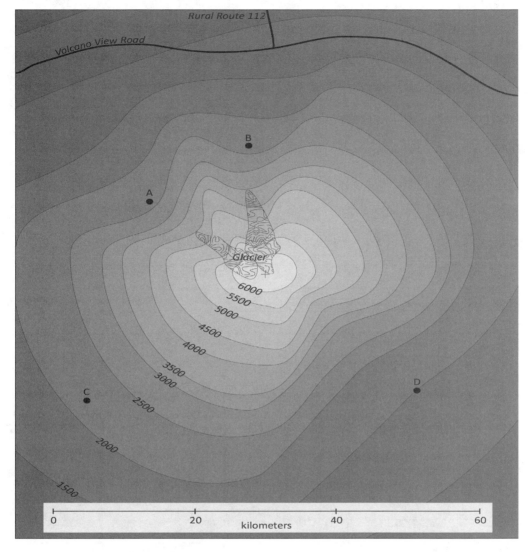

FIGURE 3–1

Figure 3–1 is a topographic model of a stratovolcano. Use your knowledge of maps from previous labs, as well as information from the recommended textbook reading, to answer questions 1–10. Note that the peak of the volcano is marked with a cross-hair.

1. In your own words, explain how a lahar is different from a pyroclastic flow. Be sure to include comments about the composition, temperature, velocity, and distance able to travel.

   _____

   _____

   _____

   _____

   _____

   _____

2. According to the textbook, about what percentage of volcano-related deaths in any given year are due to lahars and pyroclastic flows?

_____

3. Assume you are a volcano hazards scientist and the volcano on Figure 3–1 is showing signs of an imminent eruption. What two locations on Figure 3–1 would you say are in the most danger of a lahar, and why?

_____

_____

_____

4. Assume the volcano on Figure 3–1 erupts, and two separate lahars threaten locations A and B. If the lahars travel at 70 km/hr, how much time will pass before they reach each location? To solve this problem, measure distance using the provided scale and use the cross-hair at the volcano's peak as a starting point. Be sure to show your work.

_____

_____

_____

_____

_____

5. Assume the volcano on Figure 3–1 erupts, and three separate pyroclastic flows threaten locations A, B, and D. If the pyroclastic flows travel at 700 km/hr, how much time will pass before they reach each location? To solve this problem, measure distance using the provided scale and use the cross-hair at the volcano's peak as a starting point. Be sure to show your work.

_____

_____

_____

_____

_____

_____

6. Consider the topography of the volcano seen in Figure 3–1. During an eruption, why would location C have a lower probability of being struck by a lahar or pyroclastic flow compared to locations A, B, or D?

_____

_____

_____

7. Assume you are a volcano hazards scientist and the volcano on Figure 3–1 is showing signs of an imminent eruption. What would you recommend happen to Volcano View Road and Rural Route 112?

_____

_____

8. Assume the volcano on Figure 3–1 erupts and a pyroclastic flow, traveling at 700 km/hr, is headed for the intersection of Volcano View Road and Rural Route 112. If you are in your car watching the eruption at this intersection, how much time will pass before you are engulfed? To solve this problem, measure distance using the provided scale and use the cross-hair at the volcano's peak as a starting point. Be sure to show your work.

_____

_____

_____

9. Assume the pyroclastic flow calculated in question 8 did engulf your car (with you inside) at the intersection of Volcano View Road and Rural Route 112. If you closed the car's vents and windows, would you survive? Why or why not?

_____

_____

_____

_____

_____

_____

10. Assume the volcano on Figure 3–1 once had a mature forest on its slopes, but it was destroyed a year ago during an eruption. None of the trees were burned or buried, however. Instead, they were simply flattened. How could a scientist use what remained of the forest to determine the magnitude and direction of the volcanic blast?

_____

_____

_____

_____

_____

_____

Problem-Solving Module #4: Significant Eruptions

Download the following file from the textbook companion site and open it within Google Earth:
- Significant Volcanic Eruptions.kmz

In the Places Sidebar, first open "Significant Volcanic Eruptions," and then open "4350 BC-1499 (78 events)." Scroll down to the selected volcano and fly to that location by double-clicking.

79 08/24: Vesuvius, Italy
- Select "Get more details from NGDC Natural Hazards Website" in the pop-up window hovering above the volcano.

1. How many skeletons were found in Pompeii? _____

2. What produced most of the fatalities from this eruption? _____

3. How many total deaths occurred? _____

450 (approx.): Ilopango, El Salvador
- Select "Get more details from NGDC Natural Hazards Website" in the pop-up window hovering above the volcano.

4. What cultural group lost cities due to this eruption? _____

5. What is the estimated number of fatalities from this eruption? _____

6. How many cubic kilometers of tephra fall and flow deposits were produced? _____

In the Places Sidebar close "4350 BC-1499 (78 events)" and open "1500–1799 (124 events)." Scroll down to the selected volcano and fly to that location by double-clicking.

1783 07/26: Asama, Japan
- Select "Get more details from NGDC Natural Hazards Website" in the pop-up window hovering above the volcano.

7. How did 93 people survive the eruption?

_____

8. What caused a temporary dam on the Agatsuma River?

_____

9. Why was there a famine in the Kanto region?

_____

1784 04/??: Grimsvotn, Iceland
- Select "Get more details from NGDC Natural Hazards Website" in the pop-up window hovering above the volcano.

10. How many total deaths occurred? _____

11. Why did famine occur?

_____

12. How was Scotland impacted by this eruption?

_____

In the Places Sidebar close "1500–1799 (124 events)" and open "1800–1899 (133 events)." Scroll down to the selected volcano and fly to that location by double-clicking.

<u>1815 04/05: Tambora, Indonesia</u>
- Select "Get more details from NGDC Natural Hazards Website" in the pop-up window hovering above the volcano.

13. Why was 1816 termed "the year without a summer"?

_____

_____

14. What happened to wheat crops as a result of this eruption, and what was the effect on wheat prices from 1815 to 1817?

_____

_____

15. What is this eruption's VEI rating? _____

<u>1856 03/02: Awu, Indonesia</u>
- Select "Get more details from NGDC Natural Hazards Website" in the pop-up window hovering above the volcano.

16. What is the morphological classification of this volcano? _____

17. How many total deaths occurred? _____

18. What happened to daylight during the eruption?

_____

In the Places Sidebar, close "1800–1899 (133 events)" and open "1950–present (211 events)." Scroll down to the selected volcano and fly to that location by double-clicking.

19. Select any volcanic eruption in the 1950–present time frame. Select "Get more details from NGDC Natural Hazards Website" in the pop-up window hovering above the volcano. State at least three facts about the eruption.

Fact #1:

_____

_____

Fact #2:

_____

_____

Fact #3:

_____

_____

20. Select any volcanic eruption in the 1950–present time frame (different than the one selected for question 19). Select "Get more details from NGDC Natural Hazards Website" in the pop-up window hovering above the volcano. State at least three facts about the eruption.

Fact #1:

_____

_____

Fact #2:

_____

_____

Fact #3:

_____

_____

Summary of Key Terms and Concepts:
- An effusive eruption is nonexplosive and produces mostly lava.
- An explosive eruption explodes violently and produces large amounts of pyroclastics.
- Felsic lava has a silica content 70% or greater, and a high viscosity.
- A geohazard is a hazard presented to people from the physical Earth. Geohazards include volcanic eruptions, earthquakes, and tsunamis.
- A lahar is a thick slurry of mud, ash, water, and other debris that flows rapidly down a volcano.
- Mafic lava has a silica content 50% or less, and a low viscosity.
- Pyroclastics are any fragmented, solid material that is ejected from a volcano, ranging in size from ash to large boulders.
- A pyroclastic flow is a rapidly moving avalanche of searing hot gas and ash.
- A shield volcano is a large, flat dome formed from many layers of low-viscosity basaltic lava.
- A stratovolcano is a large, potentially explosive cone-shaped volcano composed of alternating layers of lava and ash.
- Viscosity is a material's resistance to flow.
- Volcanic ash is a pyroclastic powder consisting of glass shards from pulverized rock particles and solidified lava droplets.
- The volcanic explosivity index (VEI) ranks volcanic eruptions based on the amount of material ejected during an eruption.

LAB #24   Earthquakes

Recommended Textbook Reading Prior to Lab:
- Chapter 14, Geohazards: Volcanoes and Earthquakes
  - 14.3 Tectonic Hazards: Faults and Earthquakes
  - 14.4 Unstable Crust: Seismic Waves

Goals: After completing this lab, you will be able to:
- Classify the types and characteristics of body and surface seismic waves.
- Interpret a seismogram and determine the likely seismic wave characteristics.
- Determine the arrival time difference between selected P waves and S waves, and use a travel time curve to determine distance to an earthquake's epicenter.
- Use a drawing compass to triangulate an earthquake's epicenter.
- Quantify earthquake magnitude with a magnitude nomogram after interpreting key variables on a seismogram.
- Calculate energy-released comparisons, as well as ground-motion comparisons, for selected earthquakes of varying magnitude.
- Identify how an earthquake intensity scale differs from an earthquake magnitude scale.
- Carry out intensity interval sketching on a map following a hypothetical earthquake.
- Judge the likely earthquake intensity of selected cities during a hypothetical earthquake.

Key Terms and Concepts:
- epicenter
- magnitude
- magnitude nomogram
- modified Mercalli intensity (MMI) scale
- P wave
- S wave
- seismograph (or seismometer)
- seismogram
- travel time curve

Required Materials:
- Drafting compass
- Drawing compass
- Ruler
- Textbook: *Living Physical Geography*, by Bruce Gervais

Problem-Solving Module #1: Earthquake Waves and the Travel Time Curve

Earthquakes generate both P waves (primary) and S waves (secondary). Both P and S waves travel through Earth's interior and are called body waves. Earthquakes also generate Rayleigh and Love waves. These waves travel on Earth's surface and are called surface waves.

General Grouping	Travel Medium	Wave Name	Typical Speed (varies depending on medium)	Motion
Body waves	Through Earth's interior	P wave	~6 km/s	Compression and dilation
		S wave	~3.5 km/s	Shearing (through Earth's interior)
Surface waves	On Earth's surface	Love wave	~2.8 km/s	Shearing (across Earth's surface)
		Rayleigh wave	~2.7 km/s	Elliptical

TABLE 1–1

A *seismograph* (or *seismometer*) is an instrument that detects, measures, and records ground shaking. A seismometer's record is called a *seismogram*. Seismograms are read like the pages of a book, from left to right, and they are always time-stamped using Greenwich Mean Time (GMT). Because P waves travel fastest, they appear first on any seismogram, followed by S waves, and then surface waves. Figure 1–1 is a hypothetical model of a seismogram.

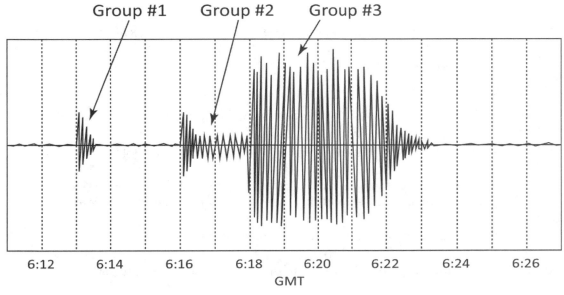

FIGURE 1–1

1. Use your textbook, along with the information in Table 1–1 and in Figure 1–1, to complete Table 1–2.

Wave Characteristic	Seismic Wave Group(s) # (see Figure 1–1)
Includes Love waves	
Has a shearing motion through Earth's interior	
Travels on Earth's surface	
Arrives at a seismometer last	
Generally grouped as surface waves	
Travels fastest	
Includes Rayleigh waves	
Travels through Earth's interior	
Classified as a surface wave	
Travels slowest	
Has the largest waves	
Travels at about 3.5 km/s	
Arrives at a seismometer first	
Has a compression and dilation motion	
Generally grouped as body waves	
Includes waves with an elliptical motion	
Produce the greatest shaking	

TABLE 1–2

Scientists use the difference between P-wave and S-wave arrival times to determine the distance to an earthquake's epicenter using a travel time curve (Figure 1–2). A travel time curve is a graph that presents the arrival times of P waves and S waves as a function of distance from a seismic source.

To use a travel time curve:
   1. Subtract the P-wave arrival time from the S-wave arrival time to determine time difference.
   2. Extend a drafting compass along the travel time curve's y-axis, from 0 up to the time difference.
   3. Keep the compass open at the determined time difference, and then move it to the right while keeping the compass point that was formerly on 0 along the P-wave curve.
   4. Stop moving the compass when the other point lies on the S-wave curve, vertically above the P-wave curve.
   5. Extend a vertical line to the graph's x-axis to determine distance to the earthquake's epicenter.

2. In Figure 1–1, how much time elapsed between the arrival of the P waves and the arrival of the S waves?

_____

3. Using the arrival time difference determined in question 2, determine the distance to the earthquake's epicenter using the travel time curve. How far away is the earthquake?

_____

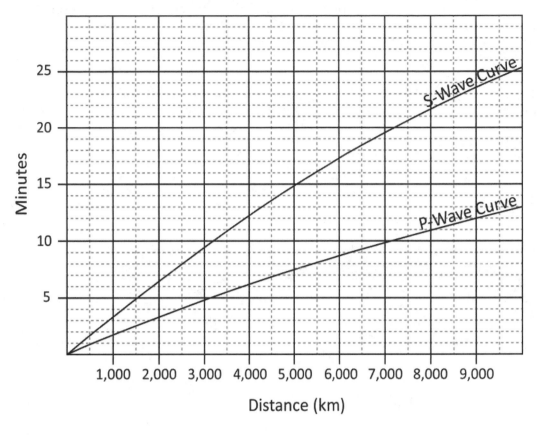

Distance (km)

FIGURE 1–2

4. Complete Table 1–3 by calculating the arrival time difference of P waves and S waves and then the distance to seven separate earthquakes.

P-Wave Arrival Time	S-Wave Arrival Time	Arrival Time Difference	Distance to Epicenter (km)
19:12:15	19:18:45		
07:34:00	07:37:30		
02:28:30	02:33:30		
12:16:45	12:20:15		
22:58:15	23:06:15		
09:01:30	09:11:30		
03:15:15	03:19:30		

TABLE 1–3

Notice in Table 1–3 that only *distance*, not *location*, has been determined. Triangulating an epicenter's location requires sketching a distance circle around each seismometer station. Where the three circles intersect is an epicenter's location.

5. Use seismogram data in Table 1–4 and your drawing compass to triangulate the location of an earthquake on Figure 1–3. Identify the earthquake's epicenter with a star where the three distance circles overlap. Be sure to use the scale provided on Figure 1–3 to adjust the width of your drawing compass.

Station	Distance to Epicenter (km)
Station #1	800
Station #2	700
Station #3	500

TABLE 1–4

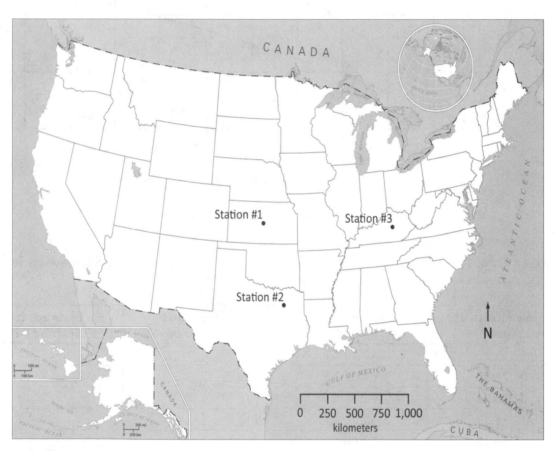

Data source: National Atlas

FIGURE 1–3

Problem-Solving Module #2: Magnitude versus Intensity

An earthquake's magnitude is a quantitative measure of its size. Of the several methods that exist to determine magnitude, "Local Magnitude" (ML) is good for quantifying nearby earthquakes. Determining ML requires knowing 1) the arrival time difference between P waves and S waves, and 2) the amplitude of the largest S wave. Amplitude is an absolute value and is determined by measuring the largest S-wave peak.

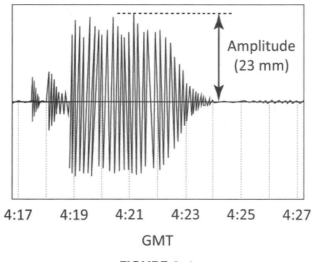

FIGURE 2–1

From Figure 2–1 we determine that an earthquake's arrival time difference is 30 seconds and its amplitude is 23 mm. These two variables can now be plotted on a *nomograph*—a graphical calculating tool that yields a desired value after two variables are aligned with a straight line. Figure 2–2 is an ML nomograph.

1. Using data from Figure 2–1, plot the arrival time difference on the nomograph's left vertical axis (notice that this automatically yields the distance to the earthquake's epicenter). Plot the amplitude on the nomograph's right vertical axis. Connect both points with a straight line. Your line intersects the middle vertical axis at the earthquake's ML. What is the ML?

_____

2. Use Figures 1–2 and 2–2 to complete the data for each earthquake listed in Table 2–1.

P-Wave Arrival	S-Wave Arrival	Arrival Time Difference	Distance to Epicenter (km)	Amplitude (mm)	Earthquake ML (Magnitude)
14:01:04	14:01:14			15	
03:12:09	03:12:15			75	
01:30:01	01:30:05			5	
17:14:10	17:14:55			35	
23:14:32	23:14:57			0.7	
08:56:17	08:56:57			100	

TABLE 2–1

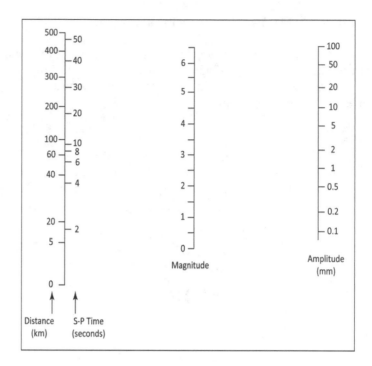

FIGURE 2–2

Every whole number increase in earthquake magnitude yields 10 times more ground shaking and 32 times more energy released. For example, a magnitude 6 earthquake moves the ground 10 times more and releases 32 times more energy than a magnitude 5 earthquake.

   Here is an example of how to determine how much more (or less) ground shaking occurred, and how much more (or less) energy was released, when comparing two different earthquakes. Assume a magnitude 6.7 earthquake occurred, and compare it to a magnitude 5.3 earthquake.

- The magnitude 6.7 earthquake shook the ground 25 times more because
    - 6.7 – 5.3 = 1.4 magnitude difference
    - $10^{1.4}$ = 25.11 (rounded to 25)

- The magnitude 6.7 earthquake released 128 times more energy because
    - 6.7 – 5.3 = 1.4 magnitude difference
    - $32^{1.4}$ = 128

3. How much more ground shaking occurs during a magnitude 6.3 earthquake compared to a magnitude 5.3? (Be sure to show your work.)

_____

4. How much more ground shaking occurs during a magnitude 6.3 earthquake compared to a magnitude 4.7? (Be sure to show your work.)

_____

5. How much more ground shaking occurs during a magnitude 6.3 earthquake compared to a magnitude 2.8? (Be sure to show your work.)

_____

6. How much more energy is released during a magnitude 7.8 earthquake compared to a magnitude 6.8? (Be sure to show your work.)

_____

7. How much more energy is released during a magnitude 7.8 earthquake compared to a magnitude 5.3? (Be sure to show your work.)

_____

8. How much more energy is released during a magnitude 7.8 earthquake compared to a magnitude 3.1? (Be sure to show your work.)

_____

An earthquake's intensity is a qualitative measure of the ground shaking at a particular site. It is based on the effects felt by people and on the observed damage to building structures. The modified Mercalli intensity (MMI) scale is the current U.S. standard and has 12 levels of increasing intensity. While it is an arbitrary ranking based on the observed effects of an earthquake, often it has more meaning than an earthquake's magnitude for people because it classifies the actual experiences of people and buildings. Table 2–2 is the MMI scale.

9. What levels of the MMI scale refer specifically to effects on people?

_____

10. What levels of the MMI scale refer specifically to effects on buildings?

_____

Modified Mercalli Intensity Value	Intensity Description
I	Not felt except by a very few under especially favorable conditions.
II	Felt only by a few persons at rest, especially on upper floors of buildings.
III	Felt quite noticeably by persons indoors, especially on upper floors of buildings. Standing cars may rock slightly. Vibrations similar to the passing of a truck.
IV	Felt indoors by many. At night, some awakened. Dishes and doors disturbed; walls make cracking sound. Sensation like heavy truck striking building.
V	Felt by nearly everyone; many awakened. Some dishes, windows broken. Unstable objects overturned. Pendulum clocks may stop.
VI	Felt by all. Some heavy furniture moved; a few instances of fallen plaster.
VII	Slight to moderate damage in well-built ordinary structures; considerable damage in poorly built or badly designed structures; some chimneys broken.
VIII	Considerable damage in ordinary buildings with partial collapse. Damage great in poorly built structures. Chimneys and factory stacks fall.
IX	Well-designed frame structures thrown out of plumb. Damage great in substantial buildings, with partial collapse. Buildings shifted off foundations.
X	Some well-built wooden structures destroyed; most masonry and frame structures destroyed with foundations. Rails bent.
XI	Few masonry structures remain standing. Bridges destroyed. Rails bent greatly.
XII	Damage total. Lines of sight and level are distorted. Objects thrown into the air.

Credit/courtesy of USGS (adapted)

TABLE 2–2

11. If a magnitude 5 earthquake occurs in an uninhabited region with no buildings, what is its MMI? Explain your reasoning.

_____

_____

_____

_____

12. In your own words, explain the difference between a quantitative value and a qualitative value.

_____

_____

_____

_____

13. Figure 2–3 is a map of western Washington with hypothetical MMI values following an M 6 earthquake. Finish the map by sketching interval lines connecting equal MMI point values.

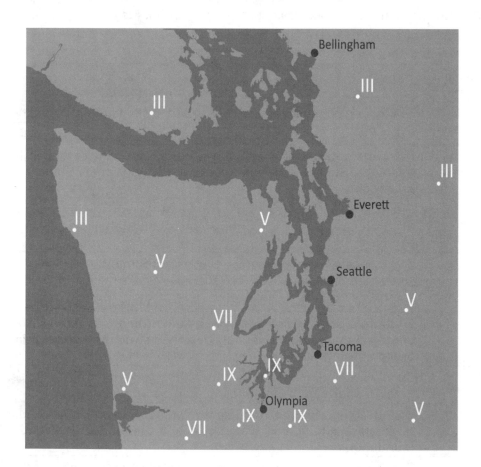

FIGURE 2–3

14. Complete Table 2–3 by identifying the city on Figure 2–3 that experienced the described intensity. Each city is used only once..

Described Intensity	City
"After the earthquake my well-built home had some cracks and my chimney lost some bricks."	
"It felt like someone hit my house with their car. I woke up, but my neighbor slept right through it."	
"Two collectable plates fell and broke, and the pendulum stopped swinging on my clock."	
"My home moved 8 inches off its foundation, and none of my doors close properly anymore."	
"I didn't feel a thing, but people on the 8th floor said they noticed some small vibrations."	

TABLE 2–3

Summary of Key Terms and Concepts:
- An epicenter is the location on the ground's surface immediately above an earthquake's focus where ground shaking intensity is the greatest.
- The magnitude scale is a quantitative earthquake ranking system based on the amount of produced ground movement.
- A magnitude nomogram is a graphical calculating tool that yields an earthquake's magnitude after the P-wave and S-wave travel time difference and amplitude are both plotted.
- The modified Mercalli intensity (MMI) scale is a qualitative measure of ground shaking and is based on the effects felt by people and on the observed damage to buildings.
- A P wave moves through Earth with a compression and dilation motion and is the fastest seismic wave.
- An S wave moves through Earth perpendicular to its direction of travel and arrives at a seismometer after a P wave.
- A seismograph (or seismometer) is an instrument used to detect, measure, and record ground shaking.
- A seismogram is the record of ground shaking produced by a seismograph (or seismometer).
- A travel time curve is a graph that presents the arrival times of P waves and S waves as a function of distance from a seismic source.

LAB #25   Mass Movement and Surface Karst

Recommended Textbook Reading Prior to Lab:
- Chapter 15, Weathering and Mass Movement
    - 15.2 Dissolving Rock: Karst
    - 15.3 Unstable Ground: Mass Movement

Goals: After completing this lab, you will be able to:
- Identify the numerous features of a mass movement using the correct morphological vocabulary.
- Classify selected mass movement types using graphics and definitions accepted by the United States Geological Survey (USGS).
- Analyze data from selected mass movement events of the twentieth and twenty-first centuries.
- Discuss the natural and human contributing variables to mass-movement events, as well as the triggering mechanisms.
- Use maps and tabular data to analyze and summarize post-wildfire debris-flow probability data for the 2011 Monument Fire in the Coronado National Forest in Arizona.

Key Terms and Concepts:
- debris flow
- karst topography
- mass movement
- mass movement cause
- mass movement speed
- mass movement trigger
- pour point
- rockfall
- rotational landslide
- slump
- soil creep
- surface karst
- translational slide

Required Materials:
- Calculator
- High-speed internet connection (for module 4) and Google Earth (free download at http://www.google.com/earth/download/ge/agree.html)
- Textbook: *Living Physical Geography*, by Bruce Gervais

Problem-Solving Module #1: Mass Movement Terminology and Types

1. Complete Table 1–1 by matching an identification letter from Figure 1–1 to a landslide definition.

Definition	Name	Letter (see Figure 1–1)
The nearly undisplaced material still in place and adjacent to the highest parts of the main scarp.	Crown	
The part of the ground overlain by the foot of the landslide.	Surface of separation	
The portion of the landslide that has moved beyond the toe of surface of rupture and overlies the original ground surface.	Foot	
A steep, nearly vertical upper edge caused by movement of the displaced material. A visible part of the surface of rupture.	Main scarp	
The undisplaced material adjacent to the side of the landslide. If left and right are used, they are referenced as viewed from the crown.	Right flank	
A steep surface on the displaced material produced by differential movements within the material.	Minor scarp	
The nearly horizontal, upper parts of the landslide along the contact between the displaced material and the main scarp.	Head	
The intersection between the surface of rupture and the original ground surface.	Toe of surface of rupture	
The slope that existed before the landslide took place.	Original ground surface	
The displaced material overlying the surface of rupture between the main scarp and the toe of surface of rupture.	Main body	
A landslide's lowest end, most distant from the main scarp.	Toe	
The surface that forms the lower boundary of the material below the original ground surface.	Surface of rupture	

Definitions credit/courtesy of USGS (adapted)

TABLE 1–1

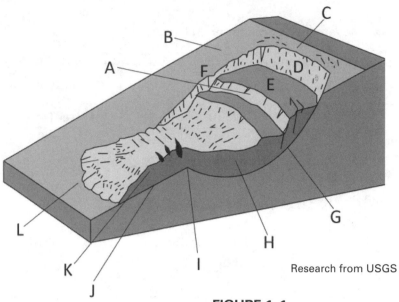

Research from USGS

FIGURE 1–1

Use your textbook to answer questions 2–6.

2. What do all mass movements have in common?

_____

_____

3. How are development activities by humans related to mass-movement disasters?

_____

_____

_____

_____

4. What will happen to weathered material when the resistance force is less than the downslope force?

_____

_____

_____

5. Why are heavy rains of particular concern in areas where mass-movement events are common?

_____

_____

_____

6. Why are wildfires of particular concern in areas where mass-movement events are common?

_____

_____

_____

7. Complete Table 1–2 by matching an identification letter from Figure 1–2 to a landslide type.

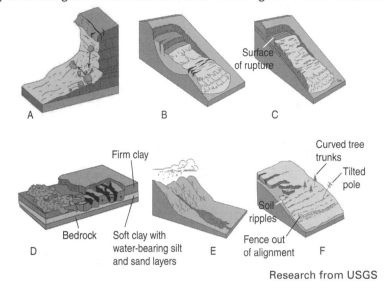

FIGURE 1–2: Landslide Types

Research from USGS

Landslide Type	Description	Letter (see Figure 1–2)
Debris flow	A form of rapid mass movement in which loose soil, rock, and organic matter combine with water to form a slurry that flows downslope. They have been informally called "mudslides." Occasionally, a rotational or translational slide may evolve into a debris flow. Dry flows can sometimes occur in cohesionless sand. Debris flows can be deadly as they can be extremely rapid and may occur without warning.	
Soil creep	Soil creep is the informal name for a slow earth flow. It consists of the imperceptibly slow, steady, downward movement of soil or rock. Movement is caused by internal shear stress sufficient to cause deformation but insufficient to cause failure.	
Rotational landslide	A landslide on which the surface of rupture is curved like a spoon and the slide movement is rotational about an axis parallel to the slope's contour. The mass may move coherently along the rupture surface with little internal deformation. The head of the displaced material may move almost vertically downward, and the upper surface of the displaced material may tilt backward toward the scarp. If the slide is rotational and has several parallel curved planes of movement, it is called a slump.	
Rockfall	Falls are abrupt, downward movements of rock and/or soil that detach from steep slopes or cliffs. The material often strikes the lower slope at an angle that causes bouncing. The falling mass may break on impact, may roll, and may continue moving until the terrain flattens.	
Lateral spread	Occurs on very gentle slopes, especially where an upper layer of strong rock or soil slides across a lower, softer layer. In rock spreads, solid ground extends and fractures, without necessarily forming a recognizable rupture surface. The underlying softer layer may squeeze upward into fractures that divide the upper layer into blocks.	
Translational landslide	The mass in a translational landslide moves down along a planar surface with little rotational movement or backward tilting. This type of slide may progress over considerable distances if the surface of rupture is sufficiently inclined. The material in the slide may range from loose soils to slabs of rock, or both. Translational slides commonly fail along the contact between rock and soil. In northern environments the slide may also move along the permafrost layer.	

TABLE 1–2   Descriptions credit/courtesy of USGS (adapted)

Problem-Solving Module #2: Contributing Variables and Triggering Mechanisms

Table 2–1 presents the natural and human contributing variables that may lead to mass-movement events. Several variables are often present at the same time and place, which, at the onset of a trigger, can prompt a mass-movement event. Table 2–1 also presents mass-movement triggering mechanisms.

Natural Contributing Variables	Human Contributing Variables
Weak, unconsolidated sediment	Excavation of slope
Sheared material	Unstable construction fill material
Jointed or fissured material	Loading of slope
Faulting	Repeated drawdown and filling of reservoir
Contrasting permeability in adjacent layers	Deforestation
Contrasting density in adjacent layers	Irrigation
Glacial meltwater outburst	Mining
Wave erosion of slope toe	Vibrations from construction or mining
Depositional loading of slope	Water leakage from water or sewer lines or septic systems
Vegetation removal by fire or drought	Diversion of currents by piers, dikes, and weirs

Mass-Movement Triggers
Intense rainfall
Rapid snowmelt
Prolonged intense rainfall
Earthquake
Volcanic eruption
Thawing
Flooding

TABLE 2–1

Use your textbook and Tables 2–1 and 2–2 to answer questions 1–8.

1. The 1919 and 1985 mass-movement events were both triggered by volcanic eruptions. Identify at least two natural contributing variables from Table 2–1—specific to volcanic slopes—that contributed to these mass-movement events.

_____

_____

_____

2. What percentage of mass-movement events in Table 2–2 was triggered by earthquakes?

_____

Table 2–2 presents 12 selected mass-movement events that occurred during the twentieth and twenty-first centuries, all of which resulted in significant socioeconomic impacts.

Year	Location	Name and Type	Trigger	Size	Socioeconomic Impact
1911	Tajikistan	Usoy Rockslide	Earthquake	2×10^9 m³ (volume)	54 deaths, Usoy village destroyed
1919	Indonesia	Kelut lahars	Volcanic eruption	Lahars flowed 185 km	5,100 deaths, 104 villages destroyed or damaged
1920	China	Mudflows	Earthquake	50,000 km² covered	>100,000 deaths, many villages buried
1933	China	Deixi landslides	Earthquake	$>150 \times 10^6$ m³ (volume)	>3,000 deaths
1941	Peru	Huaraz Debris Flow	Failure of moraine dam	10×10^6 m³ (volume)	6,000 deaths, 25% of the town of Huaraz destroyed
1958	Japan	Kanogawa landslides, mudflows, and debris flows	Intense rainfall	Unknown	1,094 deaths, 19,754 homes destroyed or damaged
1962	Peru	Nevados Huascaran debris avalanche	Unknown	13×10^6 m³ (volume)	5,000 deaths, town of Ranrahirca destroyed
1970	Peru	Nevados Huascaran debris avalanche	Earthquake	50×10^6 m³ (volume)	18,000 deaths, town of Yungay destroyed, town of Ranrahirca partially destroyed
1985	Colombia	Nevado del Ruiz debris flows	Volcanic eruption	Unknown	23,000 deaths, 4 towns destroyed
1999	Venezuela	Landslides and debris flows	Intense rainfall	Unknown	30,000 deaths, hundreds of buildings and roads destroyed
2005	Pakistan and India	Landslides, rockfalls, and rock avalanches	Earthquake	Unknown	25,500 deaths
2010	Brazil	Debris flows	Rain	Unknown	350 deaths, 61 houses destroyed

Credit/courtesy of USGS (adapted)

TABLE 2–2: Selected Mass-Movement Events, Twentieth and Twenty-First Centuries

3. What country has suffered the largest number of fatalities from the mass-movement events presented in Table 2–2?

_____

4. What were the two largest mass-movement events in terms of volume, and what was their trigger?

_____

_____

5. Considering your answer to question 4, explain why the following statement is either correct or incorrect: "The larger the volume of material unleashed during a mass-movement event is, the greater is the number of fatalities."

_____

_____

_____

6. What Peruvian town was damaged or destroyed twice within a decade, and what would you recommend as a course of action to avoid such an impact in the future?

_____

_____

_____

7. Are more deaths attributable to the "intense rainfall" trigger or the "volcanic eruption" trigger?

_____

_____

8. One of the human contributing variables to mass movement is deforestation. What does this activity do to a slope's stability?

_____

_____

_____

_____

Problem-Solving Module #3: Post-Wildfire Debris-Flows Probability

On June 12, 2011 the Monument Fire started in the Coronado National Forest in Arizona. Over the next month 30,526 acres burned within the Huachuca Mountains. Since post-wildfire areas are often sites of debris flows, a probability study was conducted following the event. The maps and data in this module are adapted from this study. Figures 3–1 and 3–2 present the drainage basins that burned. Figure 3–1 presents debris-flow probabilities at 18 different *pour points* (where drainage basins experience the highest flow of debris). Figure 3–2 presents the estimated volume of debris flow at these same pour points.

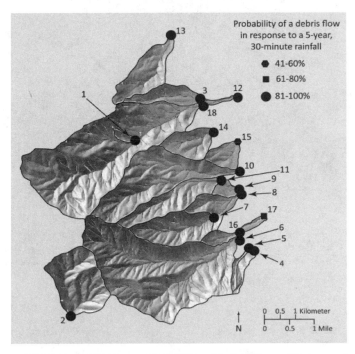

USGS Open File Report 2011–1181 – "Probability and Volume of Potential Postwildfire Debris Flows in the 2011 Monument Burn Area, Southeastern Arizona," Barbara C. Ruddy & Kristine L. Verdin

FIGURE 3–1

Use Figure 3–1 to answer questions 1–4.

1. True or False? The western side of the Monument Fire burn area is most at risk for debris flows.

2. True or False? Pour point 15 is at greater risk for a debris flow than pour point 17.

3. True or False? Because their basins are similarly shaped, pour points 12 and 17 have equal flow probabilities.

4. True or False? Pour point 1, while part of a small basin, has the same flow probability as pour point 10.

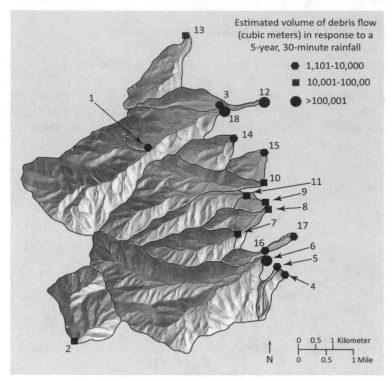

USGS Open File Report 2011–1181 – "Probability and Volume of Potential Postwildfire Debris Flows in the 2011 Monument Burn Area, Southeastern Arizona," Barbara C. Ruddy & Kristine L. Verdin

FIGURE 3–2

Use Figure 3–2 to answer questions 5–8.

5. How many cubic meters of debris are expected to flow from pour point 15 following a 5-year, 30-minute rainfall?

_____

6. How many cubic meters of debris are expected to flow from pour point 6 following a 5-year, 30-minute rainfall?

_____

7. Why do you think pour points 6 and 18 are expected to produce some of the largest debris flows compared to almost every other basin?

_____
_____
_____
_____
_____

8. Pour point 12 is part of a relatively small drainage basin, and yet it is expected to have a very large debris flow following a 5-year, 30-minute rainfall event. Why do you think this is possible?

_____
_____
_____
_____
_____

Table 3–1 presents debris-flow probability and volume following three rainfall events: a 2-year event (once every 2 years), a 5-year event (once every 5 years), and a 10-year event (once every 10 years). Use Figures 3–1 and 3–2 and Table 3–1 to answer questions 9–14.

9. How does the amount of rainfall compare over all three events?

_____

_____

Pour Point	Debris Flow in Response to a 2-year, 30-minute Rainfall (25–35 mm)		Debris Flow in Response to a 5-year, 30-minute Rainfall (33–45 mm)		Debris Flow in Response to a 10-year, 30-minute Rainfall (38–52 mm)	
	Probability (%)	Volume (m³)	Probability (%)	Volume (m³)	Probability (%)	Volume (m³)
1	98	2,080	99	2,430	100	2,680
2	95	28,000	99	32,900	100	36,500
3	81	7,280	93	8,400	97	9,240
4	96	4,480	99	5,180	99	5,690
5	93	2,370	98	2,750	99	3,020
6	98	170,000	99	196,000	100	216,000
7	95	19,800	98	22,900	99	25,200
8	87	26,800	95	30,900	98	33,900
9	76	18,000	91	20,700	95	22,700
10	89	42,600	96	49,100	98	53,900
11	84	16,100	94	18,600	97	20,500
12	92	161,000	97	185,000	99	203,000
13	71	12,000	88	13,900	94	15,200
14	91	8,380	97	9,660	99	10,600
15	26	3,780	50	4,350	69	4,770
16	66	3,140	86	3,630	93	3,990
17	46	3,440	71	3,970	84	4,360
18	96	144,000	99	167,000	99	183,000

TABLE 3–1

10. What happens to the probability of a debris slide (at any pour point) when the amount of rainfall increases?

_____

11. Are there any exceptions to the following statement (and if so, what are they)? "As the amount of rainfall increases, the volume of debris at any pour point also increases."

_____

_____

12. Examine the data for pour points 6, 12, and 18. How does Figure 3–2 graphically express these data, and what is the value?

_____

_____

_____

13. Examine the data for pour point 15. How does Figure 3–1 graphically express these data, and what is the value?

_____

_____

_____

14. Examine the data for pour points 6, 12, and 18. If you had to judge which of the three presents the greatest hazard, which would you choose and why?

_____

_____

_____

_____

_____

_____

Problem-Solving Module #4: Surface Karst

1. Why do limestone rocks dissolve in rainwater?

_____

_____

2. Why are warm places more likely to exhibit karst topography than cold places?

_____

_____

	Solution Sinkholes	Cover-Collapse Sinkholes	Cover-Subsidence Sinkholes
Where They Occur	Where limestone is exposed or only thinly covered with soil	Where a cavity develops in limestone and overlying cover material cannot support its own weight	Where soil is incohesive and permeable
Size and Shape of Sinkholes	Large, bowl-shaped depressions	Large, with vertical walls and circular shapes	A few feet in diameter and depth (where sandy soil is 50 to 100 feet thick)
Formation Process	Gradual downward movement of land and development of a depression	Abrupt and often catastrophic collapse	A gradual, relatively broad and extensive land subsidence over many years (where overburden is incohesive sand)
Additional Defining Characteristics	Large cavities are uncommon because soil subsides as limestone dissolves. Surface runoff commonly carries clays to the depression bottom where they can form a relatively impermeable seal and thereby allow a pond or marsh to form.	Unlikely to occur in areas with deeply buried rock Common in areas where a limestone aquifer is part of a dynamic water table	Upward migration of cavities (called "piping") is common as sand drops into cavities that have formed along joints within the limestone.

TABLE 4–1

Download the following file from the book companion site and open it within Google Earth:
- Florida Sinkholes.kmz

This map shows the state of Florida as a color-coded map demarcating places with specific types of sinkholes. Use this map, as well as the information in Table 4–1, to answer questions 3–11.

3. What is the likely size and shape of a sinkhole that develops around location marker A?

_____

4. What is the likely size and shape of a sinkhole that develops around location marker B?

_____

5. What is the likely size and shape of a sinkhole that develops around location marker C?

_____

6. What is the likely size and shape of a sinkhole that develops around location marker D?

_____

7. Describe the rock at location C.

_____

8. Why would it be unlikely that a person at location D would be taken by surprise by the development of a sinkhole?

_____

9. Why would it be likely that a person at location B would be taken by surprise by the development of a sinkhole?

_____

10. Which location is likely to experience piping?

_____

11. Why is it unlikely that large cavities would form at location C?

_____
_____

Summary of Key Terms and Concepts:

- A debris flow (or *earth flow*) is a fast-flowing slurry of mud mixed with large objects, such as rocks and vegetation.
- Karst topography occurs when carbonate rocks such as limestone dissolve in naturally acidic rainwater.
- Mass movement occurs when any Earth material is set in motion by gravity.
- Mass movement is caused when downslope force exceeds resistive force. Factors such as earthquakes, rain, and road cut can trigger mass-movement events.
- Mass-movement speed is the speed that Earth material moves downslope. It ranges from slow soil creep to rapid and deadly avalanches.
- Mass-movement triggers are events that initiate the movement of Earth material downslope. Triggers can include intense rainfall, rapid snowmelt, prolonged intense rainfall, earthquakes, volcanic eruptions, thawing, and flooding.
- A pour point is the location where a drainage basin experiences the highest flow of debris.
- A rockfall is the sudden rapid free-fall of rocks off a cliff or steep slope.
- A rotational landslide is a landslide on which the surface of rupture is curved like a spoon and the slide movement is rotational about an axis parallel to the slope's contour.
- A slump is a mass-movement type where regolith detaches and slides downslope along a spoon-shaped plane and comes to rest more or less as a unit.
- Soil creep is the imperceptible downslope movement of soil and regolith.
- Surface karst includes limestone pavement, sinkholes, collapse sinkholes, disappearing streams, cockpit karst, and tower karst.
- During a translational slide the mass moves down along a planar surface with little rotational movement or backward tilting.

LAB #26 Fluvial Characteristics and Landforms

Recommended Textbook Reading Prior to Lab:
- Chapter 16, Flowing Water: Fluvial Systems
  - 16.1 Stream Patterns
  - 16.2 Downcutting with Streams: Fluvial Erosion
  - 16.4 Building with Streams: Fluvial Deposition
  - 16.5 Rising Waters: Stream Flooding

Goals: After completing this lab, you will be able to:
- Identify and discuss drainage basins and stream orders using selected maps.
- Employ the scientific method to determine an ideal hydroelectric dam site by calculating and averaging stream discharges.
- Carry out flood-recurrence interval calculations using prepared data tables.
- Carry out flood-probability calculations using prepared data tables.
- Construct a floodplain profile for a selected area of Burlington, Iowa and discuss how this tool can be used by various stakeholders.
- Reflect on and judge the best place to purchase a home in Burlington, Iowa, with respect to flood risk.
- Examine and discuss the Flood Insurance Rate Map (FIRM) for Burlington, Iowa, as well as flood insurance premiums for selected locations.

Key Terms and Concepts:
- alluvium
- dendritic drainage
- discharge
- drainage basin
- flood
- floodplains
- headwaters
- stream
- stream order
- tributary

Required Materials:
- Calculator
- Textbook: *Living Physical Geography*, by Bruce Gervais

Problem-Solving Module #1: Drainage Basins and Stream Orders

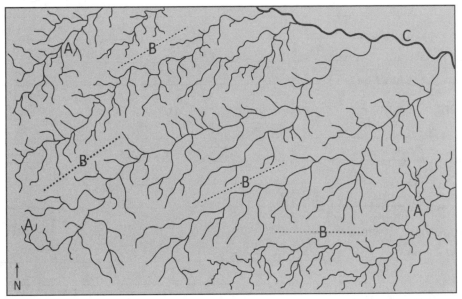

FIGURE 1–1

Research from NASA

1. Figure 1–1 is a model of a small portion of the Madre de Dios watershed in southwestern Peru. Find and circle all seven drainage basins (also known as watersheds).

Use one the following terms to complete each sentence for questions 2–7.

- discharge zone
- tributary streams
- drainage divides
- dendritic drainage pattern
- continental divide

- sub-basins
- internal drainage areas
- trunk stream
- mouth
- radial drainage pattern

2. The three locations identified by letter A on Figure 1–1 are examples of

_____

3. The four locations identified by letter B on Figure 1–1 are examples of

_____

4. Letter C on Figure 1–1 is a _____.

5. A highland that separates a drainage basin that flows into one ocean from another drainage basin that flows into a different ocean is called a _____.

6. Streams that flow outward from a central point are said to exhibit a

_____

7. Streams that resemble the branching pattern of a tree are said to exhibit a

_____

8. What is the stream order system?

_____

_____

_____

_____

9. What are first-order streams?

_____

_____

_____

_____

10. When do second-order streams form?

_____

_____

_____

Stream order rules:
   • Headwaters are first-order streams. Higher-order streams are second-order, third-order, and so on.
   • Downstream segments are defined at confluences.
   • If two streams are not the same order at a confluence, the higher order is maintained for the downstream segment.
   • If two streams are the same order at a confluence, the downstream segment is assigned the next-higher order.

11. Figure 1–2 is a simplified model of a river basin. Rank the streams from 1–5 in the provided identification boxes.

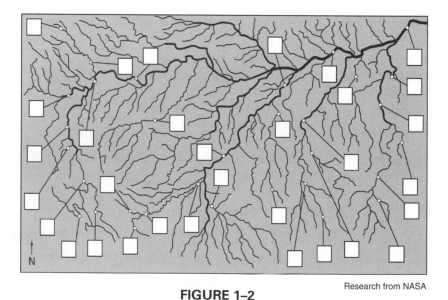

FIGURE 1–2

Research from NASA

Problem-Solving Module #2: Stream Discharge

Assume you live in a state where people recently passed a referendum to construct a large hydroelectric dam. It is determined that two different rivers—the Muddy River and the Rocky River—have potential sites for the dam's location. Both sites are located on fourth-order streams. Hydroelectric engineers tell everyone that the proposed dam should be located on the river with the larger annual discharge.

The Muddy River site has flooded many times over the past 50 years. The Rocky River site has flooded only once in the past 50 years. Nobody knows for sure which river has the larger annual discharge, but about half the people think it's the Muddy River, and about half think it's the Rocky River. You are called in to determine the answer using the scientific method.

1. State your hypothesis about which river has the larger annual discharge.

   _____

   _____

2. What data do you need to collect in order to test your hypothesis, and why is the temporal scale of your data important?

   _____

   _____

3. You begin your work by calculating the annual discharge of both rivers for a single year. Complete Table 2–1 by using the streamflow discharge equation:

$$Q = A \cdot V$$

   - Q = discharge in cubic meters/ second (m^3/s)
   - A = area of river (width × depth)
   - V = flow velocity in meters/second (m/s)

	Muddy River				Rocky River			
	Width (m)	Depth (m)	Velocity (m/s)	Q (m³/s)	Width (m)	Depth (m)	Velocity (m/s)	Q (m³/s)
January	1,534	5.9	1		1,008	8.5	1.4	
February	1,534	6	1		1,008	8.6	1.5	
March	1,535	6.2	1.1		1,010	8.7	1.5	
April	1,536	6.3	1.1		1,010	8.8	1.6	
May	1,537	6.5	1.2		1,011	8.9	1.6	
June	1,537	6.5	1.3		1,012	9	1.7	
July	1,535	6.4	1.1		1,009	8.9	1.6	
August	1,534	6	1.1		1,008	8.8	1.5	
September	1,533	6	1.1		1,007	8.6	1.5	
October	1,532	5.8	1		1,006	8.3	1.5	
November	1,533	5.8	1		1,006	8.3	1.4	
December	1,534	5.9	1		1,007	8.4	1.3	
	Annual Discharge Total				**Annual Discharge Total**			
	Average Monthly Discharge				**Average Monthly Discharge**			

TABLE 2–1

4. Assuming that the data in Table 2–1 is representative of many decades worth of discharge facts for both rivers, is your hypothesis supported or not supported by the information presented in Table 2–1?

_____

_____

5. Based on your annual discharge calculations, on which river should the hydroelectric dam be placed?

_____

6. In your own words, compose a sentence or two that corresponds with Step #6 of the scientific method as it relates to the river with the larger annual discharge. Recall that this step is about further inquiry, and it includes speculation about new questions, new ideas, and more/different data collection.

_____

_____

_____

_____

Problem-Solving Module #3: Flood Recurrence Interval and Probability

1. What is a flood recurrence interval?

_____

_____

2. What is a 100-year flood?

_____

_____

3. If a 100-year flood occurs this year, what is the chance of it occurring next year?

_____

The recurrence interval for a flood is calculated using the following formula:

$$T = (n + 1)/m$$

- T = the recurrence interval in number of years
- n = the number of years of record
- m = the rank of the flood (the largest flood on record is ranked 1)

4. Complete Table 3–1 by first specifying the rank and then calculating the recurrence interval for all the floods. Assume there are 147 years of records and these five are the biggest floods on record.

Year	Discharge (m/s)	Rank	Recurrence Interval (T)
2013	5,287		
1978	5,774		
1947	4,806		
1932	6,697		
1893	5,334		

TABLE 3–1

5. Discuss the findings you discovered in Table 3–1 by making a general statement that considers the rank of a flood and its recurrence interval.

_____

_____

6. Assume a 5,883 m/s flood is ranked #1 for the Cobblestone River within a 132–year flood record. What is the recurrence interval for this flood?

_____

7. Now, assume that the Cobblestone River experiences a 6,810 m/s flood. Recalculate the recurrence interval for the 5,883 m/s flood.

_____

8. What happened to the recurrence interval for the 5,883 m/s flood?

_____

9. Why are flood records going far back in time better for calculating recurrence intervals than records that span, say, only 30 years?

_____

_____

10. What is "annual flood probability"?

_____

Flood probability is calculated using the following formula:

$$P = (1/T) \cdot 100$$

- P = flood probability (as a percent)
- T = recurrence interval

11. Use the flood probability equation to complete Table 3–2.

Recurrence Interval in Years (T)	% Chance of Occurrence in a Given Year (P)
500	
100	
50	
25	
10	
5	
2	

TABLE 3–2

Problem-Solving Module #4: Floodplains

1. What are floodplains?

_____

_____

2. Why are floodplains often attractive places for human settlement and agricultural activity?

_____

_____

_____

Figure 4–1 is a portion of the Burlington, Iowa USGS 7.5 minute US TOPO. It is a map-view of a location with roads, highways, and railroads removed. Map views illustrate locations from a top-down perspective. A transect laid across the map is labeled "A" at its northern point and "B" at its southern point. The transect begins and ends at 650 feet above sea level and cuts across many contour lines.

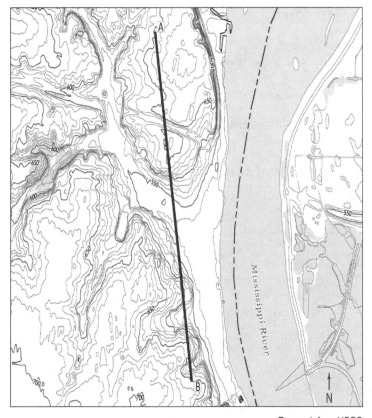

Research from USGS

FIGURE 4–1

Sometimes scientists need to visualize locations from a side perspective. This is called a profile-view. Profile-views are quickly sketched using the following 5 steps:

1. Align a scrap piece of paper to transect A–B.
2. On the scrap paper, mark the location of each index contour that it intersects.
3. Align the marked scrap paper along the base of a graph.
4. Place elevation dots within the graph that correspond to the index contour marks.
5. Connect the elevation dots with a smooth line.

3. Using transect A–B from Figure 4–1, draw a profile on Figure 4–2.

FIGURE 4–2

4. Consider the profile sketch of transect A–B that you made on Figure 4–2. At what elevation would the most alluvium be located, and how might a farmer benefit from knowing this information?

_____

_____

5. How might a hiking club benefit from the profile sketch of transect A–B that you made on Figure 4–2?

_____

_____

6. How might a potential home buyer hoping to avoid buying flood insurance benefit from the profile sketch of transect A–B that you made on Figure 4–2?

_____

_____

Figure 4–3 is the same portion of the Burlington, Iowa USGS 7.5 minute US TOPO illustrated in Figure 4–1. This time, however, the roads, highways, and railroads are visible.

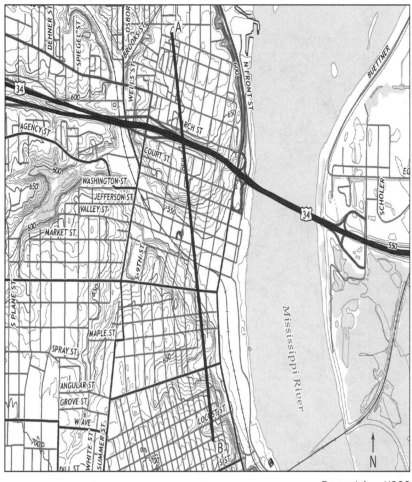

Research from USGS

FIGURE 4–3

7. Consider transect A–B on Figure 4–3. If you had to buy a home along this transect and were concerned about the cost of flood insurance, would you choose a home on Maple Street or Valley Street? Explain.

_____

_____

8. Consider the profile you constructed on Figure 4–2, as well as transect A–B on Figures 4–3 and 4–4. What will likely happen to the railroad track in the event of a 100-year flood?

_____

Figure 4–4 is adapted from the Flood Insurance Rate Map (FIRM) specific for this section of the Mississippi River. FIRM maps are available from the Federal Emergency Management Agency's (FEMA) Map Service Center (MSC). FIRM maps empower individuals, communities, and other stakeholders with information needed to mitigate flood risk.

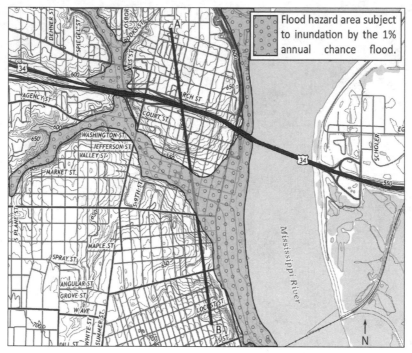

Research from USGS/FEMA

FIGURE 4–4

9. What is the recurrence interval for the flood scenario illustrated in Figure 4–4?

_____

10. Considering Figure 4–4, does the prediction you made in question 8 look likely?

_____

Table 4–1 lists two commercial addresses in Burlington. Only three blocks separate these two establishments.

Address	Flood Hazard Risk Profile	Estimated Flood Insurance Annual Premium (Building and Contents)
106 Washington St, Burlington, IA	High Risk, Special Flood Hazard Area (SFHA)	$1750–$13743
610 N 4th St, Burlington, IA	Moderate-to-low risk area	$641–$6057

TABLE 4–1

11. Which commercial establishment must be located at a higher elevation? _____

Summary of Key Terms and Concepts:

- Alluvium is sediment deposited by a stream.
- A dendritic drainage pattern is a system of streams within a drainage basin that resembles the branching pattern of a tree.
- Discharge is the volume of water flowing past a fixed point within a stream channel. It is expressed in cubic meters or cubic feet per second.
- A drainage basin is a geographic region drained by a trunk stream and its tributaries.
- A flood is an inundation by water in a region not normally covered by water. A flood results when a stream's discharge exceeds its channel capacity.
- Floodplains are attractive places to settle but present a flood hazard.
- Headwaters are the region where a stream originates.
- A stream is a channel of water that flows downhill by the force of gravity.
- Stream order is a numerical system used to classify stream size based on the number of tributaries flowing into it.
- A tributary is a small stream that merges with other streams.

LAB #27   Alpine Glaciation

Recommended Textbook Reading Prior to Lab:
- Chapter 17, The Work of Ice: The Cryosphere and Glacial Landforms
  - ☐ 17.2 About Glaciers
  - ☐ 17.3 Carving with Ice: Glacial Erosion
  - ☐ 17.4 Building with Ice: Glacial Deposits

Goals: After completing this lab, you will be able to:
- Using Google Earth, identify and explain processes associated with selected glacial erosional and depositional landforms.
- Evaluate changes in the terminus of Iceland's Sólheimajökull glacier and correlate these changes to mean summer temperature data.
- Use the scientific method to compare the size of 20 selected glaciers in 1966 to their size in 2005.
- Interpret cumulative mass balance data of Earth's glacierized regions, and discuss your findings using meters water equivalent (MWEQ).

Key Terms and Concepts:
- alpine glaciers
- alpine glacier deposits
- arête
- cirque
- cirque glacier
- col
- crevasse
- fjords
- glaciers
- glacial drift

- glacial retreat
- glacial steps
- glacial toe
- glacial valleys
- hanging valley
- horn
- ice sheets
- lateral moraine
- mass balance
- outwash plain
- paternoster lakes

- proglacial lake
- supraglacial lake
- tarn
- terminal moraine
- till
- toe (or terminus)
- valley glacier
- zone of ablation
- zone of accumulation

Required Materials:
- Calculator
- High-speed Internet connection (for Module 1) and Google Earth (free download at http://www.google.com/earth/download/ge/agree.html)
- Microsoft Excel (or similar software program)
- Textbook: *Living Physical Geography*, by Bruce Gervais

Problem-Solving Module #1: Glacial Erosional and Depositional Landforms

Download the following file from the textbook companion site and open it within Google Earth:
  • Glacial Landforms.kmz

Use the above Google Earth file to answer questions 1–24. Refer to your textbook for the correct glacial landform names.

1. Fly to location marker A in Glacier National Park. What is this landform?

_____

2. The relatively resistant portions of bedrock that lie along the floor of the valley where location marker A is located are called

_____

3. Fly to location marker B in Glacier National Park. What is the definition and name of this landform?

_____

_____

4. Fly to location marker C in Glacier National Park. Why is this landform a tarn instead of a supraglacial lake?

_____

_____

5. Fly to location marker D in Canada's Jasper National Park. What is the name of this landform, and what kind of valley glacier carved it?

_____

_____

6. Fly to location marker E in Canada's Jasper National Park. What is the name of this landform, and how was it created?

_____

_____

7. Fly to location marker F in Canada's Mount Robson Provincial Park. What is the name of this landform, and what kind of valley glaciers carved it?

_____

_____

8. Fly to location marker G in Canada's Mount Robson Provincial Park. What is the name of this landform, and how did it form?

_____

_____

_____

9. Fly to location marker H in the Himalaya Mountains. What is the name of this landform, and how deep can it become?

_____

_____

10. Why is there a depth limit to the landform located at location marker H?

_____

_____

_____

11. Fly to location marker I in the Himalaya Mountains. What is the name of this landform, and what type of moraines fused together to create it?

_____

_____

12. Fly to location marker J in the Himalaya Mountains. Is this landform a proglacial lake or a tarn, and why?

_____

_____

_____

13. Fly to location marker K in the Himalaya Mountains. What is this part of a valley glacier called, and how do you know?

_____

_____

_____

14. Fly to location marker L in the Himalaya Mountains. What is this landform called, and how is it an example of glaciofluvial processes?

_____

_____

_____

15. Fly to location marker M in the Karakoram Range. What is this landform called, and what is it composed of?

_____

_____

16. Fly to location marker N in the Himalaya Mountains. What kind of valley glacier is this?

_____

17. Fly to location marker O in Greenland. What is this landform, and how is its presence explained by Earth's last glacial period?

_____

_____

_____

18. Fly to location marker P in Greenland. This is unsorted rock debris deposited by a glacier that does not form a moraine. What is the general term used to describe this material?

_____

19. Fly to location marker Q in Greenland. What kind of end moraine is this, and how do we know?

_____

_____

20. Fly to location marker R in Greenland. Is this a valley glacier or an ice cap, and how do we know?

_____

_____

_____

21. Fly to location marker S in Greenland. Is this a zone of accumulation or ablation, and how do we know?

_____

_____

_____

22. Fly to location marker T in Greenland. Is this a zone of accumulation or ablation, and how do we know?

_____

_____

_____

23. Fly to location marker U in Greenland. Is this an ice sheet or a glacier, and how do we know?

_____

_____

_____

24. Why is the landform at location marker U not an ice shelf?

_____

_____

_____

Problem-Solving Module #2: Measuring Changes in Glacier Size

Scientists study changes in glacier size using a variety of techniques. Here are three examples:
  • Measuring the advance or retreat of a terminus
  • Measuring area change
  • Measuring mass balance change

Measuring the advance or retreat of a glacier's terminus is a research technique that has been used since the late nineteenth century. Presented in Figure 2–1 is the terminus record for Iceland's Sólheimajökull glacier. Notice that summer mean temperature (°C) is presented on the same graph.

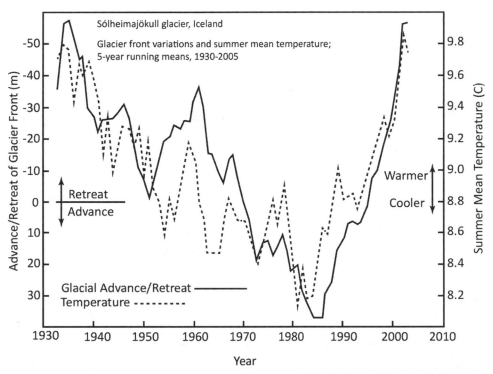

U.S. Geological Survey Professional
Paper 1386–A–2, Glaciers page A–118

FIGURE 2–1

Use Figure 2–1 to answers questions 1–11.

1. Is a solid or dashed line used to present the terminus record of the Sólheimajökull glacier?

    _____

2. Should you use the right or left *y*-axis to obtain the terminus record of the Sólheimajökull glacier?

    _____

3. What graphic is used to present summer mean temperature at the Sólheimajökull glacier?

    _____

4. Should you use the right or left *y*-axis to obtain the summer mean temperature at the Sólheimajökull glacier?

    _____

5. Overall, did the Sólheimajökull glacier advance or retreat between 1935 and 1952, and by how much?

_____

6. During the 1935 to 1952 period, how did the summer mean temperature change, and by how much?

_____

7. Overall, did the Sólheimajökull glacier advance or retreat between 1952 and 1962, and by how much?

_____

8. During the 1952 to 1962 period, how did the summer mean temperature change, and by how much?

_____

9. Overall, did the Sólheimajökull glacier advance or retreat between 1985 and 2003, and by how much?

_____

10. During the 1985 to 2003 period, how did the summer mean temperature change, and by how much?

_____

11. Describe the relationship between the advance or retreat of the Sólheimajökull glacier's terminus and summer mean temperature.

_____

_____

_____

Assume you work for the Northern Rocky Mountain Science Center. Your job is to determine the extent of glacier recession within Glacier National Park as part of a study examining the effects of climate change. You access photographic data of 20 glaciers from 1966 and compare their area to photographs of the same glaciers taken in 2005. Based on this quick look, you guess that the glaciers have lost 15% of their area. Since you are a scientist, you follow this preliminary inquiry with a thorough examination using the scientific method.

12. State your hypothesis about the extent of glacier recession within Glacier National Park.

_____

_____

_____

13. What data do you need to collect in order to test your hypothesis?

_____

_____

_____

14. Process the data in Table 2–1 by calculating the total area of the 20 selected glaciers for 1966 and 2005. Use Microsoft Excel or another similar software program to expedite your calculations.

Glacier Name	1966 Area (m²)	2005 Area (m²)
Agassiz Glacier	1,589,174	1,039,077
Ahern Glacier	589,053	511,824
Blackfoot Glacier	2,334,983	1,787,640
Carter Glacier	273,834	202,696
Chaney Glacier	535,604	379,688
Grinnell Glacier	1,020,009	615,454
Harrison Glacier	2,073,099	1,888,919
Ipasha Glacier	321,745	212,030
Kintla Glacier	1,728,828	1,136,551
Logan Glacier	503,298	302,146
Old Sun Glacier	421,254	370,257
Piegan Glacier	280,107	250,728
Pumpelly Glacier	1,489,137	1,257,211
Rainbow Glacier	1,284,070	1,164,060
Salamander Glacier	225,621	172,916
Sexton Glacier	400,444	276,780
Sperry Glacier	1,339,244	874,229
Swiftcurrent Glacier	261,410	223,519
Thunderbird Glacier	358,284	238,331
Two Ocean Glacier	428,828	275,022
Total Area		

Data credit/courtesy of USGS

TABLE 2–1

15. What is the area difference of the 20 selected glaciers from 1966 to 2005? _____

16. What is the percent of area lost between 1966 and 2005? _____

17. Is your hypothesis supported or not supported by the data?

_____

_____

_____

18. Compose a sentence that summarizes the findings of your study.

_____

_____

_____

19. In your own words, compose a sentence or two that corresponds with Step #6 of the scientific method as it relates to the above study of glacier recession within Glacier National Park. Recall that this step is about further inquiry, and includes speculation about new questions, new ideas, and more/different data collection.

_____

_____

_____

_____

_____

Mass balance is the balance of ice for a glacier over a period of time. A glacier with a zero mass balance has inputs (snowfall) and outputs (melting, sublimation, and iceberg calving) that are equal. If inputs match outputs, the glacier is balanced within the current climate and will not grow or shrink—it will simply maintain its size while continuing to flow downslope.

A glacier that is out of balance within the climate will grow or shrink. If ice gain exceeds loss, a positive mass balance exists—the glacier will grow and therefore advance downslope. If ice loss exceeds gain, a negative mass balance exists—the glacier will shrink and therefore retreat upslope.

Scientists measure a glacier's mass balance by recording input and output data over time and stating their findings in "meters water equivalent" (MWEQ). Notice that the value is "meters *water* equivalent," not "meters *snow* equivalent"—meaning that any gain or loss of glacial ice is first theoretically melted down into liquid. After this volume of liquid is acquired, it is simply divided by the glacier's area to obtain MWEQ.

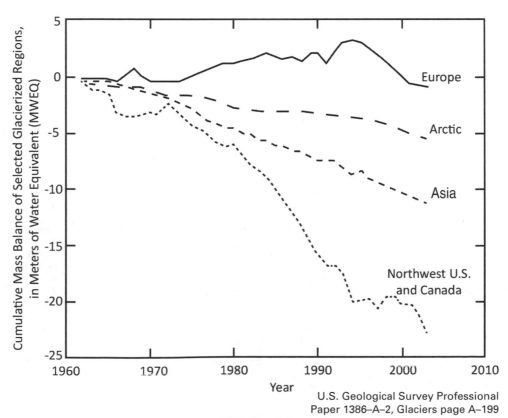

U.S. Geological Survey Professional
Paper 1386–A–2, Glaciers page A–199

FIGURE 2–2

Use Figure 2–2 to answer questions 20–24.

20. Between 1960 and 2000, which glacierized region experienced the least change in MWEQ?

_____

21. Between 1960 and 2000, which glacierized region experienced the most change in MWEQ?

_____

22. Between 1970 and 2000, what was the cumulative mass balance change within the Asia region, and is this a positive or negative mass balance?

_____

_____

23. Between 1970 and 2000, what was the cumulative mass balance change within the northwest United States and Canada region, and is this a positive or negative mass balance?

_____

_____

24. Describe what is generally happening to the cumulative mass balance trend of the selected glacierized regions illustrated in Figure 2–2.

_____

_____

_____

Summary of Key Terms and Concepts:
- There are several different types of alpine glaciers, including valley glaciers, piedmont glaciers, cirque glaciers, and ice caps.
- Alpine glacier deposits include lateral, terminal, and end moraines.
- An arête (pronounced ahr-i-TEY) is a steep-sided, sharp ridge created by cirque or valley glaciers in mountains.
- A cirque is a bowl-shaped depression with steep headwalls formed by a cirque glacier.
- A cirque glacier is a glacier found at the head of a valley, forming a bowl-shaped depression called a cirque.
- A crevasse is a crack that develops in the top 60 meters of a glacier.
- A col is a low area or pass over a ridge formed by two cirque glaciers.
- Fjords are glacial valleys that have been flooded by the sea.
- Glaciers are large streams or sheets of ice that flow downslope under gravity through basal sliding and plastic deformation.
- Any material that is deposited by glaciers or glacial streams is called glacial drift.
- Most alpine glaciers are in retreat due to atmospheric warming.
- Glacial steps are relatively resistant portions of bedrock along the floor of a glacial valley.
- The glacial toe is the leading edge and lowest elevation of a glacier. The position of the glacier's toe is continually moving upslope or downslope in response to many complex factors within and outside the glacier.
- A glacial valley (or glacial trough) is a U-shaped valley carved by a valley glacier.
- A hanging valley is a tributary glacial valley that feeds into a larger glacial valley with a deeper valley floor.

- A horn is a steep, pyramid-shaped mountain surrounded by at least three cirques.
- Ice sheets are large, flats sheets of ice that cover a significant portion of a continent. Ice sheets are found today only on Greenland and Antarctica.
- A lateral moraine consists of till that accumulates on the side of a glacier.
- Mass balance refers to the balance of ice within a glacier over a set period of time. A glacier with a zero mass balance has equal inputs (snowfall) and outputs (melting, sublimation, and iceberg calving).
- An outwash plain is a flat area of sediments deposited by a stream exiting a glacier.
- Paternoster lakes are a series of small lakes that form in a glacial valley.
- A proglacial lake is a lake that forms at or near the toe of a glacier.
- A supraglacial lake is a lake that forms on the surface of a glacier or ice shelf during summer as the surface of the ice melts.
- A tarn is a mountain lake that forms within or just below a cirque.
- A glacial toe (or terminus) is the leading edge and lowest elevation of a glacier.
- A terminal moraine is an end moraine marking the farthest advance of a glacier's toe.
- Till is unsorted rock debris deposited by ice. Moraines are composed of till.
- A valley glacier is a glacier that occupies a mountain valley.
- The zone of ablation is the area downslope from the equilibrium line where ablation (ice loss) exceeds ice accumulation.
- The zone of accumulation is the area upslope of the equilibrium line where ice gain from snowfall exceeds ice loss.

LAB #28   Ice Sheets and Mean Sea Level (MSL)

Recommended Textbook Reading Prior to Lab:
- Chapter 17, The Work of Ice: The Cryosphere and Glacial Landforms
  - 17.2 About Glaciers
  - 17.5 Geographic Perspectives: Polar Ice Sheets and Sea Level

Goals: After completing this lab, you will be able to:
- Evaluate 11 years of NASA data about Antarctica and Greenland in order to evaluate a hypothesis about their changing mass.
- Present NASA's data about the changing ice mass of Antarctica and Greenland in graphical format.
- Calculate the changing mass of Antarctica and Greenland in gigatons.
- Evaluate glaciological changes over time to the Wordie Ice Shelf using cartographic data from the USGS and the British Antarctic Survey.
- Determine annual rates of change to past ice front positions on the Wordie Ice Shelf.
- Evaluate glaciological changes over time to a section of the Larsen Ice Shelf using cartographic data from the USGS and the British Antarctic Survey.
- Calculate annual rates of change to past ice front positions on the Larsen Ice Shelf.
- Study linear trend plots of sea level records from NOAA in order to construct a hypothesis about changing mean sea level (MSL).
- Graphically present 20 years of sea level change from NASA's Jason-2/OSTM Mission.
- Evaluate your hypothesis about changing mean sea level (MSL) based on NASA data.

Key Terms and Concepts:
- Antarctica's negative mass balance
- cryosphere location
- Greenland's negative mass balance
- ice sheet
- ice shelf
- rising sea levels

Required Materials:
- Calculator
- Textbook: *Living Physical Geography*, by Bruce Gervais

Problem-Solving Module #1: Are Antarctica and Greenland Losing Mass?

NASA's GRACE (Gravity Recovery and Climate Experiment) Mission measures gravity anomalies on Earth. Gravity is dependent on the distance and mass of objects. Consider Earth's surface—it is not a perfectly smooth geoid but instead has mountain ranges, ocean floors, valleys, and plains. These topographic features have varying masses. The orbital paths of the GRACE satellites are influenced by these mass differences, and scientists are thus able to map Earth's gravity anomalies.

Because ice accumulates and melts, areas covered with ice can exhibit dynamic masses. NASA's GRACE mission has accumulated mass data for Antarctica and Greenland since January 2003. This tool is one of many techniques that scientists use to collect data about the changing mass of glacial ice.

Assume you are a climate scientist and are wondering if Earth's two ice sheets—Antarctica and Greenland—have lost mass over the past 11 years. Several people argue that they have not lost mass, and they show you many satellite pictures to support their point. Because you are a scientist, you decide to investigate the question using the scientific method and the latest data from the GRACE mission.

1. State your hypothesis about the mass of Earth's two ice sheets.

   _____

   _____

2. What GRACE mission data do you need to collect in order to test your hypothesis?

   _____

   _____

Table 1–1 presents Greenland and Antarctica mass data from the GRACE mission from 2003 through 2013. Notice that mass change is relative to the average mass of the ice sheet over the entire time period.

	Antarctica Ice Mass Change (Gt) (relative to the average over entire time period)	Greenland Ice Mass Change (Gt) (relative to the average over entire time period)
January 2003	461.96	1210.61
January 2004	241.63	998.60
January 2005	164.38	764.91
January 2006	150.47	589.80
January 2007	61.04	354.13
January 2008	−160.78	94.47
January 2009	−155.17	−62.69
January 2010	−250.25	−362.35
January 2011	−295.85	−820.15
January 2012	−448.39	−1312.09
January 2013	−696.14	−1723.89

TABLE 1–1

3. Graphically present the data in Table 1–1 by plotting mass change for Antarctica on Figure 1–1, and mass change for Greenland on Figure 1–2. Remember that mass change is relative to the average mass of the ice sheet over the entire time period.

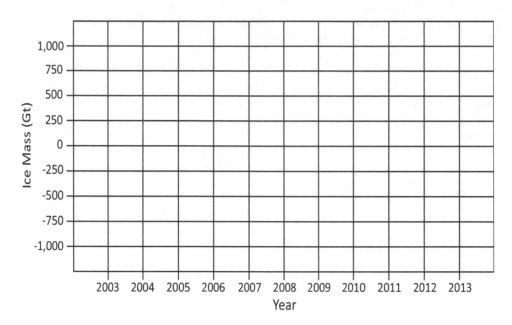

FIGURE 1–1: Ice Mass Change for Antarctica

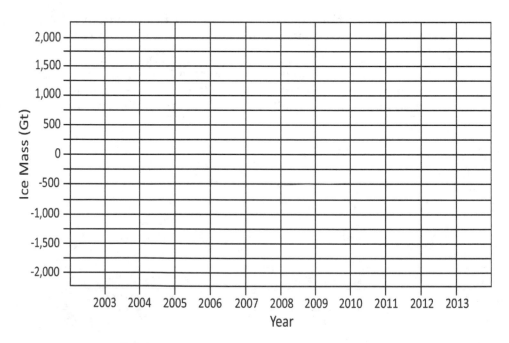

FIGURE 1–2: Ice Mass Change for Greenland

4. Is your hypothesis supported or not supported by the data?

_____

Notice that GRACE mission data are presented in Gt. This stands for gigatons, or 1 billion tons.

5. From January 2003 to January 2013, how many Gt of mass did Antarctica lose? (Show your work.)

_____

_____

6. On average, how many Gt of mass did Antarctica lose each year over the 11–year period? (Show your work.)

_____

_____

7. From January 2003 to January 2013, how many Gt of mass did Greenland lose? (Show your work.)

_____

_____

8. On average, how many Gt of mass did Greenland lose each year over the 11-year period? (Show your work.)

_____

_____

9. Which ice sheet has lost more mass over the 11-year study period? _____

10. In your own words, compose a sentence or two that corresponds with Step #6 of the scientific method as it relates to the above study of ice mass change in Antarctica and Greenland. Recall that this step is about further inquiry and includes speculation about new questions, new ideas, and more/different data collection.

_____

_____

_____

_____

Problem-Solving Module #2: Antarctica's Coastal Changes

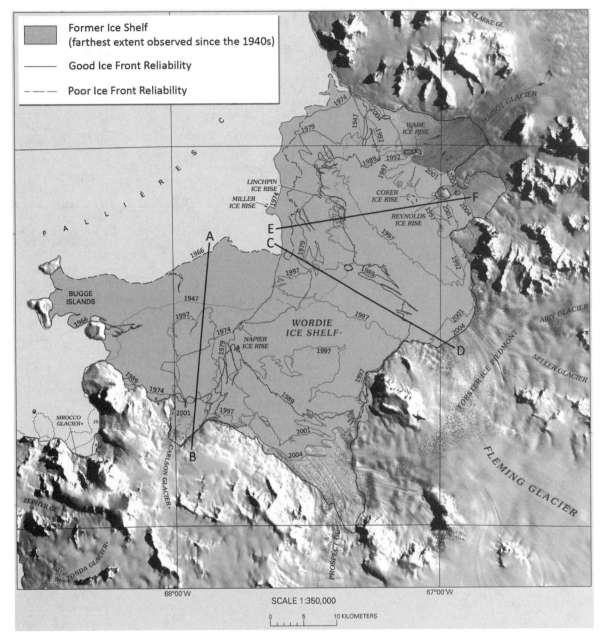

FIGURE 2–1

Figure 2–1 illustrates glaciological changes to the Wordie Ice Shelf, which floats off the coast of the Antarctica Peninsula. Three transects (A-B, C-D, and E-F) have been added to the map to facilitate its examination. Use Figure 2–1 to answer questions 1–17.

1. Should we speak about the Wordie Ice Shelf in the present or past tense, and why?

_____

_____

Use transect A-B to answer questions 2–7.

2. Did the ice shelf grow or shrink between 1947 and 1966? _____

3. Did the ice shelf grow or shrink between 1966 and 1974, and by how many kilometers?

_____

4. What year did the ice shelf reach its farthest extent? _____

5. How many kilometers farther out did the ice shelf extend in 1966 compared to 1997? _____

6. At its farthest extent, how many kilometers did the ice shelf extend from land? _____

7. Which glacier feeds most directly into the ice shelf along transect A-B? _____

Use transect C-D to answer questions 8–13.

8. What year did the ice shelf reach its farthest extent? _____

9. Did the ice shelf grow or shrink between 1979 and 1989, and by how many kilometers?

_____

10. How many kilometers farther out did the ice shelf reach in 1974 compared to 2004? _____

11. How many kilometers farther out did the ice shelf reach in 2001 compared to 2004? _____

12. At its farthest extent out, was the ice shelf front reliability good or poor? _____

13. What do the Airy, Seller, and Fleming glaciers create when they merge? _____

Use transect E-F to answer questions 14–17.

14. At its farthest extent out, was the ice shelf front reliability good or poor? _____

15. What year was the ice front reliability poor? _____

16. How many kilometers farther out did the ice shelf reach in 1974 compared to 2004? _____

17. From 2001 to 2004, did the ice shelf grow or shrink, and by how many kilometers? _____

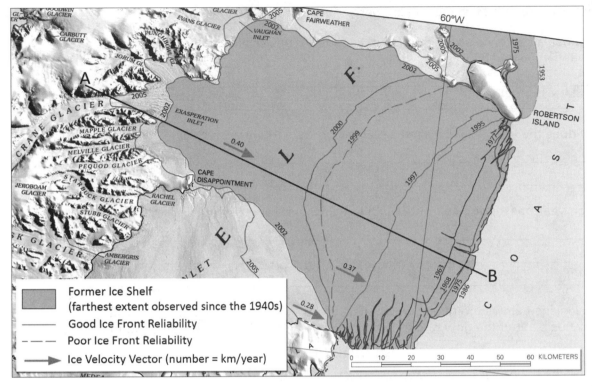

Research from USGS and
The British Antarctic Survey

FIGURE 2–2

Figure 2–2 illustrates glaciological changes to the Larsen Ice Shelf, which also floats off the coast of the Antarctica Peninsula. One transect (A-B) has been added to the map to facilitate its examination. Use Figure 2–2 to answer questions 18–30.

18. Should we speak about this section of the Larsen Ice Shelf in the present or past tense, and why?

_____

_____

Use transect A-B to answer questions 19–30.

19. Between 1963 and 1986, did the ice shelf grow or shrink, and by how many kilometers?

_____

20. Between 1986 and 1997, did the ice shelf grow or shrink, and by how many kilometers?

_____

21. What was the rate of change, in km per year, between 1986 and 1997? _____

22. Between 1997 and 1999, did the ice shelf grow or shrink, and by how many kilometers?

_____

23. What was the rate of change, in km per year, between 1997 and 1999? _____

24. Between 2000 and 2002, did the ice shelf grow or shrink, and by how many kilometers?

_____

25. What was the rate of change, in km per year, between 2000 and 2002? _____

26. Compose a sentence about the rate of change for this section of the Larsen Ice Shelf between 1986 and 2002.

    _____

    _____

27. How does the year 2000 ice shelf advance compare to the year 1997?

    _____

    _____

28. Which year has a poor ice front reliability? Speculate about why this might occur.

    _____

    _____

    _____

29. If an ice shelf slows the rate at which glaciers flow into the sea, what is a sound hypothesis about the flow rate today of the Crane, Mapple, Melville, and Pequod glaciers?

    _____

    _____

    _____

30. If increasing volumes of ice from the Crane, Mapple, Melville, and Pequod glaciers (as well as many others around the world) reach the open sea, what is likely to happen to mean sea level (MSL)?

    _____

Problem-Solving Module #3: Rising Mean Sea Level (MSL)

Assume you are a climate scientist and are wondering if Earth's global mean sea level (MSL) is rising. You begin investigating this question by examining linear trend plots of sea level records from cities around the world. Figure 3–1 shows four samples of these records from locations around the world.

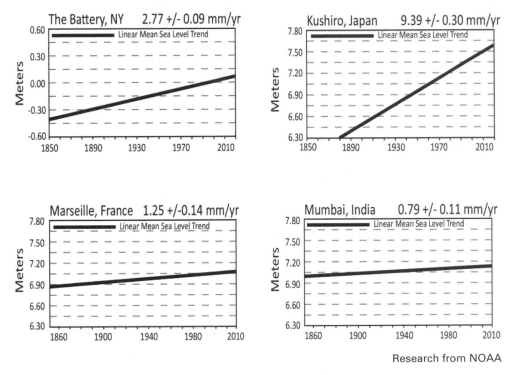

Research from NOAA

FIGURE 3–1

1. Based on the trend plots in Figure 3–1, state your hypothesis about Earth's global mean sea level trend.

   _____

   _____

2. In addition to ground-based data showing sea level trends from individual cities around the world, why would a scientist want to see satellite data showing average annual sea-surface height?

   _____

   _____

   _____

   _____

   _____

Table 3–1 presents 20 years of sea level change from NASA's Jason-2/OSTM Mission. Remember that sea level change is relative to the average height of Earth's ocean over the entire time period.

	Global Sea Level Change (mm/ year) (relative to the average over entire time period)
January 1993	−15.89
January 1994	−8.26
January 1995	−6.81
January 1996	−7.81
January 1997	−5.02
January 1998	5.70
January 1999	6.46
January 2000	12.11
January 2001	14.12
January 2002	19.25
January 2003	23.65
January 2004	25.45
January 2005	29.09
January 2006	31.66
January 2007	32.55
January 2008	32.76
January 2009	36.45
January 2010	42.33
January 2011	36.85
January 2012	45.98
January 2013	55.94

TABLE 3–1

3. Graphically present the data in Table 3–1 by plotting global sea level change on Figure 3–2.

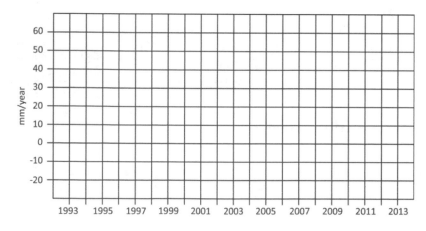

FIGURE 3–2

4. Is your hypothesis supported or not supported by the data?

_____

_____

5. In your own words, compose a sentence or two that corresponds with Step #6 of the scientific method as it relates to Earth's global mean sea level (MSL). Recall that this step is about further inquiry and includes speculation about new questions, new ideas, and more/different data collection.

_____

_____

_____

_____

_____

_____

Summary of Key Terms and Concepts:
- Antarctica's negative mass balance is due to the increasing rate of outlet glacier flow.
- About 99% of the cryosphere is found in Greenland and Antarctica.
- Greenland's negative mass balance is due to increased melt days and increased rates of outlet glacier flow.
- An ice sheet is a large, flat sheet of ice that covers a significant portion of a continent. Only Greenland and Antarctica have ice sheets.
- An ice shelf is the portion of an ice sheet or an outlet glacier that extends over the ocean.
- Rising sea levels are caused in part from melting ice sheets on Greenland and Antarctica. These ice sheets have potential to cause a 1-meter rise of sea level by 2100.

LAB #29 Desert Landforms and Processes

Recommended Textbook Reading Prior to Lab:
- Chapter 18: Water, Wind, and Time: Desert Landforms
    - 18.1 Desert Landforms and Processes
    - 18.2 Desert Landscapes

Goals: After completing this lab, you will be able to:
- Using Google Earth, identify various desert landforms and explain the processes associated with their development.
- Classify the driving forces of desertification and match these forces to specific examples.
- Classify the proximate causes of desertification and match these causes to specific examples.
- Determine how to effectively communicate and present cartographic land degradation data for the West African country of Senegal.
- Create land degradation maps for the West African country of Senegal.
- Evaluate spatial patterns of land degradation in the West African country of Senegal.

Key Terms and Concepts:
- aeolian
- bajada
- barchan dune
- butte
- desertification
- driving force of desertification
- erg
- inselberg
- longitudinal dune
- mesa
- playa
- playa lake
- proximate cause of desertification
- saline lake
- star dune
- transverse dune

Required materials:
- Calculator
- High-speed Internet connection (for Module 1) and Google Earth (free download at http://www.google.com/earth/download/ge/agree.html)
- Textbook: *Living Physical Geography*, by Bruce Gervais

Problem-Solving Module #1: Desert Landforms

Download the following file from the textbook companion site and open it within Google Earth:
- Desert Landforms.kmz

Use the Google Earth file to answer questions 1–15.

1. Fly to location marker A. What is this landform called, and what kind of mineral deposits should we expect to find on the ground?

_____

_____

2. Fly to location marker B. What is this landform called, and how did it form?

_____

_____

3. Fly to location marker C. What is this landform called, and how is uplift an important process in its formation?

_____

_____

_____

4. Fly to location marker D. What is this landform called, and why did it form?

_____

_____

5. Fly to location marker E. What is this landform called, and why does it exist when the surrounding rocks and sediments all have eroded away?

_____

_____

6. Fly to location marker F. What is this landform called after a heavy rainfall, and how long does it typically take any water to evaporate?

_____

_____

7. Fly to location marker G. What is this landform called, and why does it contain high concentrations of dissolved minerals?

_____

_____

8. Fly to location marker H. What is this extensive area called, and why can't such a landform develop in humid climates?

_____

_____

9. Fly to location marker I. The crests of these dunes are situated parallel to the prevailing wind direction. What kind of dune is this, and what is the prevailing wind direction? Remember that winds are named for the direction from which they blow. *Hint: The prevailing wind direction is* not *southwest.*

_____

_____

10. Fly to location marker J. What kind of dune is this, and what happens to the prevailing winds in this area that leads to this dune's formation?

_____

_____

11. Fly to location marker K. What kind of dune is this, and do such dunes require more or less sand on the desert floor compared to barchan dunes?

_____

_____

12. Fly to location marker L. What kind of dune is this, and what is the prevailing wind direction? Remember that winds are named for the direction from which they blow. *Hint: The prevailing wind direction is* not *southeast.*

_____

_____

13. Why are the answers in question 9–12 aeolian landforms?

_____

_____

_____

14. Fly to location marker M. This is Owens Lake. What city drained this lake in the early twentieth century, and what was the water used for? *Hint: See the textbook, Section 18.3.*

_____

_____

15. Fly to location marker N. This is Mono Lake. What city began diverting water from this lake between 1940 and 1980? *Hint: See the textbook, Section 18.3.* How far away is that city (in kilometers) from the lake? *Hint: Use the ruler tool on the Google Earth toolbar.*

_____

_____

16. Fly to location marker O. This is the Aral Sea. What country diverted water from this lake in the mid-twentieth century, and what was the water used for? *Hint: See the textbook, Section 18.3.*

_____

_____

Problem-Solving Module #2: Driving Forces and Proximate Causes of Desertification

1. If "desertification" does not mean losing land due to an encroaching desert or sand dunes, what does it mean?

_____

_____

A "driving force" of desertification is a social or physical process that *facilitates or encourages* land degradation in semi-arid areas. Driving forces include the following factors:

- Demographic
- Economic
- Technological
- Climate
- Policy and institutional
- Cultural

2. On Table 2–1, match each of the above driving forces of desertification to its examples.

Driving Force of Desertification	Examples
	• New irrigation equipment and techniques • Innovative earthmoving practices • Improved transportation efficiency • Deficient irrigation maintenance • Inefficient water use
	• Market growth • Commercialization • Urbanization • Industrialization
	• Lack of concern about dryland ecosystems • Perception of water as free and abundant • Frontier-settlement mentality • Individual lack of concern and poor practices
	• Market liberalization • Commercial crop subsidies • Tax incentives • Faulty traditional land-use tenure
	• Warming average temperatures • Shifting wind patterns • Longer dry seasons
	• Migration • Fertility • Mortality • Population density

TABLE 2–1

A "proximate cause" of desertification is a social or physical process that *creates* land degradation in semi-arid areas. Proximate causes include the following:

- Agricultural activities
- Infrastructure extension
- Wood extraction
- Increased aridity

3. On Table 2–2, match each of the above proximate causes of desertification to its examples.

Proximate Cause of Desertification	Examples
	• Increased climate variability • Decreasing rainfall • Prolonged drought • Intense fires
	• Fuel-wood harvesting • Fence-post creation • Medicinal herb digging/extraction • Plant collecting
	• Livestock production • Extensive ruminant grazing • Water-intensive crop expansion
	• Dams, canals, and roads • Human settlements • Commodity extraction (oil, quarries, and ores)

TABLE 2–2

4. Select an example of a driving force, and explain how it might work synergistically with an example of a proximate cause.

_____

_____

_____

_____

_____

Problem-Solving Module #3: Desertification in Senegal

Figure 3–1 is a map showing the 14 regions of Senegal, a country in West Africa. Desertification is an ongoing challenge here as increasing numbers of people derive their livelihood from semi-arid land. Organizations such as the United Nations, the European Union, and the African Union have all examined, and proposed solutions to, the problem of desertification in Senegal. Over a dozen other countries are also struggling with this challenge.

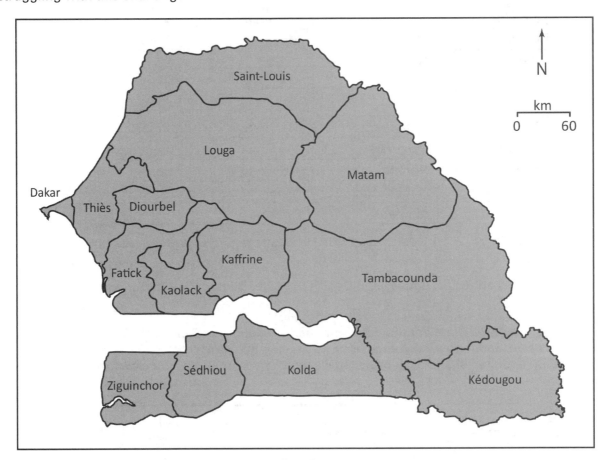

FIGURE 3–1

Assume you are a scientist that is examining land degradation in Senegal. After several years of field work, you and your colleagues have many volumes of data specific to each of Senegal's 14 regions. This data is in a variety of formats, such as field notes, tabular data, satellite pictures, and soil samples. Table 3–1 is a sample of your tabular data. It contains causes and degrees of land degradation in Senegal. You are assigned the job of cartographer—graphically presenting this data on maps of the country.

Region	Excessive Wood Gathering	Vegetation Cover Reduction	Topsoil Loss
Dakar	No data	No data	No data
Diourbel	Not effected	Moderate	Moderate
Fatick	Extreme	Minor	Minor
Kaffrine	Minor	Moderate	None
Kaolack	Moderate	Moderate	Minor
Kédougou	Not effected	Minor	None
Kolda	Minor	Moderate	None
Louga	Minor	Moderate	Moderate
Matam	Not effected	Moderate	Minor
Saint-Louis	Moderate	Moderate	Moderate
Sédhiou	Not effected	Moderate	None
Tambacounda	Not effected	Minor	None
Thiès	Moderate	Extreme	Extreme
Ziguinchor	Minor	Moderate	None

Data credit/courtesy of UNFAO

TABLE 3–1: Causes and Degrees of Land Degradation in Senegal

1. On Figure 3–2, graphically present the data from the first column of Table 3–1. Organize the data into groups first, and then assign each group a shading hue. Present this information in the map's legend, and then shade each of Senegal's regions according to your cartographic scheme.

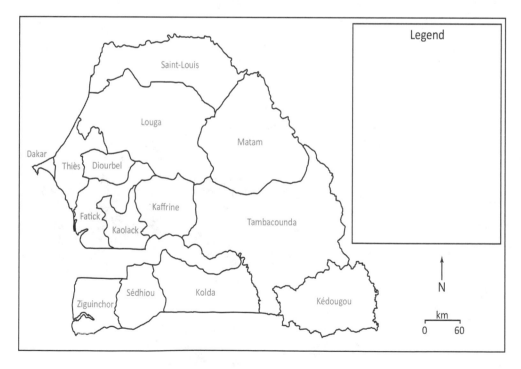

FIGURE 3–2: Land Degradation Caused by Excessive Wood Gathering

2. Describe any general spatial patterns that emerged from the data that you mapped in Figure 3–2.

_____

_____

_____

_____

3. If the Senegalese government asked for your scientific advice about where to focus their desertification mitigation efforts regarding excessive wood gathering, would you tell them to concentrate in the north, east, south, or west of their country? Explain why.

_____

_____

_____

4. On Figure 3–3, graphically present the data from the second column of Table 3–1. Organize the data into groups first, and then assign each group a shading hue. Present this information in the map's legend, and then shade each of Senegal's regions according to your cartographic scheme.

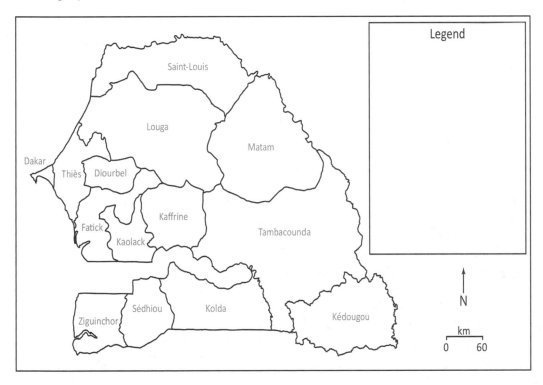

FIGURE 3–3: Land Degradation Caused by Vegetation Cover Reduction

5. Describe any general spatial patterns that emerged from the data that you mapped in Figure 3–3.

_____

_____

_____

6. If the Senegalese government asked for your scientific advice about where to focus their desertification mitigation efforts regarding vegetation cover reduction, would you tell them to concentrate in the north, east, south, or west of their country? Explain why.

_____

_____

_____

7. On Figure 3–4, graphically present the data from the third column of Table 3–1. Organize the data into groups first, and then assign each group a shading hue. Present this information in the map's legend, and then shade each of Senegal's regions according to your cartographic scheme.

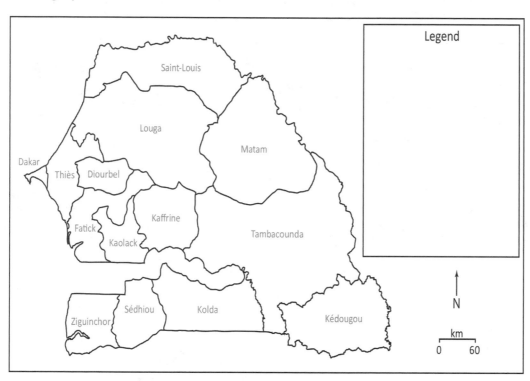

FIGURE 3–4: Land Degradation Caused by Topsoil Loss

8. Describe any general spatial patterns that emerged from the data that you mapped in Figure 3–4.

_____

_____

_____

_____

9. If the Senegalese government asked for your scientific advice about where to focus their desertification mitigation efforts regarding topsoil loss, would you tell them to concentrate in the north, east, south, or west of their country? Explain why.

_____

_____

_____

Summary of Key Terms and Concepts:

- Aeolian means "of or relating to wind."
- Bajadas are broad sloping plains created from merged alluvial fans that come from adjacent valleys.
- A barchan dune is a crescent-shaped sand dune with the crescent tips pointing downwind.
- A butte is a mid-sized flat-topped hill with cliff-face sides.
- Desertification is the process of degrading semi-arid land by climate change and human activities.
- A driving force of desertification is a social or physical process that facilitates or encourages land degradation in semi-arid areas.
- Ergs are extensive fields of active sand dunes and are most common within the subtropical high latitudes.
- Inselbergs protrude from the desert floor and form where a mass of rock resists erosion while softer surrounding rocks succumb to erosion.
- A longitudinal dune is an elongated sand dune with ridge crests parallel to the prevailing direction of wind.
- A mesa is an extensive flat-topped elevated area with one or more cliff-face sides.
- A playa is a flat, dry lakebed in a desert valley with interior drainage.
- A playa lake is a shallow, temporary lake formed in a desert basin after heavy rainfall.
- A proximate cause of desertification is a social or physical process that creates land degradation in semi-arid areas.
- A saline lake is a permanent body of salty water occupying a desert playa.
- A star dune is a star-shaped dune formed as the prevailing wind changes direction through the year.
- A transverse dune is a long, narrow, sand dune with the ridge crest perpendicular (or transverse) to the prevailing wind.

LAB #30 Coastal Landforms, Waves, and Tides

Recommended Textbook Reading Prior to Lab:

- Chapter 19, The Work of Waves: Coastal Landforms
  - 19.1 Tides, Waves, and Near-Shore Currents
  - 19.2 Coastal Landforms: Beaches and Rocky Coasts

Goals: After completing this lab, you will be able to:

- Using Google Earth, identify and explain processes associated with coastal landforms and processes.
- Identify the component portions and areas of ocean waveforms.
- Explain the difference between a deep-water wave and a shallow-water wave.
- Classify a wave as a deep-water, shallow-water, or in-transition wave by calculating the ratio of its wavelength to water depth.
- Calculate deep-water wave velocities using periods and wavelengths.
- Calculate shallow-water wave velocities using ocean depths.
- Calculate arrival times for a tsunami for various locations around the Indian Ocean.
- Distinguish between Mean Lower Low Water (MLLW) and Mean Sea Level (MSL) in reference to tidal datums.
- Build tidal prediction graphs for Bar Harbor, Maine, and describe the plotted tidal patterns.

Key terms and concepts:

- barrier island
- baymouth bar
- deep-water wave
- embayment
- emergent coast
- groin
- headland
- jetty
- longshore current
- longshore drift
- marine terrace
- Mean Lower Low Water (MLLW)
- Mean Sea Level (MSL)
- sandspit
- sea stack
- seawall
- shallow-water wave
- submergent coast
- tide
- tombolo
- wave crest
- wave-cut bench
- wave height
- wavelength
- wave period
- wave trough

Required materials:

- Calculator
- High-speed Internet connection (for Module 1) and Google Earth (free download at http://www.google.com/earth/download/ge/agree.html)
- Textbook: *Living Physical Geography*, by Bruce Gervais

Problem-Solving Module #1: Coastal Landforms

Download the following file from the textbook companion site and open it within Google Earth:
  • Coastal Landforms.kmz

Use the above Google Earth file to answer questions 1–13.

1. Fly to location marker A. What is this landform called, and what can we say about the rock's resistance to erosion compared to adjacent locations?

   _____

   _____

2. Fly to location marker B. Name this coastal landform, and explain how it is different from a tombolo.

   _____

   _____

   _____

3. Fly to location marker C. What is this landform called, and what protects it on two sides?

   _____

4. Fly to location marker D. This is a seawall in Japan. What is it designed to do?

   _____

5. Fly to location marker E. What is this landform called, and what is it designed to do?

   _____

6. Fly to location marker F. What is this landform, and how is it related to a sea arch?

   _____

7. Fly to location marker G. What is this landform called, and what is it designed to do?

   _____

8. Fly to location marker H. This is a marine terrace. What does its presence indicate has happened to the coastline?

   _____

   _____

9. Fly to location marker I. What is this landform, and how did it form?

   _____

10. Fly to location marker J. What is this landform called, and what four physical geographic conditions must be met in order for it to form? *Hint: See textbook, Section 19.2.*

   _____

   _____

   _____

   _____

11. Fly to location marker K. What is this landform called, and how is it formed? What has formed behind this landform?

_____

_____

_____

12. Fly to location marker L. This is a wave-cut bench. What tectonic process will allow it to become a marine terrace? *Hint: See textbook, Section 19.2.*

_____

_____

13. Fly to location marker M. This is a sea arch (click on the photo links to see various images). How was this formed, and what will it become when it collapses?

_____

_____

Problem-Solving Module #2: Waves

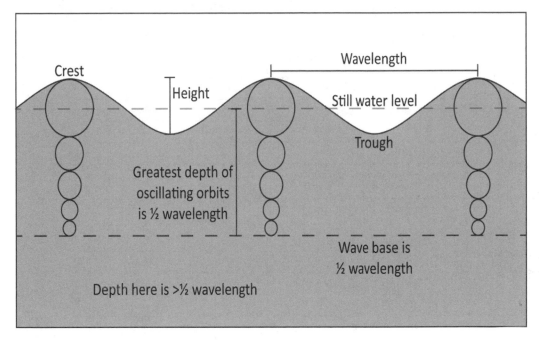

FIGURE 2–1

Use Figure 2–1 to define the following terms in your own words.

1. Wave height

_____

_____

2. Wavelength

_____

_____

3. Crest

_____

4. Trough

_____

A deep-water wave is a wave in water deeper than ½ its wavelength. Figure 2–1 shows deep-water waves. A shallow-water wave is a wave in water shallower than 1/20th (0.05) of its wavelength. Shallow-water waves begin to "feel bottom" as their lowest oscillating orbits are flattened by the rising ocean floor as a wave approaches a coastline. For example, consider a wave with a wavelength of 18 meters:
- In water > 9 meters deep, this is a deep-water wave (18/2 = 9).
- In water < 90 cm deep, this is a shallow-water wave (18 × 0.05 = 0.9 of a meter, or 90 cm).
- In water between 9 meters and 90 cm deep, it is in transition as it approaches a coastline.

5. Complete Table 2–1. Remember that classifying a wave as deep-water, shallow-water, or in-transition is always determined by calculating the ratio of its wavelength to water depth.

Wavelength (m)	Classification	Water Depth (m)
5	Deep-water wave	> 2.5
5	Shallow-water wave	
5	In-transition wave	
78	Deep-water wave	
78	Shallow-water wave	
78	In-transition wave	
14	Deep-water wave	
14	Shallow-water wave	
14	In-transition wave	
103	Deep-water wave	
103	Shallow-water wave	
103	In-transition wave	

TABLE 2–1

Tsunamis are waves generated by the sudden displacement of water. They have wavelengths between 10 to 500 *kilometers*, travel at jet-speed, and obliterate coastal communities when they come ashore. Given these characteristics, it may seem odd that tsunamis are classified as "shallow-water waves."

6. Complete Table 2–2.

Tsunami Wavelength (km)	Tsunami Wavelength (m)	Depth of Water Required for Deep-Water Classification (m)	Average Ocean Depth (m)
	50,000		4,267
77			4,267
	143,000		4,267
200			4,267

TABLE 2–2

7. Why is it impossible to classify tsunamis as "deep-water waves"?

_____

A wave's period is the time for consecutive crests to pass a fixed point. Wave period is normally measured in seconds. If we know a deep-water wave's period (T) and its wavelength (L), recorded in meters, we can calculate its velocity in meters/second using the formula below. In the formula, remember that "V" means velocity in meters per second.

$$V = L / T$$

For example, a deep-water wave has a period of 8 seconds and a wavelength of 200 meters. The velocity of this wave is 25 m/s, or 90 km/hr, because:

- V = 200 m/8 seconds
- V = 25 m/s
  and
- (25 m/s)(60 sec/min) = 1,500 m/min
- (1,500 m/min) (60 min/hr) = 90,000 m/hr
- (90,000 m/hr) / (1,000 m/km) = 90 km/hr

8. Complete Table 2–3.

Deep-Water Wave Wavelength (L)	Deep-Water Wave Period (T)	Deep-Water Wave Velocity (m/s)	Deep-Water Wave Velocity (km/hr)
10	2		
95	7.2		
290	13.6		
452	16.3		

TABLE 2–3

9. Describe the general relationship between the values in the first two columns in Table 2–3.

_____

Determining the velocity of shallow-water waves requires using a different formula. All we need to know is a wave's depth (d) in meters. In the formula, remember that 3.13 is a constant and that "V" means velocity in meters per second.

$$V = 3.13 \sqrt{d}$$

For example, a shallow-water wave in 3.5 m deep water has a velocity is 5.9 m/s, or 21.2 km/h, because:

- the square root of 3.5 = 1.87, so
- V = 3.13 × 1.87
- V = 5.9 m/s
  and
- (5.9 m/s) (60 sec/min) = 354 m/min
- (354 m/min) (60 min/hr) = 21,240 m/hr
- (21,240 m/hr) / (1,000 m/km) = 21.2 km/hr

10. Complete Table 2–4.

Shallow-Water Wave Depth (d)	Shallow-Water Wave Velocity (m/s)	Shallow-Water Wave Velocity (km/hr)
1.7		
2.6		
3		
3.2		
4		

TABLE 2–4

11. Describe the general relationship between the values in the first two columns in Table 2–4.

_____

Assume you work as an oceanographer at a tsunami warning center. Your job is to warn coastal communities of approaching tsunamis so evacuations can begin. One afternoon a very large earthquake occurs along the Great Sumatran Fault. Buoys in the Indian Ocean sense a tsunami and transmit the data to satellites and then to you. You need to call your colleagues around the Indian Ocean to tell them how much time they have before the tsunami strikes their coastlines. _Note: For this exercise, assume the Indian Ocean's depth is the average depth of Earth's oceans._

12. What formula should you use to calculate the velocity of this tsunami?

_____

13. How fast is this tsunami traveling in m/s and km/hr? Be sure to show your work.
    Hint: See Table 2–2 for Earth's average ocean depth.

_____

_____

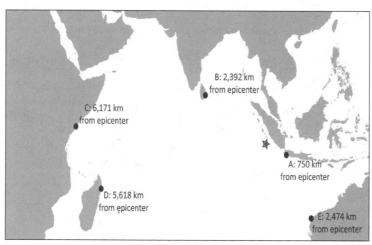

Research from NOAA

FIGURE 2–2

14. A Boeing 747-400 has a cruise speed of 920 km/hr. In percentage terms, how fast is the tsunami compared to the cruising speed of a Boeing 747-400?

_____

_____

15. Use an atlas and the information on Figure 2–2 to complete Table 2–5.

Location	Country	Hours and Minutes Before Tsunami Arrives
A		
B		
C		
D	Madagascar	7 h, 38 m
E		

TABLE 2–5

Problem-Solving Module #3: Tidal Datums

The National Ocean Service uses a 19-year-long temporal window (called a Tidal Datum Epoch) to observe tidal heights and reduce these data to obtain mean values for tidal datums. Tidal datums are standard elevations. They are determined by recording and calculating elevations for specific phases of a tide. There are over a dozen tidal datums available, but two common ones are Mean Lower Low Water (MLLW) and Mean Sea Level (MSL). The following definitions are taken directly from NOAA.

- **Mean Lower Low Water (MLLW):** "The average of the lower low water height of each tidal day observed over the National Tidal Datum Epoch"
- **Mean Sea Level (MSL):** "The arithmetic mean of hourly heights observed over the National Tidal Datum Epoch"

1. Tables 3–1 and 3–2 present real, future NOAA tide predictions (in meters) for Bar Harbor, Maine, on October 6 and 7, 2015. Notice that the data in Table 3–1 are relative to the Mean Lower Low Water (MLLW) datum, while the data in Table 3–2 are relative to the Mean Sea Level (MSL) datum. For Tables 3–1 and 3–2, identify if a tide is "High" or "Low" in the last column of each table.

Date	Day	Time	Prediction (m)	High or Low
October 6, 2015	Tuesday	12:12 a.m.	0.13	
October 6, 2015	Tuesday	6:27 a.m.	3.09	
October 6, 2015	Tuesday	12:37 p.m.	0.37	
October 6, 2015	Tuesday	6:49 p.m.	3.26	
October 7, 2015	Wednesday	1:14 a.m.	0.18	
October 7, 2015	Wednesday	7:28 a.m.	3.09	
October 7, 2015	Wednesday	1:38 p.m.	0.36	
October 7, 2015	Wednesday	7:49 p.m.	3.24	

**TABLE 3–1: Tide Predictions for Bar Harbor, Maine, October 6 and 7, 2015
(Meters Relative to the Mean Lower Low Water—MLLW—Datum)**

Date	Day	Time	Prediction (m)	High or Low
October 6, 2015	Tuesday	12:12 a.m.	−1.6	
October 6, 2015	Tuesday	6:27 a.m.	1.36	
October 6, 2015	Tuesday	12:37 p.m.	−1.36	
October 6, 2015	Tuesday	6:49 p.m.	1.53	
October 7, 2015	Wednesday	1:14 a.m.	−1.55	
October 7, 2015	Wednesday	7:28 a.m.	1.36	
October 7, 2015	Wednesday	1:38 p.m.	−1.36	
October 7, 2015	Wednesday	7:49 p.m.	1.51	

**TABLE 3–2: Tide Predictions for Bar Harbor, Maine, October 6 and 7, 2015
(Meters Relative to the Mean Sea Level—MSL—Datum)**

2. How many high tides and low tides does Bar Harbor, Maine experience on a daily basis?

_____

3. If you make a graph of Table 3–1 (tides relative to the MLLW datum), would you place the "0 meters" value at the bottom, middle, or top of the *y*-axis?

_____

4. If you make a graph of Table 3–2 (tides relative to the MSL datum), would you place the "0 meters" value at the bottom, middle, or top of the *y*-axis?

_____

5. On Figure 3–1, create a graph of the data on Table 3–1. Be sure to demarcate and label the *y*-axis.

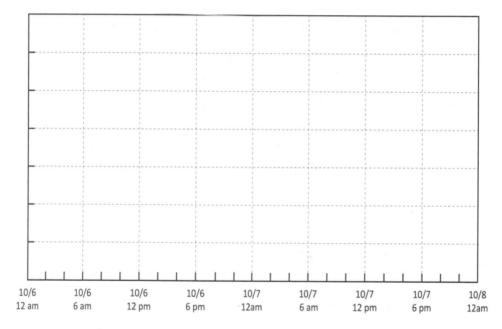

| 10/6 | 10/6 | 10/6 | 10/6 | 10/7 | 10/7 | 10/7 | 10/7 | 10/8 |
| 12 am | 6 am | 12 pm | 6 pm | 12am | 6 am | 12 pm | 6 pm | 12am |

FIGURE 3–1: Tide Prediction Graph for Bar Harbor, Maine, October 6 and 7, 2015 (Meters Relative to Mean Lower Low Water—MLLW)

6. Describe the tidal pattern that you graphed in Figure 3–1.

_____

_____

_____

_____

7. On Figure 3–2, create a graph of the data on Table 3–2. Be sure to demarcate and label the x- and y- axes.

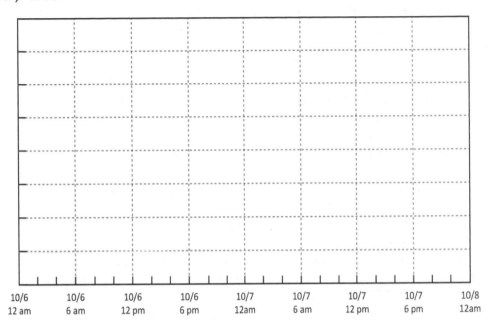

10/6   10/6   10/6   10/6   10/7   10/7   10/7   10/7   10/8
12 am   6 am   12 pm   6 pm   12am   6 am   12 pm   6 pm   12am

FIGURE 3–2: Tide Prediction Graph for Bar Harbor, Maine, October 6 and 7, 2015 (Meters Relative to Mean Sea Level—MSL)

8. Describe the tidal pattern that you graphed in Figure 3–2.

_____

_____

_____

_____

9. Explain what "0 meters" means for the MLLW tidal datum compared to the MSL tidal datum and which one illustrates a low water level that is physically lowest. Which tidal datum would you rely on if you were a boat captain in Bar Harbor, Maine and wanted to avoid running aground? Explain why.

_____

_____

_____

_____

_____

_____

Summary of Key Terms and Concepts:

- A barrier island is an offshore sand bar that runs parallel to the coast.
- A baymouth bar is a continuous sandspit formed by longshore drift, creating a brackish water lagoon behind it.
- A deep-water wave is a wave in water deeper than ½ its wavelength.
- An embayment is a low sandy beach protected by headlands.
- An emergent coast is a coast where the sea level is dropping or the land is rising.
- A groin is a linear, concrete, or stone structure that extends from a beach into the water and is designed to slow the erosion of sand from a beach.
- A headland is a rocky prominence of coastal land.
- A jetty is a human-built wall placed at the mouth of a harbor to prevent sand from closing the harbor entrance.
- A longshore current is a current that flows parallel to the beach in the direction of wave movement.
- Longshore drift is the process by which sediment on a beach is moved down the length of a beach in the direction of wave movement.
- A marine terrace is a wave-cut bench that has been elevated above sea level.
- Mean Lower Low Water is "the average of the lower low water height of each tidal day observed over the National Tidal Datum Epoch."
- Mean Sea Level is "the arithmetic mean of hourly heights observed over the National Tidal Datum Epoch."
- A sandspit is an elongated dry bar of sand that extends from a beach out into the water usually parallel with the shore.
- A sea stack is a steep or vertical column of rock found near coasts.
- A sea wall is a concrete wall designed to protect backshore environments from wave erosion during large storms.
- A shallow-water wave is a wave in water shallower than 1/20th (0.05) of its wavelength.
- A submergent coast is where sea level is rising or the land is sinking.
- Tides are the rise and fall of sea level due to the gravitational effects of the Sun and Moon and centrifugal force by Earth's rotation.
- A tombolo is a sand bar that connects an island to the mainland or to another island.
- A wave-cut bench is a flat coastal platform created by erosion from waves and exposed at low tide.
- A wave crest is the highest part of a wave above the still water line.
- Wavelength is the horizontal distance between successive wave crests.
- Wave height is the vertical distance between a wave's crest and trough.
- A wave trough is the lowest part of a wave below the still water line.
- A wave's period is the time for consecutive crests to pass a fixed point and is normally measured in seconds.